The Life of Baptists
in the Life of the World

The
LIFE
of
BAPTISTS
in the
LIFE
of the
WORLD

80 Years of the Baptist World Alliance

Walter B. Shurden, Editor

BROADMAN PRESS
Nashville, Tennessee

Dewey Decimal Classification: 286.09
Subject Heading: BAPTISTS—HISTORY
Library of Congress Catalog Card Number: 85-1401

Printed in the United States of America

Addresses are reprinted with the permission of the Baptist World Alliance.

Library of Congress Cataloging in Publication Data
Main entry under title:

The Life of Baptists in the life of the world.

Bibliography: p.
1. Baptists—Addresses, essays, lectures.
2. Baptist World Alliance—Addresses, essays, lectures.
3. Church and the world—Addresses, essays, lectures.
I. Shurden, Walter B.
BX6215.L53   1985   286'.1   85-1401
ISBN 0-8054-6582-0 (pbk.)

To
Duke K. McCall
President, Baptist World Alliance, 1980-1985
President, The Southern Baptist Theological Seminary
September 15, 1951 - January 31, 1982

Preface

This sourcebook is released with the conviction that Christians called Baptists have something of value to say to the entire Christian community as well as to the larger secular world. To be sure, Baptists also have much to hear. The experience should be dialogue, not monologue. There is no place for sectarian arrogance in the multi-faceted body of Christ or in an increasingly pluralistic world. But while, as Ecclesiastes says, there is "a time to keep silence, and a time to speak," this book provides Baptists of the world a pulpit, "a time to speak."

All of the documemts printed here were presented by international Baptist leaders at one of the fourteen Baptist World Congresses between 1905-1980. These people did not speak *for* the Baptist World Alliance (BWA) any more than they spoke *for* their individual Baptist communions or local Baptist churches. They spoke as Baptist individuals. Rather than lessening the importance of those addresses, however, the fact that they spoke as individuals increases the significance of the papers. This is so because of the consensus which emerges about what it means to be a Baptist in the twentieth century.

Two addresses from each of the fourteen Baptist World Congresses are printed. Except in four instances, the first address from each Congress is the presidential address. In three cases, the president did not deliver an address because of death or illness.[1] And because of its significance, the "Declaration on Human Rights" is substituted for the presidential address of 1980.

Most of the presidential addresses or their substitutes deal with similar themes. Several of them provide excellent insights into the history and purpose of the Baptist World Alliance. Others relate the BWA and the Baptist people to the world of that day. They provide a clear picture by elected world Baptist leaders of the relevance of Baptist principles for the life of the world.

The second address from each Congress includes various types of material. Some represent the best in world Baptist preaching. This is true of Harold Cooke Phillips's 1947 sermon at Copenhagen, Gardner Taylor's 1950 incomparable sermon at Cleveland, and William Jones's 1980 sermon at Toronto. Others of these addresses focus on specific Baptist distinctives. J. D. Freeman's address on individualism in 1905, Herbert Gezork's address on "four sturdy pillars" of Baptists in 1955, and Russell Aldwinckle's 1965 address on freedom elucidate various dimensions of the Baptist witness. Theological and ethical issues are confronted by other papers. In 1928, for example, when church union was a major issue in Canada and elsewhere, F. W. Patterson spoke of Baptists' relationship to other Christians. And in 1939, when war was threatening much of the world, S. W. Hughes of London spoke on "World Peace."

Recently, a Roman Catholic press advertised one of its books as a resource for helping Catholics to "discover and recover" the Roman tradition. That is a compelling need among Baptists as well. Some Baptists, who have never learned it, need to "discover" the Baptist tradition and the crucial role of the BWA in that tradition. Others, who once learned it, need to "recover" the Baptist way. I hope that the documents printed here will facilitate those tasks.

Contents

General Introduction

On July 17, 1905, 3,500 Baptists from around the world met in London, England, at Exeter Hall and formed the Baptist World Alliance (BWA). This was almost three hundred years after the organization of the earliest Baptist church on English soil in 1612. At the time of the first world gathering, Baptists of the world numbered 6.2 million people. Fifty years later that figure had zoomed to 22 million. By 1980, the time of the last Baptist World Congress, the number had become almost 30 million.

Given the fact that the BWA celebrates eighty years of service in 1985, one is surprised that very little in book form has been written on this important organization. While a number of good articles have been written, we still await a first-rate scholarly history which provides an in-depth and comprehensive analysis of the Alliance.

In 1939 Mrs. J. N. Prestridge wrote a brief twenty-two page pamphlet on the beginnings of the BWA. In truth, however, the work was little more than a eulogy for Mrs. Prestridge's husband and his role in helping found the organization. In 1955 Blanche Sydnor White wrote *From London to London* in celebration of the fiftieth anniversary of the BWA. The focus of White's book is on worldwide Baptist missions rather than the actual history of the Alliance.

F. Townley Lord, president of the BWA from 1950-1955, wrote the best comprehensive account of the BWA to be published thus far. Published in 1955, Lord's work covers only the first fifty years of the Alliance. Carl W. Tiller, former BWA staff member, wrote *The Twentieth Century Baptist,* released for the 1980 Toronto meeting of the BWA. Replete with valuable information on the Alliance, its purpose, its leaders, and its contributions, Tiller's work was not intended as a major scholarly contribution. It is, however, creatively presented in newspaper fashion and extremely helpful.

Two doctoral dissertations have made major contributions toward understanding the BWA and its work. Clyde Jowers wrote a dissertation in 1964 at the New Orleans Baptist Theological Seminary entitled, "The Promotion of Religious Liberty by the Baptist World Alliance." It is a very good study, but, of course, focuses on only one aspect of the BWA. Craig Sherouse, in 1982, broadened Jowers' theme and wrote an excellent dissertation at The Southern Baptist Theological Seminary on the subject of "The Social Teachings of the Baptist World Alliance, 1905-1980." Deserving of publication, this dissertation is basic to any investigation of the BWA.

While Sherouse primarily sought to provide "an analysis and critique of the ethical reasonings and involvement of the Baptist World Alliance," he made a major contribution also in delineating the BWA's historical origins. Arguing that the BWA evolved out of nineteenth century ecumenism, Sherouse insists that no single individual can carry the title of "the founder" of the Alliance. He recognizes, of course, the crucial influence of W. W. Landrum, R. H. Pitt, J. N. Prestridge, A. T. Robertson, John Clifford, and J. H. Shakespeare. "However," says Sherouse, "the formation of the BWA was not an individual project but was rather the cooperation of the three strongest groups of Baptists with each other and with the broader movement of nineteenth century church history."[2] The three strongest Baptist groups to which Sherouse refers were the Southern Baptist Convention, the Northern Baptist Convention, and the British Baptist Union.

Recognizing the autonomy and independence of local Baptist churches and of general Baptist organizations, the BWA "exists as an expression of the essential oneness of Baptist people in the Lord Jesus Christ."[3] Composed of Baptist denominations or as the BWA Constitution states, "any organization of Baptist churches . . . which desires to cooperate in the work of the Alliance . . ." the BWA, in 1980, consisted of 120 such bodies. In turn, these 120 denominational Baptist bodies included 117,357 local Baptist churches and almost 30,000,000 church members.[4]

The objectives of the BWA are clearly spelled out in Article II of the BWA Constitution. They are:

1. Promote Christian fellowship and cooperation among Baptists throughout the world.
2. Bear witness to the gospel of Jesus Christ and assist unions and conventions in their divine task of bringing all people to God through Jesus Christ as Savior and Lord.
3. Promote understanding and cooperation among Baptist bodies and with other Christian groups, in keeping with our unity in Christ.
4. Act as an agency for the expression of biblical faith and historically distinctive Baptist principles and practices.
5. Act an an agency of reconciliation seeking peace for all persons, and uphold the claims of fundamental human rights, including full religious liberty.
6. Serve as a channel for expressing Christian social concern and alleviating human need.
7. Serve in cooperation with member bodies as a resource for the development of plans for evangelism, education, church growth, and other forms of mission.
8. Provide channels of communication dealing with work related to these objectives through all possible media.[5]

To anyone who reads the above eight objectives carefully, it is clear what the BWA *is not*. It is *not* a Baptist super church. It is *not* a worldwide Baptist judicial or legislative body seeking to violate cherished Baptist principles of congregational autonomy or the rights of individual believers by imposing its will upon an individual, a local church, or a convention of churches. The BWA is designed to protect, not usurp, cardinal Baptist convictions.

Functionally, what is the BWA? First, it is a *forum for fellowship*. Every five years the BWA meets in order to strengthen the global ties of Baptists. These five-year meetings are called Baptist World Congresses or General Meetings. Baptist representatives come from every corner of the world. The symbol of the BWA is significant: two hands clasped, reaching out to each other from around the world signify the goal of worldwide fellowship. The BWA is a bridge-builder over the walls of culture, race, language, nation, and sex. If reconciliation were the sole function of the BWA, one could surely see the gospel incarnate in the organization. But the BWA is not just a forum for fellowship.

It is, second, an *agency of compassion*. With its comparatively limited financial resources, the BWA has an enviable record of stewardship in providing relief for people around the world who suffer from famine and war and homelessness. Children who need to be immunized against dreaded diseases, refugees who need "a place," victims of earthquakes and floods—these are among the beneficiaries of the BWA.

Third, the BWA is a *voice for liberty.* From its inception in 1905, the BWA has been an advocate for religious liberty and basic human rights. The Alliance is a negotiator for imprisoned and persecuted Christians.

Fourth, the BWA is an *instrument for evangelism.* As the constitutional objectives state, the BWA is assisting general Baptist bodies "in their divine task of bringing all people to God through Jesus Christ as Saviour and Lord" and serving "as a resource for the development of plans for evangelism . . . [and] church growth."

Finally, the BWA is a *channel of communication.* It seeks to keep Baptists informed on what is happening to their denominational kinsmen around the world. To achieve this purpose, the BWA publishes *The Baptist World,* a publication which serves as a window on the world of Baptists. But the BWA not only communicates to Baptists about the Baptist world; it also articulates and communicates Baptist distinctives to the world. The documents in this volume both reflect and elaborate upon these basic functions of the Baptist World Alliance.

Notes

1. These three cases were Robert Stuart MacArthur in 1923, John MacNeill in 1934, and J. H. Rushbrooke in 1947. E. Y. Mullins was not able to give his presidential address in 1928 in Toronto, but George W. Truett read the paper Mullins had written.

2. Craig Alan Sherouse, "The Social Teachings of the Baptist World Alliance, 1905-1980" (Unpublished Ph.D. dissertation, The Southern Baptist Theological Seminary: Louisville, Kentucky, 1982), p.50.

3. "The Constitution of the Baptist World Alliance," in Cyril E. Bryant and Ruby J. Burke, editors, *Celebrating Christ's Presence Through the Spirit: Official Report of the Fourteenth Congress* (Nashville: Broadman, 1981), p. 283.

4. Ibid., pp. 284, 314.

5. Ibid., pp. 283-284.

1
London
1905

Introduction

Alexander Maclaren (1826-1910), outstanding expository preacher and renown Baptist minister of Manchester, England, was selected to preside at the first international meeting of Baptists. His presidential message was brief but immensely significant. Maclaren alluded to his message as "threadbare." No description could be more inappropriate.

Because he wanted no misunderstanding as to where Baptists stood "in the continuity of the historic church," he called upon his hearers to stand and repeat the Apostles' Creed. Maclaren did not provide a title for his first BWA presidential sermon. After reading the address, however, one need not guess at his subject: "In the Name of Christ . . . By the Power of the Spirit." This historic Baptist address is printed here exactly as it appeared, editorial comments included, in the proceedings of the *B.W.A. Report* for 1905.

Baptists, as other Christian denominations, have had to explain their reason for existing within the broader Christian communion. J. D. Freeman, pastor of Bloor Street Baptist Church in Toronto, Canada, sought to do this in his sermon, "The Place of Baptists in the Christian Church." Maintaining that "the Baptist denomination is not an accident nor an incident, nor an experiment," Freeman enumerated basic Baptist distinctives, demonstrating how they derived from what he described as "the essential Baptist principle."

In the Name of Christ . . . By the Power of the Spirit
Alexander Maclaren

Dear brethren, my first word cannot but be the expression of my deepest gratitude for the great honour done me by placing me in this chair. I thank my fellow-countrymen, the Baptists of England, amongst whom it has been my pride and my pleasure to work all my life. There is no honour to be compared with the honour of living in the hearts and the confidence of the people who know you best and have known you the longest. (Applause.) And whilst I have had drops of that benediction all my life, it has come upon me in a full flood now at the end. And I thank no less our brethren beyond the seas, who, with less knowledge, of course, have shown even greater faith—(laughter)—and have confirmed the choice of my brethren who know me best. I thank you with all my heart, and I shall do my best to prove myself not altogether unworthy of your confidence and your affection. (Applause.) But if you chose to elect to the office of President a man who has entered upon the sixtieth year of his pastorate—(applause)—you must have him with the defects of his qualities; and one of these—I do not know whether it comes under the category of quality or defect—is the incapacity to deliver a long inaugural address. I have therefore asked the committee to allow me so far to forego the privileges and responsibilities of the Presidency as to content myself with a few words that I venture to speak this morning. I am sure you will understand that if it had been with me as in days and years gone by, nothing would have given me greater pleasure than to have dilated at unreasonable length—(laughter and applause)—upon some of the many topics that force themselves upon our minds in connection with this Congress.

What Are We Here For?

To glory in our own denominational strength? To rejoice in looking one another in the face and asking each other of our welfare? To demonstrate to the world what we are, and what we stand for? Yes, all these things; they are all good, all necessary, and much good in these aspects will no doubt come from this Congress. To compare methods? To learn from one another? Yes. But, dear brethren, when a man comes near to the end of his ministry, near to the beginning of his rest, the perspective has a way of altering, and some things that had hitherto looked very large dwindle, and some things that were perhaps not sufficiently prominent in one's ministry or one's experience begin to stand out with strange clearness and greatness. And so I want to touch, if I can, on the deepest thing of all in the two or three words that I venture to offer to you. And I beseech you to remember the two crystal phrases which carry everything I want to say—"In the name of Christ," "By the power of the Spirit." There we touch the bed-rock, the bottom of everything, and all will be right if we are right in these two relations—the relation to the living Christ, the relation to the indwelling Spirit; and all will be wrong, however orthodox or earnest or eloquent or learned or up-to-date or wise in methods our Churches may be, if these things fail. "These are commonplaces." Yes. And everything that is great and true is commonplace; and there is not a threadbare commonplace of Christian teaching and experience but would start up into power—power very inconvenient to some of us—and would grip us with teeth of iron if we once honestly tried to make it the basis of our lives and to put it into practice. So during the few moments I have to speak to you I make no apology for giving you a threadbare message; for it is the message that lies at the bottom of all our organisation, and that alone will give strength and efficiency to all our work. "In the name of Christ." Thinking over this meeting last evening, a thought occurred to me which I have ventured to impart to my brethren, the various vice-presidents of this Congress. And I am thankful to say that they have all heartily concurred in it. And I want to submit it to you. I should like that there should be no misunderstanding on the part of the English public, or the American public either—before whom we are taking a prominent position, for a day at any rate—as to where we stand in the continuity of the historic Church. And I should like the first act of this Congress to be the audible and unanimous acknowledgment of our Faith. So I have suggested that, given your consent, it would be an impressive and a right thing, and would clear away a good many misunderstandings and stop the mouth of a good deal of slander—if we here and now, in the face of the world, not as a piece of coercion or discipline, but as a simple acknowledgment of where we stand and what we believe, would rise to our feet and, following the lead of your President, would repeat the Apostles' Creed. Will you?

[The whole gathering then instantly rose and repeated, slowly and deliberately, after Dr. Maclaren the whole of the Apostles' Creed.]

And now, brethren, [continued the Doctor, one word more,] as to the second of the two crystallised crystals that I quoted, "By the power of the Spirit." Revival is in the air. Thank God for it. The Christian Church of to-day is more fully possessed with a longing for the experience of that higher life which comes from the indwelling Spirit than ever it was before, and Christian theology is following the leadings of Christian experience. And having in the ages of the Fathers and the Greek Church directed all its strength and subtlety to the evolving of the doctrine of the Father and the relations to the Son, and in the Mediaeval and Reformation and Puritan periods having directed its main strength to the thought and to the realisation of the experience of the Person and work of the

Atoning Christ—we have come now, in the natural evolution (for there is a Divine evolution) of doctrine—and I believe all sections of the Christian Church are beginning to feel that we *have* come more and more—to that last great thought, "The spirit of life in Christ Jesus hath made me free from the law of sin and death." And I look forward to a time when, both in reference to what I have called the evolution of Christian doctrine and in reference to the experiences of the Christian life, there will be far more prominence given to the indwelling of the Spirit of life and holiness and power than ever before. And my prayer is that this Conference may do something to bring all our brethren nearer to the only Source of life and power and peace and ability of character—the touch of the fiery Spirit, the Spirit of burning, and the Spirit of Holiness. We are crying out for revival. Dear friends, the revival must begin with each of us by ourselves. Power for service is second, power for holiness and character being first. And only the man who has let the Spirit of God work its will upon him and come into him, and do what it will with him: only he has a right to expect that he will be clothed and invested with the Holy Ghost and with fire. Do not get on the wrong tack. Your revival, Christian minister, must begin in your study and on your knees. Your revival must be for yourselves—with no thought of service. But if once we have learned where our strength is, we shall never, never be so foolish as to go fourth in our own strength, or we shall be beaten—as we deserve to be. How long would it take to pick the ore out of the matrix with a hammer and with a chisel? Ah! but pitch it into the burning furnace, and by night you will be able to draw it out in a few seconds—molten, radiant, flashing. And if we will only plunge ourselves into that blessed baptism of fire, then we shall burn like the bush and not be consumed. There is not other secret of power and no other source of strength for a Christian Church. Congresses may be multiplied a million-fold, and all our instruments may be in perfect order, but unless the fire comes the sacrifice will be unconsumed. Dear brethren, it was in my heart to say these few plain words to you this morning. I beseech you to take them as they are meant to be spoken—as a message of love from an old man, who will never probably have again such an opportunity as this, and as a witness that, looking back upon a ministry longer than God's Providence has granted to many—though I may be conscious of many imperfections and faults—yet there are two things that I still maintain, and would press upon you as being the pillars of our Churches and the secrets of our success, "In the name of Christ," "By the power of the Spirit." (Loud applause.)

The Place of Baptists in the Christian Church
J. D. Freeman

The place of the Baptist people in the Christian Church is to be determined by the potency of the Baptist principle for Christian service. The Baptist people are what their essential principle has made them. What they have wrought has been accomplished under its impulse. If they have helped to somewhat clarify the thinking and spiritualise the life of the Christian Church, if they have rendered a distinguished service in setting wide the bounds of civil and religious liberty, if they have been path-finders in evangelism and file-leaders in missionary activity, it is because, as a people, they have been dominated by one grand and overmastering religious idea. In that they have lived their life; from that they have received their character; by that they have obtained their place.

The Baptist denomination is not an accident, nor an incident, nor an experiment; it is the normal development and permanent embodiment of a great Christian principle.

The essential Baptist principle, as I apprehend it, is this: *An acute and vivid consciousness of the sovereignty of Christ, accompanied by a stead-fast determination to secure the complete and consistent recognition of His personal, direct and undelegated authority over the souls of men.*

This, for us, is the master-fact of religious experience. It is the nerve centre of our denominational sensibility. It is the spinal column of our theology. It is the bed-rock of our Church polity. It is the mainspring of our missionary activity. It is the sheet-anchor of our hope. It is the crown of our rejoicing. "For to this end Christ both died and lived again, that He might be Lord both of the dead and the living." From this germinant conception all our distinctive denominational principles emerge. As the oak springs from the acorn, so our many-branched Baptist life is developed from this seed of thought. Baptistic Christianity lives and moves and has its being in the realm of the doctrine of the sovereignty of Christ.

In the terms of this conception we express our root idea of Christianity. In its last analysis Christianity means to us the union of a human life with Jesus Christ; this union, involving on the one hand a relation of personal saviourhood and sovereignty, and on the other a relation of personal trust and love and loyalty. This is Christianity stated in terms of its irreducible minimum.

Now, this conception is one that carries with it, inseparably, the *radical and far-reaching Baptist doctrine of individualism.* To Christ, and to Christ alone, the individual must stand or fall. There can be no proxy in the matter. There can be no sponsorial performance of religious obligations. It is no more possible for one person to believe or disbelieve in another's behalf than to go to heaven or hell for him. There must be personal repentance, personal faith, personal confession of Christ's name. This doctrine of individualism has found conspicuous expression and application along two bright and indelible lines of Baptist witness-bearing. In the first place it has made us always and everywhere

From Anti-Ritualistic People.

From first to last we have uttered our steady protestation against all soul reliance upon ceremonial observances. We could do no other. Our fundamental principle lays the axe at the root of all sacramentalism and sacerdotalism. The undelegated sovereignty of Christ renders it for ever impossible that His saving grace should be manipulated by any system of man mediation. That union with Christ which is the soul of Christianity is a union effected by the sovereign operation of the Holy Ghost in the immediate bestowment of Divine grace. Any interposition of ecclesiastical machinery, whether sacraments or priesthoods, or discipline or ritual, is a manifest impertinence. It is necessarily and always a usurpation and a wrong. "There is one God; one Mediator also between God and man, Himself man, Christ Jesus." It is not by way of consecrated water or oil, or bread or wine, that grace comes to man. Salvation is not by magic. It is by the direct impact of the Christlife upon the human soul. Wherever man puts out the dry fleece of an appealing faith it is soaked by the direct descent of the dew of grace. In the light of the mediatorial Lordship of Christ, all doctrines of baptismal regeneration and priestly absolution become not merely meaningless fictions, but unconscious defamations of the crown rights of the Son of God. That has been our Baptist testimony throughout the ages. Hierarchies there have been and are, whose colossal pretensions obscure this truth, and whose far-flung shadows fall dark upon the paths of men. As long as the last shade of a shadow of the doctrine of man-meditated grace lingers on the earth, our Baptist mission remains unfulfilled.

In the second place, our doctrine of individualism, under the sovereignty of Christ, has made us the unswerving and strenuous, if sometimes lonely,

Champions of Soul-Liberty.

In our postulate of soul-liberty we affirm the right of every human being to exemption in matters of faith and conscience from all coercion or intimidation by any earthly authority whatsoever. Our demand has been not simply for religious toleration, but religious liberty; not sufferance merely, but freedom; and that not for ourselves alone, but for all men. We did not stumble upon the doctrine. It inheres in the very essence of our belief. Christ is Lord of all. Every attempt to put the conscience in thrall to human authority is *Lése-Majesté* to the King of kings, and a negation of the privileges and responsibilities conferred by Him upon the individual soul.

The conscience is the servant only of God, and is not subject to the will of man. This truth has indestructible life. Crucify it and the third day it will rise again. Bury it in a sepulchre and the stone will be rolled away, while the keepers become as dead men.

With reference to this great principle we can clearly claim a thoroughgoing consistency. Steadfastly refusing to bend our own necks under the yoke of bondage, we have scrupulously withheld our hands from imposing that yoke upon others. Baptists are the one considerable religious body in the world, with three centuries of history behind them, who can claim to have been a non-persecuting people from first to last. Of martyr blood our hands are clean. We have never invoked the sword of temporal power to aid the sword of the Spirit. We have never passed an ordinance inflicting a civic disability on any man because of his religious views, be he Protestant or Papist, Jew or Turk or infidel. In this regard there is no blot on our escutcheon.

It has been in behalf of soul-liberty, primarily, that we have ever stood for

Separation of Church and State.

In our deep conviction, the union of these two institutions represents the most baneful misalliance of the ages. Whether the State be grafted upon the Church or the Church upon the State, the fruit therefrom is alike "Ate with impoisonment and stung with fire."

"One of the anomalies of history is that Protestants, coming out of the Roman Catholic Church, with loud complaints against her tyrannies, so speedily and so greedily copied and emulated her repressive measures." Over the whole field swept by, the Reformation movement Protestant State Churchism soon reigned supreme. Luther and Melancthon imposed it upon Germany; Zwingli and Calvin riveted it upon Switzerland; Knox and his associates fastened it upon Scotland; Thomas Cromwell and Henry the Eighth bound the accursed incubus upon the life of England, to which it clings relentlessly and oppressively until this day. At this very moment minions of the State Church, booted and spurred, are endeavouring to ride the Nonconformist conscience of England under the saddle of an unrighteous school law, in the hope of driving the lambs of Nonconformity into the fold of the Establishment. True, they do not find it easy going. Already they are pounding hard in the saddle. Unless all signs fail, saddle and riders will soon be in the ditch, while Nonconformity, a little sore perhaps, but still sturdy and fit, will be found keeping the middle of the road.

We who are delegates to this Congress from over the seas, desire to express the deep satisfaction we feel, in that, at this crisis, it has fallen to the English Baptists to give to Nonconformity its outstanding champion and acknowledged leader in the person of their own hero, prophet, and patriot, Dr. John Clifford. No cause could ask a more gallant and intrepid leader. No leader could command a more intense and absolute love-loyalty. In the year of grace 1905 John Clifford is the Prime Minister of England.

And what could be more fitting than that a Baptist should lead in such a cause as this? Baptists created the conscience of this country on the subject of soul-liberty. They wrought in advance of their age. As far back as 1611 they formulated the doctrine of non-magisterial interference in religious matters. The earliest work on soul-liberty published in the English language was issued by them in 1614. During the next fifty years so numerous were their publications on this subject that one of their bitterest opponents said, "The presses groan and sweat under the load." And all the while they fought a lonely fight. Their doctrine was sneered at as "a religious paradox" and "a raving delirium." It was execrated as "a pestilent error" and "a damnable heresy." But they faltered not. The constant Baptist witnessing fell like a steady rain upon the iron hills of State Church pride, and upon the rich wild tracts of a partially developed Nonconformity. Decade after decade, century after century, it has soaked this soil, until to-day a mighty river of intelligent, passionate, popular conviction in favour of absolute religious liberty rolls through this land. Upon that river all our ships some day shall ride, and by it all our fields be fertilised.

The brightest chapter of Baptist achievement has, however, been enacted, not in the Old World, but in the New. The old spirit of religious intolerance crossed the Atlantic in the *Mayflower*. The Pilgrim Fathers were no lambs fleeing from the slaughter. With them it was a question of whose ox was being gored. Their own ox had been gored long enough. They would provide him with a new pasture and an exclusive stamping-ground. But they had no thought of dehorning him in the interest of universal soul-liberty. The Puritans who settled the Massachusetts Bay colony in 1628 were another people, but of a similar spirit, and the two soon blended. Together they established, not a State Church so much as a Church State, in which citizenship was conditioned upon Church membership. There, then, for a season, was the spectacle of Congregationalism established by law, coercing all into conformity therewith, forbidding all dissent, and enforcing its prohibitions by penalties of disfranchisement, fine, imprisonment, scourging and banishment. But the monstrosity was short-lived. The mixture of iron and clay soon crumbled. By nothing was its downfall hastened so much as by the "passive resistance" of Baptists within the colony, and their constructive work beyond its bounds. In 1636 Roger Williams, fleeing from oppression in Massachusetts, settled Providence, and obtained a charter which provided that no person was to be in any wise molested, punished, or called in question for any religious opinion.

It may be remembered that Lord Baltimore, a Roman Catholic, under charter from Charles I., had in 1635 settled a colony in what is now known as Maryland, on what purported to be a basis of religious liberty, but it was liberty with a string to it, and a short string at that. It provided liberty for Christians only. In granting the charter Charles had expressly provided that members of the Church of England should be protected in the exercise of their religion. In 1649, at the instance of Lord Baltimore, to his credit be it said, equal security was guaranteed "to all believers in Jesus Christ." This was a great advance upon the Massachusetts situation, but how far it was from liberty of conscience may be seen by the proviso that "Whatsoever person shall blaspheme God, or shall deny, or shall reproach the Holy Trinity, or any of the three Persons thereof, shall be punished by death." In the Rhode Island Colony, however, there were no restrictions, and there, for the first time in the history of the world, was a civil government whose corner stone was absolute soul-liberty.

Bancroft, speaking of the part played by Roger Williams in the cause of liberty, writes thus: "At the time when Germany was desolated by the implacable wars of religion; when even Holland could not pacify vengeful sects; when France was still to go through the fearful struggle of bigotry; when England was gasping under the despotism of intolerance, almost half a century before William Penn became an American proprietary; and while Descartes was constructing modern philosophy on the method of free reflection, Roger Willimas asserted the great doctrine of intellectual liberty and made it the corner-stone of a political institution. . . . The principles which he first asserted amid the bickerings of a colonial parish, next sustained in the general Court of Massachusetts, and then introduced into the wilds of Narragansett Bay, he found occasion in 1644 to publish in England and to defend as the basis of the religious freedom of mankind; so that borrowing the language employed by his antagonists in derision, we may compare him to the lark, the pleasant bird of the peaceful summer, that, 'affecting to soar aloft, springs upward from the ground, takes his rise from pale to tree, and at last utters his clear carols through the skies of the morning." He was the first person in modern Christendom to establish civil government on the doctrine of the liberty of conscience, the equality of opinions before the law; and in its defence he was the harbinger of Milton, the precursor and the superior of Jeremy Taylor."

The time allotted to this paper will not permit me to further trace in detail the story of the struggle in the New World. Suffice it to say that owing to the lynx-eyed vigilance with which the Baptist people watched against the possibility of a State connection with the Church, the Constitution of the United States, as adopted in 1787, declared: "No religious test shall ever be required as a qualification to any office in the United States." Lest this should prove inadequate as a safeguard of liberty, it was amended, upon the petition of the Virginia Baptists, to read: "Congress shall make no law respecting an establishment of religion, or prohibiting the free exercise thereof." That is America's chiefest contribution to the art of government and the science of politics. It is, to a very large extent, a Baptist achievement.

The world must not be permitted to forget what the Baptist doctrine of soul-liberty, broadening into the conception of personal liberty and finding expression in the ordinances of civil liberty, has wrought for the political emancipation of mankind. "Individuality in relation to God and Christ and salvation, the Scriptures and judgment and eternity, conducts by an irresistible sequence to freedom of thought and speech and Press, to popular government, to unfettered scientific investigation, to universal education. Soul-liberty cannot be dissevered from civil freedom." All modern reforms in government, broadening from the few to the many, can be traced to the recognition more or less of this great principle.

No man ever appreciated this fact more fully than William Knibb, the Apostle of Jamaica, who carried the fiery cross of freedom through these British Islands, who applied the torch of his burning enthusiasm to the train which had been laid by Wilberforce, Clarkson, Buxton and Sharpe, that galaxy of British liberty-lovers, and blew up the whole abominable institution of slavery, making true the saying that is written, "Slaves cannot breathe the air of England."

The moment Knibb heard that the Reform Bill had passed the British House of Commons he exclaimed: "Now I will have slavery down'd; I will never rest day or night till I see it destroyed root and branch." As evidence that his opposition to slavery was the outcome of his interpretation of the great Commission, take this extract from his first speech in England after his return from Jamaica: "I daily and hourly feel that the questions of colonial slavery and of missions are now inseparably connected; that British Christians must either join with me in an attempt to break the chains with which the African is bound, or leave the work of mercy and the triumphs of the Redeemer unfinished, and abandon the simple and oppressed Christian slave to those whose tender mercies are cruelty." During this impassioned speech one of the cautious officials of the Baptist Missionary Society is stated to have pulled the tail of Knibb's coat by way of admonition, but Knibb went on: "Believing as I do that the African and Creole slave will never again enjoy the blessings of religious instruction or hear of the benefits of the Gospel, which Christ commanded to be preached among all nations, unless slavery be overthrown, I now stand forth as the unflinching and undaunted advocate of immediate emancipation, and if the friends of missions will not hear me, I hope the God of missions will. Having in His strength entered on this contest, I will never cease to plead for the people I love, till aided by British Christians and Afric's God, we wave the flag of liberty over departed colonial slavery, shout with melodious harmony its funeral dirge, and proclaim as we leave the spot in which we have entombed the greatest curse that has ever stained the annals of nations: 'Glory to God in the highest, and on earth peace, good-will towards men.' " This vow, registered in such dramatic fashion, was literally fulfilled in that memorable midnight celebration, when Knibb, attended by a multitude of emancipated blacks, digged a grave, flung into it the manacles and other symbols of hated slavery, now driven out for ever from under the British flag, and concluded the burial rite by singing the Gloria and Doxology, whose triumphant tones swept through the island with "melodious harmony."

That is but one example of the fruit which has ripened on the branches of our Baptist tree. The taste of it to-day is sweet on every tongue.

Stanzas from a little poem by Tennyson seem appropriate here.

> "Once in a golden hour
>   I cast to earth a seed,
> Up there came a flower,
>   The people said, a weed.

> "To and from they went
>   Through my garden bower,
> And muttering discontent,
>   Cursed me and my flower.

> "Then it grew so tall
>   It wore a crown of light,
> But thieves from o'er the wall
>   Stole the seed by night.

> "Sowed it far and wide,
>   By every town and tower,
> Till all the people cried,
>   'Splendid is the flower.'

> "Read my little fable:
>   He who runs may read,
> Most can grow the flowers now,
>   For all have got the seed."

We are glad they've got it. We rejoice to see the splendid passion flower of soul-liberty blossoming far and wide in the fields of modern thought, but we think our brethren of the sister denominations can afford to acknowledge that they found the seed in our Baptist garden.

I must hasten now to point out how our essential Baptist principle has made our place a place of witnessing in behalf of

A Spiritual Church.

By a "spiritual Church" we mean a Church responsive in all its members to the mind of Christ, and yielding personal, loyal obedience to His sovereign will.

Since the Church is Christ's body, membership in the Church should depend upon, follow and express a previous personal relation to Him as the incorporating and directing Head. To admit to the body those who are not joined to the Head by a living faith, is to commit a mischievous incongruity. Hence we cannot permit the State to say who shall be members in the Church. Caesar must not determine what belongs to God. Hence we dare not say with the Westminster Confession, that "the Church consists of all those throughout the world, who profess the true religion, *together with their children.*" We dare not baptize those who can give no sign that they have been born again. Baptism is the symbol of regeneration, and must be reserved for those who, in personal confession of His name, put on the Lord Jesus Christ.

This principle of a regenerated Church membership, more than anything else, marks our distinctiveness in the Christian world to-day. It is a matter of amazement to us to find ourselves noticed, not so much for insistence on the spirituality of the Church, as for the scrupulous observance of an appointed form. The latter is but incidental to our position; the former is of its very essence. If we stand for believers' baptism and no other, it is not simply because we think we have the better of our Paedobaptist brethren in a matter of exegesis, but because both logic and experience teach its importance as a safeguard to the Church from the intrusion of unregenerate life. If we hold to immersion it is because the Master chose that form as the symbol of that death and resurrection by which He achieved His sovereignty, as well as of that death to sin and resurrection to newness of life by which the believer comes under His sovereign sway. The purpose throughout is spiritual.

It is noteworthy that the practice of infant baptism is falling more and more into disuse among the evangelical denominations, while the old grounds for its administration have been largely surrendered. In the interests of a spiritual Church it should, we believe, be discontinued entirely, discarded as an outworn tradition, and shunned as a garment spotted by the flesh.

As I bring this paper toward conclusion, there are two other matters that I must touch upon, if ever so lightly and briefly. One is the place which our essential Baptist principle has given us in the great modern movement of

World Evangelisation.

The nineteenth century, with all its marvels, witnessed nothing more wonderful than the rise and spread of the Foreign Missionary movement. The spirit of that movement found its incarnation October 2, 1792, when twelve men of Baptist faith organised the first society of modern times for the avowed purpose of giving the Gospel to the heathen world. The little town of Kettering was the Bethlehem of this movement, while the collection of £13 2s. 6d., taken up in the parlour of Widow Wallis, provided the swaddling clothes in which they wrapped the holy child.

It was by no accident that this movement came of Baptist birth. World-evangelisation is a corollary to the doctrine of the Lordship of Christ. In William Carey the doctrine found a new interpretation and expression. By him it was clarified and restated in terms of the Great Commission. The older doctrine of Divine sovereignty had sterilised the Church. Hyper-Calvinism, running near to fatalism, had chilled evangelical enthusiasm. It had bidden the young manhood of the Church "sit down," declaring that when it pleased God to convert the heathen He would convert them without human help. From such a theological obscurantism, with its sad consequence of religious quietism, Carey brought deliverance. He gave the Church a new horizon, kindled within her a new light, created within her a new soul. Carey was no mere ecclesiastical mechanist, he was a great prophet and inspirationist. It was a new thought of God and of man that he gave to the world, or rather an old thought brought to newness of life. His contribution was splendidly revolutionary. It is with us still a thing of life and power and blessing. "Time cannot wither, nor custom stale the infinite variety" of its beneficence in the Christian Church at large. In the exaltation of her ideals, in the enlargement of her sympathies, in the intensification of her zeal, in the sanctification of her life, in the purification and simplification of her doctrine, the Christian Church owes more to William Carey and his mission than to any other man or movement since the days of Paul. Upon the trellis of the Foreign Mission enterprise the vine of the Church has run over the wall. It has given her, spiritually, a southern exposure, through which she has felt at her heart the thrill of a new vitality, while bearing on her outmost branches a burden of precious fruit for the vintage of the skies.

The last matter upon which I shall touch is closely allied with this— namely, our place of steadfast

Loyalty to the Authority of the Christian Scriptures.

The sovereignty of Christ and the supremacy of the New Testament as the rule of life are practically one doctrine. Whether we ground the authority of the New Testament in the fact that Christ gave it to us, or in the fact that it gives us the Christ, the result is the same. The Christian consciousness and the Christian Scriptures are not, and cannot be, with us, two separate sources of authority. They are one in Christ. The New Testament creates the Christian consciousness and appeals to the consciousness it creates. It also corrects the Christian consciousness and progressively justifies itself therein. Hence it is and ever must remain for us the word of final authority. It is the imperial sceptre of the Son of God. It has been said that the chiefest contribution of the Baptist people to the Christian Church has been her succession of great preachers. That would not be strange if true. The Baptist principle has continually driven our preachers in upon the Scriptures. Standing there they have felt the Rock of Ages beneath their feet. Standing there they have beheld the glory of the Lord. They have gazed upon the cross red with the blood of redemption. They have beheld the throne of God with the Lamb in the midst thereof. The Baptist preacher has never needed to go peeping cautiously about to see what other men were doing, or to put his ear to the ground to listen for the Word from human lips. It has been for him to hear what God the Lord would say and to speak the Word from His mouth. Hence through all the messages of our great preachers there has ever throbbed the deep, awful, gracious note of Calvary. Their testimony has been sown with the fire of the Holy Gospel, and it has filled all the Church with light.

With humble thankfulness we claim as ours John Bunyan, the immortal dreamer of Bedford Gaol; Christmas Evans, "the one-eyed man of Anglesea," and a prophet sent from God; Andrew Fuller, who held the rope with a giant's grip while Carey went down into the well; Charles Haddon Spurgeon, who in this city excercised the most fruitful ministry since apostolic times; and Alexander Maclaren, the prince of all expository preachers of any age or country, the incomparable stylist of the nineteenth-century pulpit, who has left a scroll of light about every text which he has touched, a poet in the garden of whose imagination the flowers have never ceased to bloom or the birds to sing, and who presides over this Congress to-day, a benediction to us all, honoured and beloved as the grand old man of the Baptist Brotherhood of the world.

Fathers and brethren, the place of Baptists in the Church of the future is destined to be a larger place than we have yet achieved. The world has not outgrown the need of Baptist principles. It was never in greater need of them than it is to-day. Our principles have not yet manifested the full force that is in them. New light and power are to break forth from them in the days to come. Loose them and let them go. They have in them, through the quickening of the sense of personal answerableness to Christ, the power to sanctify the family and make the home a place of richer spiritual culture. They have in them the power to secure for the Church a more intelligent, comprehensive, and universal consecration of her members. They have in them the power to mitigate the antagonisms of commercial life. Setting before capitalist and tradesman alike the higher standards that necessarily accompany the sense of personal responsibility to Christ, they will go far to break the tyranny of both combined capital and organised labour. They have in them the promise of succour and deliverance for millions who now groan under the oppressions of the autocratic Governments of the world. In a word, they bid each man who lives under the blue sky to stand upon his feet and hearken to his Lord and Master, Jesus Christ, and go with Him up to the heights of noblest manhood.

May God make us worthy of the trust committed to our hands. May we prove the divinity of our principles by the increasing splendour of our achievements. May we be good soldiers of Jesus Christ and strong helpers of mankind. Then, when the day is done, we shall have a royal diadem to cast at Jesus' feet. Our principles with our achievements we shall weave into a crown. As jewels for that crown we shall gather all the names that have shone starlike and clear in the galaxy of Baptist history, and with a joy unspeakable and full of glory we shall raise all our voices to "Hail the power of Jesus' name" and lift all our hands to "Crown Him Lord of All."

2
Philadelphia
1911

Introduction

John Clifford (1836-1923) dominated British Baptist life in the first quarter of the twentieth century. After you read his BWA presidential sermon of 1911, which he gave at age 75, you will understand why. Only the title of the sermon—"The Baptist World Alliance: Its Origin and Character, Meaning and Word"—is wooden and prosaic. The sermon itself pulsates with passion, revealing a razor-edged intellect, a tender conscience, and a loving spirit, all immersed in the relevance and profundity of Baptist ideas and ideals. Few Baptists can read it without a new appreciation for their denominational heritage. When he concluded the sermon, "the audience broke into prolonged applause and cheers." Joshua Levering responded to the sermon by admonishing the preachers present to "forget your own sermons and go to your people and read it."

One of the distinctives of Baptists has been their understanding of the ordinances. In Philadelphia, A. T. Robertson (1863-1934), who taught New Testament at The Southern Baptist Theological Seminary for forty-four years, preached a sermon indicating the Baptist interpretation of the ordinances. Insisting that Baptists "are the champions par excellence of spiritual Christianity," Robertson pointed out that Baptists have avoided both "over-emphasis and indifference" in relation to baptism and the Lord's Supper.

The Baptist World Alliance: Its Origin and Character, Meaning and Work
John Clifford

Dear Brethren and Friends:

I cannot enter upon the duties of this office without first of all thanking you with all my heart for the honor you have conferred upon me. Frankly,

I must say, it was one of the great surprises of my life when the Baptist World Congress held in London in 1905, elected me to the Presidency of this newly created Alliance. In the natural order of things the chairman to succeed our revered and most illustrious chief, Dr. Alexander MacLaren, should have been chosen from amongst our brethren of the Great Republic of the West. But in the overflow of your generous confidence you called me to this position, and thereby gave me the high privilege and sacred responsibility of presiding over this, our Second World Congress; and now with a gratitude too deep for words for that election, and for the trust reposed in me during the six years I have held this post, I cast myself upon your assured sympathy and brotherly love.

Dear Friends:

We meet in the name and by the grace of the Lord Jesus Christ our Saviour. We are cheered by His promised presence and the conscious leadership of His Spirit. Our fellowship is with the Father and with the Son, and we gladly add, with millions of our Baptist brethren scattered throughout the whole world. We are only a few gathered in this City of Brotherly Love; but we represent, and at this hour, are associated with, multitudes in confession and yearning, in aspiration and effort for the coming of the Kingdom of God and the coronation of the King of kings. For this is not only the week of our assembling, but it is also, and this is our first thought, a week of universal prayer in our homes and churches;— truly a great week; perhaps the greatest week in the experience of our Baptist brotherhood. Never before have we so thoroughly realized our essential unity. Never before has there been such a strong sense of comradeship, linking together the workers in the crowded towns and cities with the lonely souls who have ascended to the heights of faith, resolved to keep the exposed fortresses of truth in the villages and hamlets of the world, in face of fiercest attack, and in scorn of all consequences. It is a quickening atmosphere we breathe; charged with the radiant energy of devotion, of dependence upon God, of faith in the might of the gospel, of invincible fidelity to the principles by which we are compacted together. "This is none other but the house of God, and this is the gate of heaven."

Nor is that all. "A great cloud of witnesses holds us in full survey." We stand in their presence. "Part of the host has crossed the flood." We are grateful for their service and rejoice in the splendid heritage they have bequeathed to us. And "part is crossing now." Fellow-pilgrims on in front, under the lead of the Captain of our salvation have only just passed out of sight, their warfare accomplished; their reward secure. But there is also a glorious company of men and women who join us through these memorable days in thankful commemoration of our brave forefathers, in glowing sympathy with the heroic sufferers for conscience' sake in distant lands, in exposition of the principles of which we are trustees, and above all, in prayer that our God will bless us, and increase us yet more and more; that He will lead us in His way, and fit us for doing His work in the years immediately before us,—so that this Congress may issue in the salvation of our fellows, the shaping of the future course of our churches, and the advancement of the kingdom of righteousness and peace and joy in the Holy Ghost.

I.

And now, my brethren, the one subject your President cannot escape from, on this, the first occasion of our meeting as an Alliance, is THE A LLIANCE ITSELF, ITS CREATION AND CHARACTER, ITS MEANING AND WORK. For this is really our first meeting as an Alliance. Our Constitution was formed in London in 1905. A series of inspiring and most helpful meetings of the European churches followed three years afterwards in the city of Berlin, but those gatherings were local in their representation, although of universal interest and influence. This, therefore, is the beginning of the public work of the Alliance, and the manifestation of the latest phase of our Baptist life.

The novelty of this organization is surprising, partly because it appears in a people delivered over, body and soul, to individualism, and in mortal terror of the slightest invasion of their personal and ecclesiastical independence; and yet to others, who have grasped the intrinsic catholicity of our fundamental principles, it is astonishing that we have been so long arriving at the present stage of our development.

For although this Alliance is a new creation, it is really the outward and visible sign of an inward and spiritual grace that has been working within us, with special energy and vitality, during the last ten or fifteen years; and witnesses to magnetic and cohesive forces operating, though latent, and powerful though silent. It is not that we have made any new discovery, or surrendered any long-cherished truths, or forsaken any primary aims, or found any new basis of agreement;—not at all; it is simply that the consciousness of the universal sweep of our ideas and ideals has become more vivid, and the conditions favorable for their expression have at last arrived. Deep in the soul of us has always dwelt the conviction that we are the possessors of a genuinely universal religion; although it has only found voice here and there. For the most part we have not known one another. We have been like members of a family who, instead of growing up under the same roof-tree, have rarely met, and have not infrequently misunderstood one another when they did meet, and therefore we have misjudged and misrepresented one another's opinions and practices. The churches have been isolated. Many of them have been beaten back into remote corners of the earth in their incessant conflicts with priestly assumptions and clerical oppressions; so that a World Alliance was as impossible fifty years ago as was a treaty for the settlement of all international disputes, without any exception whatever, at the same date.

But a new day has dawned. The barriers are broken down. The post and the press, the telegraph and the telephone, the rail and the steamboat unite us. St. Petersburg finds itself in Philadelphia, though with difficulty enough to remind us that the sons and daughters of freedom have not finished their work. Swedes and Norwegians join hands with New Zealanders and Victorians. Frenchmen and Germans exult in their brotherhood in Christ, and yearn for the day when their countries will not teach war any more. Spain and Italy converse with the ancient Latin races from Central America, and the Britisher rejoices to find himself by the side of the emancipated representatives from Georgia and Carolina. So we come together! So our Alliance is *possible.* Moulded under different conditions, dwelling under different flags, trained in different climes and by different teachers with different methods, we come together rejoicing, that in the new nature, we have received through the grace of God, there is neither Greek nor Jew, Englishman nor American, black nor white, bond nor free, but that all are one in Christ, and Christ is all in each and in all.

Speaking of the United States, Mr. Bryce says: "America is a commonwealth of commonwealths, a republic of republics, a State which, while one, is nevertheless composed of other States even more essential to its existence than it is to theirs." So this Congress is an Alliance of other alliances, civic, county, colonial, and national; a union of representatives of churches which has its strength in the individual churches represented, and which are immeasurably more to the Alliance than the Alliance can possibly be to them.

Yet the appearance of this Alliance is a fact full of promise, the embodiment of ideas and forces operating over vast areas of Baptist life, and prophetic of the place we have to take in the leadership of the religious life of mankind. It could not well have come earlier. It has come now; and we hail it as the morning star of a new day, the first flower of a new spring, the opening of a new epoch in our history.

II.

What is new is that this is a *World* Alliance of Baptists. We have other unions; but they are restricted. This is all embracing. They unite two or three churches in a locality, a hundred in a county, or thousands in a nation; this represents all, and is really and not factitiously ecumenical.

It is not our immense numbers that creates this union; though we must have more than eight millions of registered members, and a host of adherents; nor is it by the authority of persons that we meet, as of a Pope claiming infallibility, or a body of Patriarchs compelling our appearance; nor is it again, in obedience to the mandate of a church, or the action of the machinery of the State. Our cohesiveness is due to our ideas. They bind us together. They are our driving and inspiring force. They are the founts of our power; the well-springs of our life, the stars that shine in the over-arching sky of our life, the suns that feed and uphold our life. Carlyle says: "Every society, every polity, has a spiritual principle; is the embodiment, tentative and more or less complete, of an ideal; all its tendencies of endeavor, specialties of custom, its laws, politics and whole procedure, are prescribed by an idea, and flow naturally from it as movements from the living source of motion. This idea, be it of devotion to a man or class of men, to a creed, to an institution, or even, as in more ancient times, to a piece of land, is ever a true loyalty; has in it something of a religious, paramount, quite infinite character; it is properly the soul of the State, its life; mysterious as other forms of life, and like these working secretly, and in a depth beyond that of consciousness." Cardinal Manning declared "ideas are the life of institutions," and Stade tells us that "the history of Israel is essentially a history of religious ideas." So the ecumenical character of this Alliance is derived from its central and formative ideas; not from one, or from two in their separateness; but from the whole body judged as a coherent and compact whole; this completing and balancing that; and the entire combination receiving that accentuation and emphasis which secures for each principle its full place and legitimate action,— their "various parts closely fitting and firmly adhering to one another," grows by the aid of every contributory link, with power proportioned to the need of each part, so as to clothe the Alliance with the attributes and functions of a universal Council.

Indeed, I claim for this Alliance that it is "catholic" with a wider catholicism than that of Rome, and "orthodox" with an orthodoxy more spiritual and biblical than that of the Eastern Church. The Council of Nice, for example, held in the year 325, was a meeting of the Catholic Episcopate. We recognize no distinction of clergy and laity,—for all believers are in the judgment of Peter, God's clergy. That Council owed its initiation to Constantine, and was mainly an attempt to pacify the State through the Church, by an imperial ruler. Our impulse comes from a common faith, working by a common love, producing a common service, and issuing in a common joy. The Nicene Creed, which makes the Nicene Council famous, was adopted in compliance with an Emperor's appeals, and penalties were imposed by him on those who refused to subscribe. No creed will be propounded by us, and yet we are far more united in the faith of the gospel than were the fathers at Nice. Only eight, or according to some authorities, not more than five out of the 318 bishops of that Council came from the West; to-day we are come glad and happy from all over the earth to share in a Pentecostal fellowship based on spiritual ideas and principles more truly universal than, any of those of the older times.

III.

But this organization is a World Alliance of *Baptists,* and that means that the catholic principles on which we base ourselves we derive straight from Jesus, are accepted on His authority, and involve in all who accept them total subjection of soul to His gracious and benignant rule. He is Lord of all, and He only is Lord of all. Our conception of Christ's authority is exclusive. We refuse to everybody and everything the slightest share in it. It is absolute, unlimited, indefeasible, admits of no question, and allows no equal. The right to rule in the religious life is in Him and in no other. In no other, be he as saintly as St. Francis, as devout as St. Bernard, as loving as John, or as practical as Paul; not in any offices, papal, episcopal, or ministerial; not in tradition, though it may interpret the goings of the Spirit of God, and illustrate the effects of obedience and disobedience; not in the Old Testament nor yet in the New, though their working values are great since they enable us to know His mind, understand His laws of conduct, and partake more freely of His spirit; not in the long annals of the life of the church; or the agreement of "the whole church" at one special moment; yet we welcome the illumination church history affords of His administration of the social life of His people, of its aim and spirit; of its difficulties and hindrances, and of the sufficiency of His grace. Jesus Christ holds the first place and the last. His word is final. His rule is supreme.

In short, the deepest impulse of Baptist life has been the upholding of the sole and exclusive authority of Christ Jesus against all possible encroachment from churches, from sections of churches, from the whole church at any special moment of its life and action, as in a Council, from the traditions of the elders, from the exegesis of scholars, and from the interesting but needless theories of philosophers. It is the momentum of that one cardinal idea which has swept us along to our present position.

And now it follows upon that, that the ideas to which we give witness root themselves, first in the teaching of the New Testament, and secondly in the soul's experience of Christ.

In our modern form as Baptists we date from 1611, and that is, from the same year as the Authorized Version of the Scriptures. This year is the ter-centenary of the first promulgation of the principles on which we build as societies as well as of the appearing of that version of the Bible which King George the Fifth describes as "the first of our national treasures."

This synchronism is suggestive. For as a matter of fact the relation of the two events is vital and not accidental. It is contemporaneity of source, like that of twins, and not mere juxta-position like that of pebbles jostling one another on a beach. The two events are related as fruits on the same tree, as flowers of the same early spring, as effects of the same energy, and lights proceeding from the same central sun. The God who inspired Bezaleel the artist of the tabernacle, also inspired William Tyndale to give the Bible to the ploughboy and peasant in the language they could understand and feel; and not less I claim did the same divine inspiration lead John Smith, Thomas Helwisse, and Leonard Busher to discover and promulgate the doctrine of the right of the human soul to freedom from the dictation of the civil magistrate in matters of religion. The first gave us the Bible; the second won for us an open road to it; that illumined the mind, this set free the conscience to follow its illumination; the new version dissipated the gloom and drove away the night, the new teaching shook and shattered to pieces the monopoly of a sacerdotal caste, and gave liberty to the soul of man. The translators in that supreme moment of the liberation of England, sent out a rendering of the Word of God in language so beautifully simple, so matchless in its cadences and majestic in its music, that it has taken its place as one of the foremost factors in our religious development: acted as a strong bond of union amongst all English-speaking peoples, and an inspiration to the service of mankind. On the other hand, the Pilgrims from Holland, by the same spirit, enriched the ages by telling out the four supreme lessons they had learnt in their exile, to the effect that "(1) In matters of religion there should be absolute liberty. (2) The Church of Christ is a company of the faithful. (3) Baptism as an initial rite of the Church should be administered only on a profession of faith, and (4) Every community of believers is autonomous, —subject only to the headship of Christ." Those two mighty forces were necessary to each other; factors working together for the same ends, for perfecting the work of the Reformation, breaking up feudalism, quickening inquiry, rousing zeal for right and truth, effecting the exodus of the Church from the Goshen in which it was enslaved, and in short making our modern world. It is scarcely too much to say that as without the Bible we should have had no Puritans or Separatists or Pilgrim Fathers, so without the Baptist doctrine that magistrates "must leave the Christian religion free to every man's conscience because Christ only is King and Lawgiver of the Church and conscience," Britain would still have been a prison for all Baptists,—as it is occasionally now for some of them, Rhode Island would not have been founded, and this vast democratic Republic would have been waiting to see the light.

In this assembly therefore we hail this commemorative year on both grounds; for our fathers were advocates of freedom because they were men of the Book. The Bible made them as it has made us. It is our only creed, as it was theirs. They were nourished on the pure milk of the Word, as we are still. They found their charter of freedom in Christ, whose unique figure they beheld in its pages, and so have we. For the statutes of their pilgrimage they turned to Him, and made it their business to study and expound them, and that this is still our spiritual instinct and habit is attested by the fact that the two greatest preachers of the last century were Biblicists and Baptists: for Dr. Hastings says that Mac-Laren's "Exposition of Holy Scripture" is the most gigantic feat of sermon making accomplished by any single man in modern times, with the exception of Spurgeon's "Metropolitan Tabernacle Pulpit." And he adds: "It is noticeable that he also was a Baptist. What is the secret?" he inquires; and his answer is: "It is simply fidelity to the written Word. It is simply the fact that both Spurgeon and MacLaren were expositors."

IV.

Another cord binding us together in an indissoluble spiritual union, and clothing this Alliance with a true catholicity is our unswerving maintenance of an exclusively regenerated church-membership. We are as I have said men of the Book, not of its letter, but of its spirit, and of the Spirit who inspired the men who wrote it. We hold to the Christ of history, and of doctrine, but also to Christ in the soul, new light for the conscience, new energy for the will, a new interpretation of life, and a new outlook for the future, and we make that spiritual experience the basis of our free and voluntary association as churches. On spiritual experience we build; not on creeds; but on "conversion," "a change of heart," the awakening of the soul to God in Christ; regeneration by the Holy Ghost, a conscious possession of the mind and spirit of Jesus, a will surrendered to God, a life dedicated to His service. We say with John Smith, that "no part of saving righteousness consists in outward ceremonies" and inculcate with Paul, "that circumcision is nothing, and uncircumcision is nothing," but "faith which worketh by love," "keeping the commandments of God," becoming a "new creation in Christ"; that is all in all.

Therefore we preach "soul liberty," and contend against all comers that the spirit of man has the privilege of direct conscious relation to God in Christ and through Christ. Nothing may come between the soul and God. Not the priest, whatever his claims; he will cloud the vision of Christ, and put a fetter on the soul's freedom; not the theologian; he may help, if he keeps his true place; but he may check individual search for truth and emasculate the man; not even the church, for it may wrap the spirit in conventions, and tie it up with red tape; not the State, it will imprison energy and check growth. The soul must be free. All the Lord's people are potential prophets and liberty is the vital breath of prophecy. To every one is given the spirit to do good with; and the first law of the spirit is that there must be no quenching of its fires. Grace is free from first to last, i. e., God is free in His advent to the soul and His work within, to redeem it, to renew it, to raise it to the heights of moral energy, and fashion it after his likeness. Freedom is inherent in the very conception of the spiritual life, and therefore there must be "ample room and verge enough" within the territories of the Church for the full expression of an eager, intense, and sanctified individualism.

We know our insistence upon freedom has its risks: but they may be avoided; whereas the stagnation and death that follow the enslavement of the human soul are inevitable. We know our distrust of over-organization, and mortal dread of machinery has deprived us of speedy successes and blocked rapid advance: but it has given free course to personality and, at last, men are learning that personality is the one thing needful and that the best made machinery cannot do the work of souls in which the Spirit of God has free play.

A friend writes to me saying: "It is a very great thing for Baptists to be joined together to help and encourage those of like faith in the maintenance of their convictions under the stress of governments and authorities which personally I think I should find it very difficult to withstand, certainly impossible for me if I could not 'endure as seeing Him who is invisible.' But I hope that the Baptist World Alliance may never become a 'Catholic' Baptist 'Council,' to dominate the *expression* of faith and ultimately to follow the other Councils, and establish a Baptist 'Papacy.' I fear that my reading of the signs of the time is that *authority* in all the phases of life is supplanting soul liberty—whilst it is soul liberty and soul intelligence we all need." Of all the churches we have least to fear in that direction.

There is no need for anxiety. The complete autonomy of the separate church is a creation of grace, and will not suffer. Each society will insist on maintaining its independence, but it will more and more exercise it so as to secure the good of the whole brotherhood, and the solid advance of the kingdom of God. The glorious liberty of the sons of God will not be impaired. The free man will be free; but he will use his liberty to further the wider aims of the voluntary association of believers to which he belongs, and for co-operation in the common service of men. The fact is, the irrepressible human soul, fed on the liberty-giving word of God, and strengthened with the free grace of God, will and must assert itself. The personal is the real. The soul is the man; the real man, and filled and fired by the Spirit of God it is like radium. It burns on and on, and still abides. It gives out its light, and remains unexhausted, insuppressible by hierarchies and oligarchies, and the whole tribe of oppressors. It may be trusted to assert its rights, that is to say, the grace of God within the soul, working there by His infinite love will follow the guidance of His indwelling Spirit into all truth and service, and discover in subjection to Christ

Jesus, the Lord; not only his fullest liberty, but also an inspiration to the suppression of the selfish self, and an encouragement to add, along with faith, a noble and manly character, and to a noble character, knowledge; to knowledge, self-control; along with self-control, power of endurance, and along with power of endurance, godliness, and to godliness, brotherly affection; and to brotherly affection, love.

V.

In speaking of the *work* of this Alliance it is important, at the outset, to recall the limitations imposed upon us by our ecumenical character. From sheer necessity we are not competent to judge one another's local work with accuracy. We lack sufficient data. We miss the special point of view. We are too far apart and we have the enormous difficulty of the "personal equation." Britishers do not know the United States and yet some of them do not hesitate from passing sentence upon the American churches, stating their problems, and showing how they could be solved, even though they have only had the opportunity of paying a flying visit to these climes; and they do it apparently unaware that their verdicts are no more than thinly disguised assertions of their own prejudices and presuppositions. Nor can Americans estimate the weight of the social pressure on Baptists in England, and the enormous resistance we have to overcome in following the light we see. You do not see the diminished returns in the till of the village shop, and the persecution in the village streets consequent upon State patronage and support of one particular church. To know that you must get into touch with our village churches as I have done for more than fifty years.

Physicians tell us there are no climatal diseases now. They are gone, or rapidly going. They used to say that diseases were tropical or subtropical, and designate certain geographical areas as the homes of cholera, malaria, sleeping sickness, and yellow fever. Now, it is found that these diseases are in all latitudes, and that the question is not *where* you are; but in what hygienic conditions you are living. No doubt it is so; and it is some advantage to know that "climate" is only one of the possible contributory causes of disease, and that the whole set of conditions must be dealt with in order to eradicate the disease. So the conditions under which principles have to be wrought into the life of the world differ immensely, and we are bound to take them into account. In one zone the disciple of Christ is perfectly immune from the microbes of despotism and intolerance; in another they infest everything he touches and nearly all that he is. England offers temptations of incredible strength to avoid our churches, or to leave them if you have become attached to them. Our law, for example, penalizes the citizen seeking to enter into or to rise higher in the ranks of State School Teachers, if he is a Baptist. In Hungary our churches cannot own, hold and administer property except on terms that fetter their free action as Christian communities. But in our Australian Colonies, and in your free Commonwealth such difficulties do not occur, or if they do arise, it is in a most attenuated form.

These and similar facts must of necessity shape the character and determine the contents of the advice given with regard to specially local conditions, and compel us to move on high and broad planes opened out to us by the historic and universal principles of the gospel of Christ on which the Alliance is built. These it is our business to maintain in their integrity and propagate with zeal, generosity, and self-sacrifice; so that we may carry them, at the earliest possible hour, to their pre-destined place in the whole religious life of mankind.

Our all-inclusive work is that of bringing in the kingdom of our God and of His Christ. That one thing we must do. It is for that we have been laid hold of by Christ, and called by His grace. We have a gospel for the world. We begin at the cross, not at the baptistery. God has sent us to preach the gospel, not to baptize men in platoons or in their unwitting infancy. We have to mediate the truth to men that the power at the back of all things is the Eternal Father, eager to enter into a direct and conscious relation with them through His Son Jesus. We preach Christ and Christ crucified. We stand at the cross, see Jesus in the awful light of Gethsemane and Calvary, "as the propitiation of our sins, and not for ours only." "Not for ours only." There is nothing limited or partial in the love of God. It sweeps the human race within its embrace. God Himself commends His love towards us, in that whilst we were yet sinners Christ died for us. "Not for ours only, but for the sins of the whole world." With one hand on the cross, we reach out with the other to the circumference of the human race. We are therefore missionary. We do not keep silence. We cannot. We have to tell all men of the Father's love and grace; that God was in Christ reconciling the world unto Himself, not imputing to men their trespasses. Necessity is laid upon us. We are debtors to all men. Whether we be beside ourselves, it is God, or whether we be sober, it is for the cause of man. For the love of Christ constraineth us, for we judge that He died for all, that we who live should not live unto ourselves, but unto Him who died for us and rose again.

It is a source of unfailing joy to us to feel that this our primary work links us with the holy church throughout the world, relates us to every believer in Jesus, in any church or in none; makes us one with the self-forgetting missionaries of all societies who hazard their lives for the sake of the gospel of Christ; and yet in our witness on behalf of the simplicity and purity, fulness and sufficiency of the salvation offered to men in Christ, we have to repeat and maintain the protest our fathers started against all the corruptions of Christianity. Everywhere we repudiate the teaching that entrance into a visible church is either salvation in itself or a condition of receiving it. If men would only believe it, our emphatic witness as to the place of baptism is entirely due to our antagonism to the notion that sacraments have any saving efficacy, and that the so-called "developments" of the "Germ" of original Christianity are at variance with the teaching of the New Testament, contradict Peter and John and Paul, cloud the vision of God, check the free outflow of the Divine mercy, debase the religious ideal, lower morals, add to the power of the priests, and derogate from the authority and glory of the Redeemer of men.

Everybody knows that this protest involved separation from other churches at the first, but does it necessitate separation still? and separation at a time when the forces making for ecclesiastical federation and unity are working with unprecedented strength?

First, this must not be doubted, that we rejoice in the efforts now being made on behalf of unity of the followers of Jesus Christ, and gladly co-operate with these endeavors. We crave it. We pray for it. We should hold ourselves guilty if we created or upheld any ecclesiastical division on mere technicalities of the faith or on insignificant details of the practice of churches. We endeavor to keep the unity of the Spirit in the bonds of peace.

But with equal frankness we say that a visible, formal, and mechanical unity has no charm for us whatever. It is not the unity Jesus prayed for; nor is it the unity that increases spiritual efficiency, augments righteousness, or advances the Kingdom of God. Nor can we forget that the welding of the churches together by bands of State gold mostly leads to slavery and not freedom, to subserviency and not manliness, to stagnation and not life. As to the unity of Rome, the unity of an ecclesiastical empire rigidly ordered under one priest as emperor, history has judged it, and condemned it, out and out. We distinctly disavow any hankering after a world-wide unity of organization on the platform of that of the Seven Hills, on the one hand, or that of Moscow on the other, confident that it would suffocate originality of thought, block boldness of initiative, quench enthusiasm and fetter souls in what ought to be the very citadel, and best defence, of freedom. Unity of life, of love, and of governing ideas and ideals, let us have by all means, but unity of "order," of "machinery" or of "creed," is not in keeping with the "unity in diversity" either of Nature or of Grace.

Besides it avails nothing to make light of the fact that we do not think as Christendom thinks on the vital elements of Christianity. The great historic churches are against us: the Roman Catholic, the Eastern, the Anglican, and some other communions; and against us on subjects that go to the uttermost depths of the soul of the gospel of Christ; and therefore "Separation" is one of the inevitable conditions of faithfulness to our experience of the grace of God, to our interpretation of the claims of Jesus Christ, and to the principles He has given as the ground and sphere of our collective life. It cannot be helped. We accept the isolation, and all the penalties it involves.

For it is most unthankful work. It means sacrifice; it shuts us out of alliances we would gladly join, and excludes us from circles of rare exhilaration and charm, but it is useful as well as necessary. Christianity owes its continuance amongst men to the insuppressible race of protesters. It would have remained in the swaddling bands of Judaism, and been cradled as a Jewish sect, if the Spirit of God had not pushed Peter into the protesting line. Nor would it have become in the first century a universal religion, had not that matchless statesman, the Apostle Paul, vigorously resisted all the traditional and conventional defenders of the racial and sectarian religion. "In Tertullian's century there seemed some prospect that every characteristic feature of the gospel would be so 're-stated' as to leave the gospel entirely indistinguishable from any other eclectic system of the moment." But Tertullian would have none of it. His protest was strong and clear. "Let them look to it," he said, "who have produced a Stoic and Platonic and dialectic Christianity. We need no curiosity who have Jesus Christ; no inquiry who have the gospel." The Lollards were protestants. John Huss, and John Wycliffe, could only save the gospel by exposing the falsehoods under which it was buried. Luther burning the Pope's bull, which was the chief expression of the current Christianity, is a dramatic demonstration of the way he made room for the saving truths of the Reformation. Robert Browne left the church, and "without tarrying for any" gave an impact to the reforming movement which it never lost. Bishop Hall wrote to Robinson, the Pilgrim Father: "There is no remedy. You must go forward to Anabaptism, or come back to us. . . . He (and the Bishop is speaking of our John Smith), tells you true; your station is unsafe." It was unsafe, and so they left it in order to give security to the truth of the gospel of God. Hitherto it has been the only way of keeping the soul of Christianity alive. There is no other effective method. Puritanism endeavored to dispense with it. Separation seemed harsh and hard. It wore the garb of self-assertion. It exposed to censure. It looked like schism; but it was the only way to escape a creeping paralysis followed by death. The Evangelicals in the Anglican Church tried it. Hating Rome and battling against it, they remained in the Protestant Church under the terms of the compromise effected between Rome and Geneva in the days of Queen Elizabeth. They were Protestants, and wished the church to be Protestant in reality as well as in name. They saw the truth of Bagehot's declaration that "the articles of the Church of England were less a compromise than an equivocation. . . . A formula on which two parties could unite and go their separate ways under an appearance of unity"; but they believed they could purify the Church of England by staying in it; but the result after 300 years is that the Roman elements are more definitely paramount than at any time since the reign of Queen Mary. The Separatists felt they could do little or nothing from within, and therefore they came out, and followed the churches of the New Testament as the model of the new society they created. Wakeman, in his "History of Religion in England," uses this significant expression as to the origin of the Free Churches: "When men became *really* instead of decorously religious, they broke away from the established order and sought the realization of their deeper faith in the organization of a more primitive type." It was separation for the sake of life and usefulness.

Hence, for generations to come, eager as we are for the unity of all believers in Christ, and resolved to remove wherever we can the grounds and causes of division, yet necessity is laid upon us, "to go forward to Anabaptism" as Bishop Hall said, and not to go back to any other church. We have to lift up our voice against that capital error of Christendom, that source of immeasurable damage to the gospel and to souls, the magical interpretation of baptism and the Lord's Supper, the treatment of the baptism of the babe as obedience to the will of the Lord Jesus, as expressed in the New Testament and as a way of salvation. We must stand aloof from it. We can have no part or lot in it. In a word, we must be in a position to give a full, clear, unconfused witness to the cardinal principles of our faith and life.

Again, we have not only to contend earnestly for the faith once for all delivered to the saints, and forming the old gospel and for the pure gospel, stripped free of the accretions of the ages; but if we are to be true to the earliest Christianity of all, and to the spirit and work of the creators of our Modern Baptist denomination, we must also advocate and work for the *Social Gospel.*

The Acts of the Apostles give evidence of the arrival of a new social ideal and impulse in the Christianity of Christ. That is admitted. Nor is it to be questioned that as early as 1527, the Anabaptists were promulgating their revolutionary ideas, demanding liberty for all men in matters of religion, applying the law of Christ to every relation of life, and specially to the ordering of the affairs of States. Strong as they were as individualists, they were by the force of the same principles, collectivists or socialists, and socialists in a hurry being nearly three centuries before their time; and therefore they had to suffer accordingly. It was natural, if premature and unexpected, for Baptist ideas carry us with tremendous momentum to the side of the "common man," as a son of God, as our brother, of value in himself incomputable and of possibilities measureless; with rights that must be defended for the sake of duties that must be done; possessed of claims on the collective resources and activities of society that must be conceded for the sake of the brotherhood of man and the Kingdom of God.

"Liberty, equality, and fraternity" were in the heart of the Baptist faith. The deliverance of the poor out of the hand of the evil-doers becomes a primary duty when you once really accept Christ's estimate of the worth of man. Poverty must be dealt with in its *causes*. Charity must not be accepted as a substitute for Justice. Justice must limit the range of charity, and leave no room for it that justice ought to fill. Social misery must be extinguished; unjust laws must be repealed. The men who have been "flattened out" by the long tramp of misery, must be rescued, healed, strengthened and set on their own feet. Whoever touches these social problems with a timorous hand, we assuredly must grip them firmly and courageously and persistently, and attempt their solution or be traitors to that word of the Lord by which we live.

We are held by the most sacred bonds to seek the fullest realization of universal brotherhood. To us war is a crime, and the promotion of international peace one of our foremost duties. The duel of nations must disappear in this century as the duel of individuals in the English-speaking countries, disappeared in the nineteenth. No doubt there are discouraging and reactionary appearances, but we must feed the deep and hidden currents of the world's life so steadily setting towards peace. In the increasing complexity of modern life we have to fight against all the encroachments of might on the rights of the weak, against commercial and social, military and ecclesiastical systems linked together for the defence of wrong. We must break them up, and prepare them for the fire in which all that injures man, God's child, and stands in the way of his redemption and total regeneration, shall be consumed.

Man must be free to work out his own salvation, to realize himself, and to enthrone God in Christ, in the whole life of mankind.

VI.

And now standing upon this eminence, let us ask what is the outlook for the Baptist people all over the earth? What is the position likely to be assigned to us in leading and shaping the religious life of mankind?

To answer that question we need ask first, towards what sea are the deeper currents of thought and action in modern civilization setting? What is the "stream of tendency" amongst the progressive peoples? Is it with our principles or against them?

The reply is unequivocal and complete.

Protestantism is to the fore. The races leading the life of the world are either distinctively Protestant, as in Britain and the United States or they are effectively using Protestant ideas as weapons against Roman Catholicism as in France and Spain. "The Dissidence of Dissent" holds the field, if not in form, in fact. Modernism is sapping Rome in its strongholds, as in Italy and Austria. Those who know Romanism most intimately are ashamed of its morals, rebel against its tyranny of the intellect, are indignant with its interdict upon united social service, and resent its treatment of leaders in science, philosophy, and religion. In Germany and in England and in some of our colonies, gigantic efforts are being made to capture the Teuton and the Saxon, but the successes they have secured are, neither in character nor number, such as to invalidate the conclusion that Protestantism is one of the chief factors moulding the coming generations of men.

The leaven of teaching concerning the intervention of the magistrate in religious affairs cast by John Smith and Roger Williams into the three measures of human meal in Holland and England and America, has been doing its work. The United States has established forever the doctrine of the neutrality of the State towards all Christian societies. France has cut the concordat in twain, and State and Church are free of each other. Portugal is doing the same this year. Welsh Disestablishment is at the doors. And though England, as usual, lags behind, yet both within and without the Anglican Church the conviction that separation is just, gains strength, and all that is wanted is the opportunity to translate the conviction into legislative deed.

In like manner the reflective forces of the age make against an exclusive and aggressive priestism. Indeed, it has received its sentence of death, and is only waiting for the executioner. It has to go. A professor trained in the higher ranges of the Anglican Church says: "A revival of any form of sacerdotal Christianity would be an appalling calamity to the human race." In the nature of things that revival cannot come. Never was the proportion of thinking men so large as now. Personality becomes more and more every day, and officialism less and less. Material and sensuous as the age is in many of its aspects, yet character was never more highly appreciated or told for more than it does at the present time.

Nor can prelacy stand against the divine right of the democracy. Although the cry of "Increase the Episcopate" is heard, yet the Bishops themselves admit that they must give the laity some share in the administration of the affairs of prelatical churches. The people cannot be excluded from churches or from nations. Their day has dawned; and it will go on to its full noon. Not churches, nor parties, not nations merely, but the people are the legatees of the future; the inheritance is theirs. Long have they been kept out of it; but every year witnesses their growing consciousness of power and their increased determination to use it. Washington and Jefferson, Hamilton and Knox, Franklin and Madison, and the men who framed your Constitution in this city uttered with something of lyric passion this great message, and fixed it forever in the Charter of Independence. France thrilled the world with its deeds in the people's name, and sealed with the blood of many of her sons and daughters the people's cause. Walt Whitman, rapt into ecstacy with the vision of the advancing people, sings:

> "I will make Divine magnetic land,
>   With the love of comrades,
>   With the life-long love of comrades."

And then again he asks:

> "What whispers are these, O lands, running ahead of you, passing
>   under the seas?
> Are all nations communing? Is there going to be but one heart to the
>   globe?"

Yonder in Russia, Tolstoy is seized by the spirit of universal comradeship in the cause of peace and purity, of righteousness and charity, and tells men in many a volume of quickening thought, expressed in strong and lucid speech that the kingdom of God is come night unto them. Nay, can you believe it; even the British House of Lords has discovered that it is an irritating anachronism, a gilded stumbling-stone in the way of progress, and the sooner it moves out of the way the better. This is the reign of the people. The issue is inevitable. They are one. They know it: and they will act as one. Instead of fighting one another, they will make common cause with each other, and rule the world in righteousness and peace.

But the most outstanding characteristics of our time is the amazing dominance of the idea of social service. The age is permeated with the obligation of brotherhood, the duty of self-sacrificing ministry, to the more needy members of the Commonwealth. We cannot escape it. Social problems are supreme. "The condition of the people" question is everywhere surging to the front. Housing and health, temperance and purity, drill for the body, education for the mind; these and kindred phases of life are never out of sight. The churches have broadened out so as to embrace them. Institutions, clubs, spring up in towns and villages to deal with them. Governments have done with *laissez faire*, and are taking them up. The British Legislature points the way with its old age pensions, and its charter for the industrial classes. As a doctor it is fighting disease. As a nurse it is watching over the invalid. As an insurance agent it is arranging help for those who are out of work; and doing it all, we cannot forget, through a political leader of splendid genius and captivating simplicity, who has been trained from childhood in Baptist ideas, who is now an active member of a Baptist church, and whether he knows it or not, is absorbed in applying the doctrines of the Anabaptist of the sixteenth century to the needs of the men of our own day. From him has come this Great Charter of the Industrial Classes; a charter conferring untold good at once, and also foretelling the arrival of a new era in the commercial, industrial, and social condition and activities of the whole world.

And all this movement is intensely moral. The illuminated and energized conscience is in it. It is ennobled by a high ethic. The Spirit has "convinced the *world* of sin and righteousness and judgment"; and in the strength of that conviction, a concerted and comprehensive attack is being made by churches and States, by individuals and societies on the strongholds of injustice and misery, and a long stride is taken to that one far-off divine event towards which the whole creation moves.

VII.

Need I trace the parallel between those manifest tendencies of this New Century and the principles which our fathers set forth and which we maintain? Is it not obvious that the ideas and aims are ours, and that whatever becomes of us as churches, this, at least, is certain, that those ideas of ours are working mightily as the formative factors of the future?

"The sum of all progress," says Hegel, "is freedom." On freedom we are built, for freedom we fight; and towards freedom the race is everywhere moving.

Man is able to enunciate his own law, and to follow it. He is made to govern himself. In a world of increasing complexity and marvelous interplay of vital and social forces, he is slowly acquiring self-government. Our churches are autonomous, and have proved themselves useful schools in the mastery of the art of self-rule.

The individual enters society, and is made by it; social responsibility educates him; social service purifies and expands him. The more complete his free and equal participation in the social organism, the richer his life, and the more valuable his gifts to the world. Our fellowships offer such aids. Monopolies are excluded. Caste is forbidden. Work for others is obligatory and inspired.

But though the parallel in those and other respects is so significant, we cannot forget that there are immense ecclesiastical organizations occupying vast fields enrolling multitudes of members, repudiating us and claiming an exclusive right to preach the way of salvation, and to direct the religious life of men.

Islam, for example, has a brilliant history; controls wide regions, attracts millions of adherents, and is once more fired with missionary zeal. Its activity is ceaseless, and its hope of conquest bright; but it must be affected by the rise of the Young Turks with their antagonism to clericalism, hatred of intolerance, sympathy with justice and equality, and bold avowal that women have souls as well as men. One of two things must follow;

either the leavening of Mohammedanism with Christian ideas or its gradual dissolution under the powerful solvent of the current principles of modern life.

It is the same with Roman Catholicism. It asserts the right to an exclusive dominion over the minds and wills of men, boasts of its universality, and has the allegiance of hundreds of millions of believers. But Dr. Cobb says: "It is quite impossible to think of the Roman Catholic Church possessing any determining voice in the religion of the future—unless she herself is first reconstructed so as to bring her on to the line of modern progress; and then she would be no longer the Roman Catholic Church, but something entirely different."

The same thing, with even more reason, may be said concerning the Holy Orthodox Church of Russia.

Then we are left to the Protestant churches in their several denominations. Of the Anglican Church, Dr. Cobb, who is himself a member of that Church, affirms: "It is the living voice we ask to be allowed to hear. It is the dead hand which we feel oppressive. . . . The Free Churches have a living voice. . . . The Church of England alone among the churches of the West has none." Without endorsing that verdict, we may say it is perfectly true that all Christian churches have some truth, and live and serve by the truth they hold, and the truth that really holds them; and by the quality and quantity of the service they are rendering to humanity: but it is clear (1) that it is the genuine Christianity that is in all the churches that will give the determining word and influence, (2) that Protestantism, specially in the Free Churches, admittedly contains and embodies more of the primitive gospel than the Roman and Greek churches, and (3) that our Baptist churches are by the principles they avow and the ideas they hold charged with a responsibility second to none for inspiring, directing and shaping the religion of the future.

For in addition to our ruling ideas we have a freedom as to verbal forms of belief and of organized collective life, though we are so immovably fixed as to principles, that leaves us wholly at liberty to adapt ourselves to the teaching of experience, and the changing needs of societies as continuously living organisms can and must. Biblical criticism does not disturb us, for we do not rest on it, but on personal experience of the grace of Christ. Modes of political government do not affect us; we can accept any, but we fare best under the most democratic; and as a matter of conviction we can only be kept out of politics by the absence of injustice, of interference with conscience, of favoritism, and of neglect of the weak and the poor. Collisions with the people cannot occur, for we are of the people, and one with them in their popular ideals and democratic aims. I do not say that Baptists are necessary for the full development and final triumph of these principles. We are not. "There is no man, nor any body of men necessary for anything, not even the Prince of Denmark to Hamlet." But I do declare with my whole soul that these principles are necessary to the strength and purity, the fulness and harmony of the religious life of men; and I am sure that the church that can give the most living, fresh, and powerful embodiment of them will find itself summoned of God to guide the races of men through the jungle of this life into the blissful Canaan God has prepared for those that love Him. It needs the best men and the best churches to carry the best cause to victory; the men and the churches of the finest manhood, of the tenderest sympathy, and most self-forgetting love; men and churches who will have no purpose but such as can be entirely subordinated to the glory of God our Redeemer; churches that come nearer to that divine ideal of which we have so many brilliant glimpses in the New Testament; churches with a full spiritual life, a large ministry—a brotherly spirit, and a broad sweep of service; churches meeting the needs of the whole life of man with a whole gospel; churches that hold that the soul to be saved is the self, all the self, and in all its relations; that we are ourselves "social settlements," communities of brothers and sisters of Jesus, willing to go into an uninteresting obscurity for the sake of men lost in the dark regions of Slumdom, or to ascend into the highest realms of culture for the sake of spiritualizing the entire life through the intellect.

Two duties then are before us, one is to keep the stock of human thought enriched by the ideas and principles of the gospel of Christ, and the other is to add to the stock of human energy engaged in the saving of men. Paul's incredible labor was as necessary to his missionary successes as the revelation which came to him, not by man nor from man, but from God. "Send them an enthusiast," said Dr. Price when the first Lord Lansdowne asked what he should do to reform the profligates of Calne. "Send them an enthusiast." Men with sloppy ignorance and sleepless energy often achieve more than individuals crammed with libraries of knowledge but void of fire and passion. The best constructed engine stands still until the steam is up. The apprehension of our capital ideas will avail nothing unless we are ready to hazard our strength, our money, our efforts for the salvation of men. The harvest truly is great, but the laborers are few. It is work that is needed. "Come over and help us" is the cry sounding in our ears from all parts of the world and specially from Southeastern Europe. Churches of our faith and order have sprung into existence in Hungary and Austria, Moravia and Bulgaria, Bohemia and Bosnia, and the Russian Empire. Thousands upon thousands have been added to the Lord. They are persecuted, but they take joyfully the spoiling of their goods, and with dauntless courage spread the fire of their evangelism far and near. They need our help. They call upon us for sympathy and guidance in the training of their eager pastors and evangelists, colporteurs and missionaries. They wait our response. It must be prompt, practical, and sufficient. It must be made now.

Let us then humbly accept our responsibility for leadership of the religion of the future and go forward to our place. Pioneers never get the best pay, but they do the best work; the work that lasts and comes out of the fire because it is not inflammable wood but gold that melted in the flames is coined afresh, and sent out again into the currency of the ages. Do not wait for others! Do that which costs. Wait for others, and you will never start. Tarry till Baptists are socially popular, and ostracism ceases, and the persecutor disappears and you will do nothing. Keep out of the firing line with your principles, and nobody will know that you have them. The bewitched forest heard the lies told by the evil spirit that the first tree that broke into blossom in the spring would be withered and destroyed, and each tree, fearing the threatened doom waited for the other to begin, and so the whole forest remained dark and dead for a thousand years. Away with fear. Be ready to endure the cross and despise shame. Rise to the courage of your best moments. Push your convictions into deeds. Scorn bribes. Stand true. Be faithful to Christ and His holy gospel, and so help to lead the whole world into the light and glory of His redeeming love.

The Spiritual Interpretation of the Ordinances
A. T. Robertson

This is one thing that Baptists stand for against the great mass of modern Christians. The Greek Church, the Roman Catholic Church, the Lutheran Church, the High Church Episcopalians, and the Sacramental wing of the Disciples attach a redemptive value to one or both of the ordinances. It is just here that the term "Evangelical Christianity" comes in to emphasize the spiritual side of religion independent of rite and ceremony. It is a curious turn in history that the one body of Christians that holds a thoroughly consistent attitude on the subject of regeneration *before* baptism should be so often charged with holding that baptism is essential to salvation. As a matter of fact, Baptists lay less emphasis on the necessity of baptism than any other denomination except the Quakers who go to the extreme of rejecting it entirely. The Quakers are right in stressing the fact that one's spiritual fellowship with God is independent of rites, but they impoverish the message of the gospel in refusing to use these ordinances which are charged with rich truth, just because so many misuse them. Those evangelical Christians who practise infant baptism lay more stress upon baptism than the Baptists do, since they will not wait till the child is converted. They practise infant baptism in hope that the child will be converted. This puts the cart before the horse and empties the ordinance of its real significance. One cannot but feel that infant baptism among the evangelical denominations is a relic of the fears that infants would perish unless they were baptized, the origin of the practice, in truth. Then they are wholly inconsistent, though preaching salvation by grace, praise God.

Now, Baptists stand out against the indifference of the Quakers, the heresy of the Sacramentalists, the nervous over-emphasis of the Paedobaptists and contend for the spiritual apprehension of the ordinances. Our position is a difficult one because men are prone to drift into reliance upon rites for salvation. It is the lazy man's religion. It is the way of the literalist. The very use of rites tends, unless resisted, to harden into formalism and sacramentalism, unless one continually strives to see the significance of the symbol. The Pharisees made an ordinance out of washing the hands before meals. A Pharisee who invited Jesus to dine marvelled that Jesus did not take a bath before the meal. Unless you take a bath before meals, you are unclean and cannot be saved. The Judaizers carried this sacramental notion into Christianity. They held that a Gentile could not be saved without circumcision. He had to become a Jew. The blood of Christ was not enough. The Holy Spirit could not give one a new heart without the help of this ancient Jewish rite. So the Pharisaic party in the church at Jerusalem had Peter up before the church for fellowship with the house of Cornelius in Caesarea. They reluctantly submitted after his story and held their peace for a while. When Paul and Barnabas returned from the first great missionary campaign, the Judaizers promptly turned up at Antioch with the ultimatum: "Except ye be circumcised after the custom of Moses, ye cannot be saved." Paul accepted the challenge without a moment's hesitation. He took the matter to Jerusalem to show that the apostles and the mother church did not endorse the radical doctrine of the Judaizers. He would not for the sake of peace agree for Titus, a Greek, to be circumcised. He did not yield for one hour to the demands of the false brethren, that the truth of the gospel might abide. The battle of Paul's life was just this. He preserved spiritual Christianity against the demands of the ceremonialists. He met terrific opposition as did Jesus, as did Stephen, and for the same reason. The intolerance of those who mistake the symbol for the reality is always bitter.

Paul won his fight with the help of the other apostles and Judaizers were driven back before the onward march of apostolic Christianity. But the same narrow spirit reappeared in the second century. It dropped circumcision and seized on baptism as the *sine qua non* of salvation. This teaching was in reality Pharisaism *redevivus.* It was also in harmony with much pagan theology. It was easy to understand and it swept the field in the course of time. Out of the heresy of baptismal regeneration or remission has sprung a brood of errors that have turned the course of Christian history away from its primitive purity. If baptism was regarded as essential to salvation, then the sick and dying should be baptized before it was too late. Clinic baptism thus arose. But the sick could not always be immersed; hence sprinkling or pouring could be done in extreme cases. Water for immersion was not always ready to hand, and, since death might come, the ordinance had to be changed to sprinkling or pouring. This situation appears as early as the middle of the second century in the *Teaching of the Twelve Apostles.* The supposed *necessity* of baptism is the explanation of the gradual use of sprinkling and pouring alongside of, and finally instead of, immersion. Thus also is explained the origin of infant baptism. If baptism is essential to salvation, then infants must be baptized. At first, and for long, infants were immersed (see the Church of England Articles), but gradually sprinkling and pouring drove out immersion.

The modern Baptist voice cried in the wilderness in the seventeenth century in England, only the multitudes did not flock to the wilderness to hear and heed. To the many, after the long centuries of perversion of the ordinances, we seem interlopers and disturbers of the settled order of things. But the Baptist voice has been heard in the world of scholarship. The lexicons, the Bible dictionaries, the critical commentaries with monotonous unanimity now take for granted as a matter of course that baptism in the New Testament is immersion and immersion alone. To the unlearned Baptists still have to prove this fact so patent to scholars.

And yet we do not carry all modern evangelical Christians with us in the restoration of the ordinance of baptism. We have won our contention, but we do not carry those who are convinced to the point of action. The tables are turned upon us in this wise. They say that we are sticklers for a mere form. What is the use? Grant all that we claim, and what difference does it make? So it comes about in modern life we are put again on the defensive and pushed over to the edge near the side of the ceremonialists, we who are the champions *par excellence* of spiritual Christianity, of a regenerated church-membership. We must expound our message yet again. We do not insist on baptism as a condition or a means of salvation. We deny both positions very strenuously. We say "no conversion, no baptism." First the new life in Christ, then the baptism as the picture and pledge of that life. We contend that the form is important just because the ordinance is only a symbol. The point in a symbol lies in the form. It is true of a picture. One wants the picture of his own wife, not just the picture of a bird, a man, or that of another woman. Baptism is a preacher. It cannot preach its full message unless the real act is performed. John the Baptist used baptism as the pledge of a new life worthy of the repentance which the people professed. He used it also to manifest the Messiah. Jesus spoke of it as a symbol of His death, the baptism which He was to be baptized with. Peter likened it to the flood in Noah's time. But it is Paul who has given the classic interpretation of the significance of baptism. He has brought out the rich message in his "mold of doctrine" as no one else has. It is a burial and a resurrection, submergence and emergence, buried with Christ and raised with Christ. It is a preacher of Christ's own death and resurrection, of the sinner's death to sin and resurrection to new life, of the Christian's own death and resurrection in the end. The very heart of the gospel message is thus enshrined in this wonderful ordinance. Leaving to one side the question of the duty of obedience to the example and command of Christ and the practice of the apostolic Christians, matters of no small moment, we press our plea on the ground of the great loss sustained by the perversion of the ordinance. Its beauty is gone. Its message is lost. It cannot tell the story that was put into it. It becomes a mere rite that may have a meaning to those who perform it, but certainly not that with which it was charged. No stretch of imagination can make sprinkling or pouring proclaim death and resurrection.

Since it is an ordinance to which Jesus submitted and which He enjoined, since it is so beautiful in itself and so rich in high teaching, we claim that modern Christians should not let mere custom or convenience, prejudice or inertia rob them of the joy of obedience to Christ and fellowship with Him in His death and resurrection through this mystic symbol. Thus all can proclaim the heart of the message of Christ's death. We should not rob Christianity of its full rights in this matter. Let baptism preach. Our contention thus finds its full justification. We do not call men non-Christians who fail to see this great truth. We joyfully greet all true believers in Christ of whatever name and are glad to march with them in the great army of the Lord Jesus. But we cannot approve the substitution of a device of man for the sacred ordinance of John and of Jesus and of Paul. Once it is clear that immersion alone is baptism, then we should not hesitate to take the next step, to be baptized.

The second ordinance preaches much the same message as that of the first, the death of Christ. It does not, indeed, speak about burial and resurrection. It is only of death that it has a message. But, if the Lord's Supper does not hold so full a message, the celebration is repeated frequently while baptism comes only once. The bread and the cup symbolize the sacrificial body and blood of Christ. The atonement is thus preached. The blood of Christ was shed for the remission of sins. This ordinance reminds us of the blood covenant of grace. We were bought with the blood of Christ. We must never forget that. We keep this ordinance in remembrance of Christ. We proclaim His death till He comes. The ordinance, like baptism, points forward as well as backward, the one to the Second Coming, the other to the Resurrection. It is a symbol also of the high fellowship which the saints will have with Jesus in the Father's

Kingdom on high. It is an ordinance rich with spiritual teaching. We do not admit the doctrine of transubstantiation nor that of consubstantiation, but we do see in the Lord's Supper much significance. Thus we symbolize our participation (communion) in the body and blood of Christ. Like baptism, the communion is a preacher. It proclaims the death of Jesus for sin, His second coming, and our participation in the blessing of His death. But there is one thing more. "We, who are many, are one bread, one body for we all partake of one bread." In a mystic sense we are one loaf in Christ. This ordinance accents our fellowship with Christ and with one another.

Paul uses baptism as a powerful plea against sin. "We who died to sin, how shall we any longer live therein? Or are ye ignorant that all we who were baptized into Christ, were baptized into His death?" Rev. F. B. Meyer has made a most effective use of Paul's argument in a diagram in which a grave is placed beneath the cross. Our old man was crucified with Christ on the cross. The burial with Christ under the cross advertises our death to sin. We come out on the other side of the cross and His grave to a new life in Christ. Paul uses the Lord's Supper in a similar plea for consecration. "Ye cannot drink the cup of the Lord and the cup of demons. Ye cannot partake of the table of the Lord, and of the table of demons." He alludes to the feasts in the idol temples, but the principle is general. How can the man who partakes of the cup of the Lord resort to the saloon, the gambling den? How can he align himself with the evil forces of this world? Baptism is a true *sacramentum,* the Christian soldier's oath of fealty to Christ in his conflict with the hosts of Satan. The Lord's Supper is the mystic fellowship of the saints with Christ and with each other in Christ.

The ordinances speak loudly against the misuse into which they have fallen. Between over-emphasis and indifference there is the golden mean of truth. The Baptist voice has always spoken in clear tones for the free intercourse of the soul with God. The ordinances preach the same glorious doctrine of soul liberty. They testify to the fact that the soul is in communion with God through Christ. It is a supreme travesty to make these ordinances stand between the soul and Christ as hindrances, not as helps, to the spiritual life. Through centuries of misunderstanding we have come thus far. Three hundred years ago the English Anabaptists then in exile in Holland made a confession of faith in which they protested against infant baptism as the Dutch and German Anabaptists had done a century before. It was not till 1640-1 that the English Anabaptists clearly grasped the Scriptural requirement of immersion alone as the true baptism. The Baptists have not cried in vain during these centuries for a return to apostolic purity in the matter of the ordinances, for the immersion of believers only. In simply truth many men of culture in other denominations wish that they instead of the Baptists had the powerful message which Baptists offer to the world. It is a message of reality and is in harmony with the modern spirit. The life is more than meat, more than ceremony. There is no reason in any ceremony that does not express a glorious reality. If we have died to sin and are living in Christ, the baptism and the Lord's Supper have a blessed significance; else they become a mockery and a misnomer. Never in all the history of the world was the Baptist message on the ordinances more needed than it is to-day. Never did it have so good a chance to win a hearing.

3
Stockholm
1923

Introduction

World War I cancelled the meeting of the BWA to be held in Berlin in 1916. After the Philadelphia meeting of 1911, the Alliance did not meet again until the 1923 Stockholm conference. Robert Stuart MacArthur, pastor of Calvary Baptist Church in New York, was elected president of the BWA in Philadelphia. He died before the Stockholm meeting so there was no presidential address in 1923.

Dominating the 1923 meeting were the concerns of a postwar world. In his "Foreword" to the 1923 Congress volume, J. H. Shakespeare described the atmosphere of the Baptist gathering in Stockholm.

At times the atmosphere was electric. It would be a cold heart which could survey with deep emotion the host of delegates from the Far East and the great mission fields, from the New world across the Atlantic, and especially from European countries long held down beneath political, ecclesiastical persecution, and only recently enfranchised.[1]

In the face of such concerns, E. Y. Mullins, president of The Southern Baptist Theological Seminary and the one whom the delegates at Stockholm elected as president of the BWA, preached a powerful sermon on "The Baptist Conception of Religious Liberty." This is a significant address not only because it delineates the Baptist position on the subject but because it symbolizes one of the ongoing concerns of the BWA from its organization in 1905. The BWA has been both a voice and an action agency for religious liberty. One writer described Mullins's 1923 sermon as "one of the greatest messages ever heard at a Baptist World Congress."[2]

W. A. Cameron, renown pastor of the Bloor Street Baptist Church in Toronto, preached the Congress sermon in Stockholm.

Cameron's sermon is an excellent example of the tone and content of most Congress sermons. Christological in content, it alludes to Baptist principles while issuing the challenge to do the work of God's kingdom. Inspirational in tone, the sermon represents the best in the preaching tradition of Baptists.

The Baptist Conception of Religious Liberty
E. Y. Mullins

With Baptists, religious liberty is born of the direct vision of God. Sometimes it has been a dream when, like John Bunyan in the darkness of prison, they have gazed through the bars at the far-off stars. Sometimes it has been a theme of eloquent discourse when they have expounded it to others. Sometimes it has been a solace when they have gone into exile for conscience sake, and sometimes a battle-cry when they have shed their blood for it. But always it has been a passion deep as life welling up from the depths of being in eternal faith and hope.

If I could express in a word the heroic spirit of Swedish Baptists seventy-five years ago, and after, I could tell you what religious liberty means. If I could give to you the distilled essence of the spirit of our Virginia fathers, and once more catch the vision of Roger Williams, of Rhode Island, who founded a commonwealth on the principle, I could set forth the truth. Nay, if I could reproduce in descriptive words the heroism of our brethren and sisters to-day in Russia, in Bessarabia, in Roumania, and many other countries, I would need no other words. It was expressed in immortal words in Oncken's reply to the Burgomaster: "Oncken," said he, when he had been arrested, "as long as I can lift my little finger I will put you down from preaching this Gospel." "Mr. Burgomaster, as long as I can see God's mighty hand above your little finger I will preach this Gospel."

Look then at the bases of religious liberty.

There are three great discoveries made by every human soul which grows normally to maturity. First, it discovers the world. To the babe the world is a part of itself. Even our own mothers are at first a mere patch of moving color and a soothing sound. But when the babe tries to pluck the flame of a candle and burns its hand, or bumps its head on the floor, it makes the first great discovery. It discovers that the world is different from itself. The self and the world become henceforth great realities. Later when the moral nature awakes the soul discovers God, the greatest of all realities. When a human soul discovers God, the foundation for religious liberty is laid.

Men have wandered from the path of duty, civilization has gone astray, because these three realities, the self, the world and God, have not been properly related. The human problem has been how to relate personality to society, the individual life to the corporate life. But how to relate man to God comes first. It is the key to all problems. The quest for economic liberty, intellectual liberty, civil liberty, all go back to religious liberty as the root.

Thomas Jefferson wrote his own epitaph before his death. It is most remarkable in the fact that, although he served as President of the United States eight years, there is no mention of that fact. The epitaph reads as follows: "Here lies buried Thomas Jefferson, Author of the declaration of American Independence—of the statute of Virginia for Religious Freedom, and Father of the University of Virginia." Jefferson had the spiritual vision to see that liberty is the fountain head of civilization and that religious liberty is the mother of all other forms of liberty.

Sir Walter Besant, in his little book "Building the Empire," shows a similar insight. In an early sentence he shocked my American sensibilities by the declaration that the British Empire includes the British Isles, Australia, New Zealand, South Africa, Canada and the United States of America. The reader is amazed until he reads further Sir Walter's statement that he is defining the Empire not as a political or physical, but as a spiritual entity. He means that Great Britain was the seed plot of liberty for all these governments. The love of religious liberty is the deepest bond of unity and friendship among nations.

Religious liberty rests upon man's original creation in God's image. The purpose of God in creation did not appear until the dust stood erect in the form of man, as a free and self-determining being. Man as a person created in God's image, free and spiritual, competent to deal directly with God, with an upward look, an endless discontent with the finite and temporal, a passionate yearning for the infinite and eternal; man, endowed with a conscience ringing in the soul like an alarm bell against wrong doing; man, with a will of his own which he can misuse and bring on moral ruin, but which he can surrender to God; man, with an intellect hungering for infinite truth and eternally discontented; man, with a heart which no earthly object can satisfy; man, self-willed and sinful and then penitent and believing, redeemed by the power of Jesus Christ, Redeemer and Lord; man, recreated in the Divine image, with the witness of the Spirit in his soul, telling him of his eternal destiny; man, as a child of God seeking to walk worthily of his calling, and heir of all the ages—this is the being and these the endowments which demand that great boon we call religious liberty.

As Baptists understand it, religious liberty excludes certain things and implies certain other things. It implies certain rights and along with these involves certain duties and privileges. Let us look at these in order.

First, religious liberty excludes a number of things. It excludes, for one thing, State authority in religion. The State depends on the use of force. Religion is moral and spiritual. The State uses coercion. Religion appeals only to freedom. The State deals with evil-doers. Religion seeks to produce righteous men and women. The State represses crime. Religion develops character.

Again, religious liberty excludes the principle of toleration in religion. To put the power and prestige of the State behind one form of religion and merely tolerate others is not religious liberty. It is religious coercion. God has not given the State any power to compel men in religion. Equal rights to all and special privileges to none is the true ideal. Some do not know the difference between toleration and liberty. If a snail could speak it would say to the tortoise "You go too fast for me." The clod would say to the snail: "You go so fast, you make me dizzy." But neither clod nor snail nor tortoise would know of the mighty flight of the eagle overhead. Religious toleration is the snail and tortoise. Religious liberty is the eagle.

Religious liberty excludes the right of the State to impose taxes for the support of one form of religion against the conscience of the people. All honor to the heroes of passive resistance who refuse to pay an obnoxious tax, which the State has no right to impose. A free church in a free State is the goal we should seek.

Again, religious liberty excludes the imposition of religious creeds by ecclesiastical authority. Confessions of faith by individuals or groups of men, voluntarily framed and set forth as containing the essentials of what men believe to be the Gospel, are all right. They are merely one way of witnessing to the truth. But when they are laid upon men's consciences by ecclesiastical command, or by a form of human authority, they become a shadow between the soul and God, an intolerable yoke, an impertinence and a tyranny.

Religious liberty excludes centralized ecclesiastical government. Men, redeemed by Christ, regenerated by His Spirit, born of Divine power and grace, are capable of dealing directly with God. Each one has a right to a voice in religious affairs. God speaks directly to men. Even the humblest believer may be a channel of the highest divine wisdom. Democracy, or self-government in the church, is the New Testament ideal. All believers are entitled to equal privileges in the church.

Religious liberty excludes priestly mediators and sacramental power of salvation. We have one priest, Jesus Christ, our great High Priest. All believers are priests entering into the most Holy Place. God's grace flows freely and directly to all who have faith and respond to His call. God has not limited the gift of His grace to any particular human channel. No group of men has any monopoly of God's grace, to withhold or bestow it upon their own conditions. God's grace is direct. It is His free gift. "Let us come boldly to the throne of grace," is the injunction of the sacred writer.

Religious liberty excludes infant baptism. Baptists refuse to treat the infant as a thing. We treat it as a potential person. We recognize its will, its intelligence, its freedom. We will not rob it of the joy of conscious obedience in baptism. Proxy faith is a counterfeit faith. The New Testament recognizes only personal faith. Train the growing child for God. Religiously we should do everything for the child, but nothing to it. Lead it to Christ. As the living flower at your feet requires the forces of the boundless universe to mould and shape it, so does the child require an infinite spiritual universe. As the flower needs the power of gravitation which grips all the systems, the sunlight that travels ninety-million miles to paint its petals, the mysterious and wondrous power of electricity, and the complicated water system of the planet, to mould and shape it, so also the child needs God's infinite truth, His boundless love, His immeasurable power and His unspeakable grace to regenerate and mould the child into Christ's image. Religious liberty requires that we let the child, as it grows up, learn the truth for itself, repent and believe for itself, obey Christ for itself, be baptized for itself, rejoice and struggle and grow for itself. To deny it these things is to rob it of its religious rights.

Consider next what religious liberty implies. First of all, religious liberty implies the greatest of human rights. Let us glance at some of these rights.

The first is the right of direct access to God. No cloud, no shadow of human authority, should come between the soul and its God. The second is man's right to search for truth in religion. Jesus recognized this. He did not compel belief by Divine authority. He so lived and taught the truth that men discovered His Messiahship for themselves. His revelations became their discoveries. Many things are revealed which men do not discover. The cause of many diseases was clearly revealed in signs and symptoms through the ages. But it required the genius and insight of a Pasteur to discover the germ. When he made this discovery he revolutionized the science of medicine. The facts of the solar system were revealed during all past ages. But not until Copernicus made his great discovery did we know that the sun is the centre. Jesus was revealed to the disciples as the Divine Son of God, but not until by faith they discovered Him did they understand Him. "Who do ye say that I am?" was His question. "Thou art the Christ, the Son of the Living God," was their answer. He dawned upon them like a sunburst. They discovered His glory and were lifted to divine heights.

So also religious liberty implies the right of free utterance and propagation of truth. The evil powers of the world have ever sought to stifle men. Heroes have led the way in the witness for the truth. Martin Luther is one of the greatest heroes of all time because at a supreme moment in the spiritual history of the race, with every earthly power arrayed against him, at the Diet of Worms, he said: "Here I stand. I can do no otherwise. God help me."

Religious liberty implies the right of equal privilege in the Church. There are no spiritual lords in the Christian religion, except the one Lord, Jesus Christ. Christ brings the common man to his rights. Under the old human systems, the Church or State was everything, the common man nothing. The Church or State was like the tree, enduring through the generations. Common men were like the leaves on the tree that fell to the ground and perished with the seasons. The State or Church was like the ocean, enduring through the centuries; common men were like the waves, rising and falling and disappearing for ever. Christ says: "Let the common man speak. Give him a voice in your affairs. Let God speak through him." Look at that group of worshippers in that first Church at Corinth. All grades and classes in society are represented. There is a Greek with classic features indicating culture. There is a Roman, rugged and strong of feature. There is a rich man, and by his side a slave. There is a city official, and there is a regenerated outcast. There are the respectable and among them the Scarlet-woman, washed and cleansed by the blood of Christ. There is a Northern barbarian, and a swarthy Ethiopian; for Corinth was a cosmopolitan city representing the ends of the earth. The Roman government was an iron band holding the world together by force. Here is a new inward spiritual bond uniting men on a new principle of a common faith and hope and love. Here is loyalty and obedience to a common Saviour, Jesus Christ, Who has shown them the way to God. Here is a new freedom, a new equality of privilege, a new brotherhood. This Corinthian Church is a new spiritual democracy. It is the seed plot of all future democracies, because it is an embodiment of religious liberty in its primary meaning of free access to God.

So also religious liberty implies the right of free association and organization for religious purposes. All men with religious beliefs and convictions have a right to organize and propagate their views. There never has been and never will be any human government, civil or ecclesiastical, with any right to curb or hinder or thwart the utmost freedom of men to associate themselves together, to organize, and to propagate the truth as they see it.

And this leads to the statement that religious liberty implies the right of men to demand of governments under which they live protection in the free exercise of their religion. That government which persecutes men for religious beliefs commits a crime against God and man. That government which is partial in its treatment of religious beliefs violates the principles of common justice, transgresses eternal and inalienable human rights, and defies the will of God.

Having considered the rights which religious liberty includes, I consider next what are the duties imposed. Among these duties are the following:

First of all, is the duty to search for and discover truth. God gave us the Bible. God made the world. There is no conflict between truths. The city of truth which science is building up from the earth, when completed and purified, will be seen to be a suburb of the city of God, which is descending from heaven arrayed in the glory of a bride adorned for her husband. Let us not fear that God's revelation in nature will conflict with His revelation in redemption. Christ is the key to both. Slowly science is fashioning a crown for Him. Slowly economics and sociology are fashioning a crown for Him. Slowly psychology and biology are fashioning a crown for Him. Slowly His people are fashioning a crown for Him. He Who went forth with a single crown will return crowned with many crowns. All the armies of truth shall follow Him, and on His vesture shall be written His name: "King of Kings and Lord of Lords."

I name next the duty of sacrifice for truth. To discover truth is one thing. To be willing to sacrifice and even die for it is another. Christ's witnesses have ever been Christ's martyr. Let us never forget:

> "Though love repine and reason chafe,
>   There comes a voice without reply,
> 'Tis man's perdition to be safe
>   When for the truth he ought to die."

Let us also remember that

> "By the light of burning martyrs Christ's bleeding feet I track,
> Toiling up new Calvaries ever, with the Cross that turns not back,
> And those mounts of anguish number how each generation learned
> Some new word in that grand credo which in prophet-hearts has
>   burned
> Since the first man stood God-conquered with his face to heaven
> upturned."

A third duty is to protect with all our souls against religious oppression. Baptists believe in religious liberty for themselves. But they believe in it equally for all men. With them it is not only a right; it is also a passion. While we have no sympathy with atheism or agnosticism or materialism, we stand for the freedom of the atheist, agnostic and materialist in his religious or irreligious convictions. To God he stands or falls. He will render his account to the Eternal Judge, not to men. So also the Jew and the Catholic are entitled to protection in the exercise of their religious liberty. Baptists do not desire to share the errors of men, but we are, and ever have been, and ever will be passionate and devoted champions of the rights of men. The supreme and inalienable right of all men is the right to direct and free and unhindered approach to God.

The next duty involved in religious liberty is loyalty to the State. The State is ordained of God. It serves a Divine end and purpose. Baptists have ever been ardent patriots. Liberty is not license. Liberty is opportunity for service. Religious liberty is the prime condition for every kind of human progress. Let a man have free access to God and hear God's voice, and he will become a champion of law and order. He will become a champion of the economic rights of men. He will become an advocate of the golden rule in all industrial relations. He will become an evangelist of brotherhood among the nations, of peace on earth and good will among them. He will oppose war because he knows that war is directly opposed to the Gospel of Christ. He will pray for his own country and for all countries. He will live and strive and pray that his own country may become a part of God's Kingdom.

Finally, religious liberty involves the supreme duty of loyalty to Jesus Christ. Not license, self-will, or human will, but God's will as revealed in Christ is the goal of history and of religious liberty. There is no danger in this religious liberty centered and anchored in Jesus Christ. Catholics are afraid of it and want to impose the authority of the Pope and the Church. Cardinal Gibbons defines religious liberty as "the right to worship God according to the dictates of a right conscience, and practice that form of religion most in harmony with man's duty to God." But a right conscience is a Catholic conscience, and the Catholic religion alone answers the above description as Cardinal Gibbons sees it. Wrapped up in that definition is all oppression. Gibbets and prisons and thumbscrews and racks are concealed in it. It can start martyr fires which would girdle the earth.

Another Catholic writer referring to the Pope says: "We acknowledge that authority; we proclaim it; we embrace it, as one surrounded by dark and turbulent waters clings to a lone spar lifting to safety above the perils of the deep. We may, indeed, hear the siren song of liberty; we may feel in our hearts the urge of our race to be free; we may be tempted to turn and walk no more in the way pointed out to us. But we know full well that liberty without authority is the kiss of death. As a kite without a string, a ship without a rudder, a meteor that has strayed from its orbit in the skies, so is man when the tie that binds him to his Creator is cut asunder. He floats through life, a wayward and meaningless atom in the universe, his destiny thwarted, his future nothing but darkness, desolation and extinction. Oh, give us faith, that virtue which reaches down from heaven to lift the universe."

But authority here advocated is that of the Pope and the Catholic church, and these are not the true authority. Jesus Christ is that authority.

Unto Him is committed the destinies of the human race. Let him have sway in men's hearts and they will realize their true freedom. Freedom only comes when a man finds his true object and is impelled by a higher motive. No man finds his soul's true object until he finds Jesus Christ. None have such spontaneity of action, such untrammeled energy and buoyancy as men who have acquired the freedom that Christ, the Son, gives. Look at Paul. He abounds in images which suggest spontaneity and exuberant joy. See him yonder when like a mighty swimmer rising above the billows of adversity and difficulty he exclaims, "I can do all things through Christ." Hear him as he spreads the wings of devotion, and in a splendid flight of mystic passion he shouts, "For me to live is Christ, and to die is gain." Observe him as he is caught in the mighty grip of moral enthusiasm and self-conquest, exulting in the joy of battle, "Thanks be to God, Who always leads me in victory through Christ." See him again as he is impelled onward, the embodiment of flaming love and quenchless hope and deathless ambition, running the Christian race as one who treads on air, and exclaiming, "Forgetting the things that are behind, I press towards the mark."

The moral career of Paul reminds one of the flight of some mighty eagle, long confined in a cage and then released. At first he is uncertain of his new feeling of freedom, but at length, becoming conscious of it, the heavy eyelids open, he looks about him, his dropping wings he gathers for flight, and then with a scream of joy he soars away to the clouds. His eagle soul has found its object, God's free air. Jesus Christ is the atmosphere of the soul. In Him the soul finds its true object and freedom. Men become the slaves of Christ, because He makes them autonomous, sets them free.

Human history has seen the downfall of many false authorities in Church and State. Crowns have been shattered and thrones sometimes broken down. But men have gathered the pieces of the broken thrones and they are erecting another greater than all, and they are making of the shattered crowns another more glorious than all. On that throne they are placing Jesus Christ, and that glorious crown they are putting on his brow, and I can hear by the ear of faith the far away rising and falling of the mighty chorus of the nations:.

> "All hail the power of Jesus' name,
> Let angels prostrate fall;
> Bring forth the royal diadem,
> And crown Him, Lord of all."

The Uplifted Lord
W. A. Cameron

It was the hour of apparent triumph. Christ's entry into the city had been hailed with joyous acclamation. Although the procession was a humble, impromptu affair, it doubtless filled the souls of the disciples with exultant hopes and with visions of their hero ruling in majesty over the kingdoms of the world. The narrow streets had echoed to the loud hosannas of the people. Nor were the disciples the only ones deceived by the enthusiasm of the hour. When the Pharisees witnessed our Lord's welcome as He entered Jerusalem, they spitefully said among themselves: "Behold, we prevail nothing; lo, the world is gone after Him."

Then came certain Greeks giving color to the same impression. When the excitement was at its height they approached Philip and expressed a desire to see Jesus. Just why they wished to see Him we do not know. It may have been to satisfy an idle curiosity, or it may have been with the hope that He would speak some message that would answer a spiritual longing which even Judaism had failed to satisfy. Their visit stirred the soul of Jesus with conflicting emotions. A strange and wondrous joy took possession of Him. For the moment, at any rate, He was elated. In deep spiritual ecstacy He cried: "The hour is come that the Son of Man should be glorified." What was it in this seemingly trivial incident that wrought the Christ to such intense emotion and that warranted the assertion of so positive and complete a triumph? With true prophetic instinct Christ saw the vision of a seeking world, inquiring its way to Him. Here was a little band of advanced scouts preceding a host which cannot be numbered. The tendency of this handful of Greeks will become the drift of the world.

It must have seemed to our Lord's bewildered followers that nations were already coming to His light, and kings to the brightness of His rising. Eagerly they seized upon the thought that the hour of His temporal sovereignty had at last arrived. They saw the kingdoms of the world and the glory of them and Christ on the throne. They saw empires wide open to such powers as His. They saw Him serving God on a royal scale and making Him an offering of a conquered world. But Christ broke the spell by that pregnant parable of a corn of wheat. "Except a grain of wheat fall into the earth and die it abideth by itself alone." Strange hour this to talk of death! But Jesus knew that there is no expansion possible for a grain of wheat until it is planted.

In Canada's capital, on the banks of the Ottawa River, there stands a statue put up by a Harvard student. It is built of bronze on a huge granite base. It is the figure of a young knight. His hair is blowing in the wind. His head is poised upward, and he has a sword drawn in his hands. His cloak flies behind him, and he is evidently climbing the granite rock.

Underneath are written these words of Sir Galahad: "If I save my life I lose it." It stands there in memory of another Harvard student, William Harper, who was walking along the bank of the river when he saw a young man and a young woman skating. They came down to a dangerous place where there was a swirl in the water. The ice was thin; it broke; and they disappeared. Harper took off his coat and went out and dived into that hole and was drowned, trying to save two people he did not know. "If I save my life I lose it." It was true even of the Son of Man. He shows how the selfless life that pours itself out, and offers itself up, and gives itself away is the life that yields the harvest of abundant blessing. For Him as for us there is no royal road. The throne upon which they would have thrust Him was, after all, the symbol of a very limited authority. The cross to which He resolutely journeyed was the true throne of the universe. It stood not at the end but at the beginning of things. If He had drawn these few Greeks by the magnetism He now possessed, when He was uplifted on the Cross, He would not draw a few but all. "And I, if I be lifted up from the earth, will draw all men unto Myself."

The Egotism of Jesus.

1. First of all, then, I bid you notice what I shall venture to call the sublime egotism of Jesus. "And I, if I be lifted up." There isn't anything quite like that in all the world. If Jesus Christ is nothing more than one man among many then here is presumption without a parallel in history. He is about to die and He claims that it is to be no ordinary death. He claims that His death would but enlarge His powers of offering Himself to men as their spiritual food. He claims that His death is to liberate stores of vital energy which are to loosen the souls of men from their most tyrannical sins. Sidney Lanier has a poem in which He offers pardon to the great and good men of the past for the faults and flaws that mar the perfection of their record. There is something in each of them to forgive. There is something to be forgiven in Buddha:

> "I pardon thee
> That all the All thou hadst for needy men
> Was nothing, and thy Best of being was
> But not to be."

There is something to be forgiven in Dante:

> "Worn Dante, I forgive
> The implacable hates, that in thy horrid hells
> Or burn or freeze thy fellows, never loosed
> By death, nor time, nor love."

There is something to be forgiven in them all:

> "All, all, I pardon, ere 'tis asked,
> Your more or less, your little mole that marks
> You brother, and your kinship seals, to man."

Then he turns to Jesus:

> "But Thee, but Thee, O sovereign Seer of Time,
> But Thee, O Poets' Poet, Wisdom's Tongue,
> But Thee, O Man's best Man, O Love's best Love,
> O perfect Life in perfect labour writ.
> O all men's Comrade, Servant, King and Priest,
>
> ....
>
> O what amiss may I forgive in Thee—
> Jesus, good Paragon, Thou crystal Christ?"

And here is the marvel of it—the poet's estimate of Christ is Christ's estimate of Himself. He finds nothing in Himself to forgive. He exhausts metaphors in the assertion of His unique and pre-eminent relation to life. "I am from above," "I am not of this world," "I am the bread of life," "I am the light of the world," "I am the door," "I am the good shepherd," "I am the way," "I am the truth," "I am the resurrection and the life." On one occasion the Pharisees were stung to madness by the immensity of His claims and they retort "Art Thou greater than our Father Abraham?" And His reply is one lifting the whole controversy almost out of the range of human thought, "Before Abraham was I am." And here is the supremely wonderful thing about Jesus, that when He makes His superlative claims we do not resent it. The Emperor Julian repeated dreams which he had had in the night, and in which he saw himself clothed with god-like prerogatives and powers. But everybody felt the colossal and insane conceit of the thing. Is it not most significant that although Christ made such claims He has ever been regarded as the ideal of humility? His lowliness is the base of all His virtues. The heart of man instinctively recognises in Him the humility of the incarnate God. When we look at Him through His own eyes, He is transfigured before us. His cross becomes His throne. Nothing has happened to invalidate a single claim made by Him. He was never more unique and never more sufficient. Still He stands, strong among the weak, erect among the fallen, clean among the defiled, living among the dead.

> "Who that one moment has the least descried Him,
> Dimly and faintly, hidden and afar,
> Doth not despise all excellence beside Him,
> Pleasures and powers that are not and that are.
> Ay, amid all men bear himself thereafter,

Smit with a solemn and a sweet surprise,
Dumb to their scorn and turning to their laughter,
Only the dominance of earnest eyes?"

The Optimism of Jesus.

2. In the second place we have in our text a suggestion of the optimism of Jesus. "I will draw all men unto Myself." It is impossible to ponder these words without feeling the sweep of that assertion. It covers all the sons and daughters of men. It includes the working man and also his employer. It includes the drunkard and also the publican. It includes the pauper and also the millionaire. It includes the pulpit and also the press. It includes the North American Continent and also every other continent. It over-leaps the barriers of race and caste and creed. It brings us into touch with the God who hath made of one blood all the nations of the earth. Very early in His ministry Christ said, "If ye love them that love you what reward have ye. Do not even the publicans the same?" There is no more selfish force in all the world than the love that limits itself to its own family or nation. During the days of feudalism there was intense loyalty among families and tribes, and the result was a perpetual warfare which split up society into scores of hostile camps. It was

"the simple plan
That they should take who had the power
And they should keep who can."

And the world has not outgrown that spirit yet because it has not learned the purpose of Christ. That purpose is not limited by personal friendships. It is not bounded by community interests. It knows nothing of party affiliations, racial prejudices, or national pride. It takes fire at the thought of bringing the whole world into the loving embrace of God. It is love set free and behold what it can do! "All men unto Myself."

The secret of that optimism was an abiding confidence in God. Our faith is clouded and intermittent. It floods and ebbs like the tide. Jesus never doubted. His vision was unclouded. His trust was absolute. He saw God. He realised God. He hid Himself in God. In God He lived and moved and had His being. He was no cheerful optimist who had shut His eyes to the sorrow and heart-break of the world. Never were eyes wider open than His. He saw suffering in its every form. He had ears which caught every shriek of agony, every cry of distress, every sigh of want. But he remains undaunted. He never loses heart. He marches breast forward. He faces facts as they are and He predicts grander facts which are to be. He sees both sides—the bright side and the dark side—and having seen both sides His face has light on it. He felt the fury of the storm and was certain of the calm which was to follow. He could measure the dimensions of the night and also see the dawning of glorious morning. His optimism was the optimism of God because He knew the secret of perfect trust.

Then too, the secret of that optimism was an unshakable confidence in man. Matthew Arnold says of Goethe that he was able to lay his finger with unerring accuracy upon the real seat of human mischief and ill and say, "Thou ailest here and here." The same might have been said of Christ. The difference between others and Jesus is this—that while they saw the disease and despaired, He saw the disease and hoped. Our Lord had an extraordinary belief in the spiritual competence and responsiveness of every man. One of our modern writers emphasises Christ's ability to impart spiritual ideas to dull and prejudiced people. I am by no means wishful to disparage Christ's "ability" as a teacher. But it does not represent itself to me as a matter of "ability" at all, but rather as a matter of Christ's belief in them. That great sermon on the spirituality of God and the universality of worship He preached to a despised and degraded Samaritan woman. It was an amazing compliment to the spiritual capacity of human nature, even when that nature was degraded and sunken. Another writer says, "He was not afraid of wasting time or truth on barren souls." It would be better to say that He was not afraid of wasting time or truth on any man for the simple reason that He did not believe that any soul was barren. In these days of radio we know that unless the transmitter and receiver are keyed together the wireless message trembles in the ether in vain. Jesus believed that the heart of God and the heart of man were keyed together, and that eternal foundations can be laid in human souls.

And, once more, the secret of that optimism was an abounding confidence in the Kingdom. In the mind of Jesus the Kingdom was the chiefest good of the soul and the hope of the world. The Kingdom is commensurate with His reign and rule and authority everywhere. It includes the new social order where is gathered together a great fellowship of art, science, literature, music, statecraft, government, family life, everything shot through with the Spirit of God. It includes the sanctified church, the sanctified state, the sanctified family, the sanctified nation, the sanctified world. The Kingdom cometh to a man when he sets up Christ's Cross in his heart. It passes on its way when that man rises from the table and girds himself and serves the person next him. It comes to every man with its offer of re-birth into newness of life. It comes to society with a new order which re-shapes the men and women who live under it. It comes as a protest against any features in prevailing conditions that do not disclose Christ-like love. It comes with a program of social redemption to be made effective in commerce, in pleasures, in international relations, and the whole of human life. It is the world-wide state, whose law is the divine

Will, whose members obey the Spirit of Jesus, whose strength is goodness, whose heritage is God.

Surely we as Baptists have a contribution to make in the building of the Kingdom. Who knows but we have come into the Kingdom for such a time as this? Many of our principles are shared with others who profess the Evangelical faith. In this we rejoice and would adopt the attitude of Tennyson when his friends told him the minor poets were using his methods.

> "Once in a golden hour
> I cast to earth a seed;
> Up there sprang a flower—
> The people said—a weed.

> "Then it grew so tall
> It wore a crown of light;
> But thieves from o'er the wall
> Stole the seed by night.

> "Hear my little fable—
> He that runs may read—
> Most can raise the flowers now:
> For all have got the seed."

But the seed is still ours and the world still needs it. What is that seed? An American scholar says, "The Baptist principle is one, and only one. It may be stated in many ways, but it has never been better put than in that old Reformation formula: 'the competency of the soul before God.'" That includes the immediacy of the soul's communion with God. It includes the spirituality of religion. It includes the rights and responsibilities of the individual. It includes freedom from the coercion of belief, from the coercion of ritual, from the coercion of ecclesiastical authority. It includes the right of private judgment—to see and state the truth as God gives the vision. It includes the liberty and equality and priesthood of all believers. It includes these and many other things. These principles are essential if we are to have a redeemed humanity upon a regenerated earth; if we are to look forward to a time when the clash of arms shall be no more; when oppression and injustice and hatred shall have ceased among mankind; when this world of struggling men and women shall indeed recognize Christ as the Light of its light and the Leader of its thought.

And if all this means anything to us assembled in this congress it ought to mean that in Christ is to be found the deepest ground of our optimistic faith. The more we commit ourselves to Him the securer will be our optimism. Christ is our great Watchman on the ramparts of the city of Humanity. Let us send up one voice to Him as He stands there with His broad outlook on human life: O Divine Watchman, what of the night? And, as we cry, the answer will come, tender and clear and strong: "My anxious disciple, the night cometh. Not yet is the perfect day. But already comes the morning. Fear not. Faint not. Fight on. Trust on. The Eastern sky is brightening with the promise of sunrise. I shall yet draw all men unto Myself."

The Magnetism of Jesus.

3. And now, finally, let me say that our text speaks to us concerning the magnetism of Jesus. The magnet is not only Christ, but Christ in the wonderful power of His unique sacrifice. Yea, He declares that it is in the power of that unique sacrifice. Yea, He declares that it is in the power of that unique sacrifice that His personal magnetism is to be found. "I, *if I be lifted up.*" The Cross swings into view. The path of humiliation is to be the path to glory. The sacrifice is not meaningless but has a redemptive purpose. He who went to Calvary was not the mere victim of man's hate and envy. He was the Lamb slain before the foundation of the world. The sacrifice is not something flung at the feet of an angry God to persuade Him to change His mind. God did not need to change His mind. The sacrifice began in His own heart before it ever expressed itself in the perfect Life or the wondrous Death. The world could only be redeemed by sacrifice and the sacrifice that redeemed us was the sacrifice of God. And when we see Christ identifying Himself with our sinful race, even to the uttermost of all that was involved in that, we know that the heart of God is thus entangled in our sorrow, and the hands of God are stretched out to save us from our sin. This is why the Cross is so melting, so subduing, so morally magnificent, so mightily attractive.

There is nothing like that magnet even on the plane of common life. Sacrifice does not imply the lessening but the enlargement of life, nor should it always be associated in the mind with the thoughts of pain and sorrow. Its greatest ingredient is rather the joy of self-giving and the triumph of achievement. Properly speaking there is no such thing as sacrifice in the sense of permanent loss and impoverishment; rightly understood it is always gain, glorious gain, more life and fuller. All the world over and in every age men have instinctively felt and recognized the grandeur of self-offering in the service of an impersonal ideal. The worst and cruellest religious observances contain something of it. In his "Tale of Two Cities" Charles Dickens makes the not otherwise very reputable Sydney Carton go willingly to the guillotine to save the husband of the woman he loved. The play in which the episode is represented is rightly termed "The Only Way." It is the only way. The only way in which God could save the world. The only way in which the soul of the race or the individual can mount to God. The Lamb in the midst of the throne has been slain on a good many altars since history began. Dickens' hero is only expressing the experience of humanity scaling the heights of divinity when he says in his dying moments: "It is a far, far better thing that I do now than I have ever done; it is a far, far sweeter rest that I go to than I have ever known." I think of Livingstone taking on himself that ancient curse of Africa. I think of Father Damien becoming a leper for those who suffered from that lamentable disease. I think of Florence Nightingale carrying the burden of wounded men lying on the battlefield. I think of the men who died in the war, men from almost every nation represented in this congress, sacrificing themselves to set right a world entangled by selfishness and impeded by sin.

> "Each drop of blood that e'er through true heart ran
> With lofty message, ran for thee and me."

Surely there is no one so dead in soul as not to feel the magnetism of such sacrifice. But when I think of the uplifted Son of God offering Himself as the supreme sacrifice, I understand how He lays His wondrous spell upon the hearts of men and draws them to Himself.

There is no spiritual attraction like the Cross. Those who find themselves proof against many other religious attractions are drawn by this one. We Baptists may not make much of it as a visible and material sign in our church and homes. We may not wear it as an ornament on our bodies. But we are not of those who wish to make it of none effect. We know full well that the secret of its power is not bound up with any ecclesiastical exposition of it. The men who find in ecclesiastical theory and myth little to attract and much to repel, but who still glory in the Cross and find the law and inspiration of their life in the faith and spirit of Him who consecrated it by His death, are in our day a multitude which no man can number.

Notwithstanding all this our religion has had too little sacrifice in it. Christ's Cross has been taken from His hands and smothered with flowers. It has become what He would have hated, a source of graceful ideas and agreeable emotions. There has been nothing of travail; nothing of struggle; nothing of climbing on hands and knees through thorns and briars. When Jesus presented the Cross for the salvation of His disciples, He was not thinking of a sentiment which can disturb no man's life, but of a calling which is both serious and high. He knew we could get along without a creed, He also knew we could not get along without a cross. Only as we follow in His steps can we in any high degree bless our generation. We help, heal and save only as the virtue goes out of us. Self-indulgent, self-centred, self-seeking, we cannot be Christ's disciples. There is no option but to follow Christ. It is a mockery to bear His name and live the selfish life. If we be dead with Him, we shall also live with

Him; if we suffer, we shall also reign with Him. It is the glory of the Cross that it speaks to us of the service He did for us; but let us not forget that it also speaks of the service He expects from us.

> "Measure thy life by loss, instead of gain,
> Not by the wine drunk, but the wine poured forth;
> For love's strength standeth in love's sacrifice,
> And he that giveth most hath most to give."

Here, then, is our challenge as we face the future. The Cross is the starting-point of the vastest activities of the world. It is the birth-place of the hope which crowns human life to-day and thrills it with divine ambitions for its onward course. It is a tremendous moral demand. Its splendid idealism may become a superb realism. Its imitation will lay upon us a terrific ethical obligation. It will open the doors of the greatest experience possible to mankind. When Samuel Rutherford was marching along in one of his grand pulpit marches, he passed away from a controversial passage to expound the Cross, and one of the Dukes of Argyle who was present, was so excited that he shouted out: "Gang on, mon, you are on the right string now!" It was a great saint of another century who declared "The church of our deathbed is the church of the future" If we will but listen we can hear the echo of the feet of the multitudes who through past centuries have come to God through the royal way of the holy Cross. And we can hear the oncoming tread of the greater multitudes of all nations in the days to come who are coming into the Kingdom by this road. My Baptist friends, I pause to listen for your feet. Are they on this road? If they are you are destined to reach that gateway that leads to victory and to God.

Notes

1. *Baptist World Alliance: Third Congress, Stockholm, July 21-27, 1923* (Nashville: Baptist Sunday School Board, 1923), p. vii.

2. Herschel H. Hobbs, "The Relevance of Our Faith As Revealed in Baptist World Congress Preaching," *Baptists of the World, 1905-1970,* edited by Josef Nordenhaug, et.al. (Fort Worth, Texas: Printed by The Radio and Television Commission, The Southern Baptist Convention, 1970), p. 92.

4
Toronto
1928

Introduction

E. Y. Mullins (1860-1928) was a formative influence in the BWA in its early years. President of The Southern Baptist Theological Seminary from 1899-1928, Mullins was to Southern Baptists what John Clifford, his contemporary, was to English Baptists—*the* acknowledged leader. Because of illness, Mullins could not attend the meeting in Toronto over which he was to preside. Standing in for him was another leading Southern Baptist minister—Dr. George W. Truett, pastor of the First Baptist Church in Dallas, Texas.

Truett not only presided for Mullins, he also delivered the address which Dr. Mullins had written. Entitled "Baptist Life in the World's Life," Mullins's sermon identified five challenges or "tests" which Baptists confronted in 1928. Those challenges, Mullins said, were (1) Baptist unity, (2) Christian unity, (3) civil liberty, (4) economic justice, and (5) the scientific spirit. The latter part of the sermon is an apology for Baptist individualism. The sermon states Baptist ideals within the context of the world situation of 1928.

Elaborating upon one of the themes of Mullins, F. W. Patterson, president of Acadia University, spoke on the timely topic of "Our Relation to Other Protestants." Church union had been a live topic of discussion among Protestants since the late nineteenth century. When Baptists gathered in Toronto on June 12, 1928, church union was the number one topic of conversation. Only three years prior to the Baptist meeting, the United Church of Canada was organized. This merger of Methodists, Presbyterians and Congregationalists in 1925 forced other Protestant bodies to declare themselves regarding ecumenism. Patterson's statement, while not officially adopted, doubtless represented the Baptist point of view correctly. His last sentence reads, "For the present, at least, we believe that we can best serve Him whose we are not by merging into a larger union, but by becoming better Baptists than we have ever been before."

Baptist Life in the World's Life
E. Y. Mullins

I invite you to consider the position of Baptists to-day in relation to the life of mankind: Baptist Life in the World's Life.

In order to do this we may look briefly at certain elements of history, especially of Reformation history. Behind Luther's Reformation there was a fourfold revolt attended by a fourfold vision. The first was the intellectual revolt against the tyranny which had for centuries kept the mind of man in swaddling clothes. It was attended by the vision of an open Bible and the open universe of God. Henceforth the mind of man is to range forth on many a grand tour of discovery. The second was the moral revolt, accompanied by the vision of a purified church and a purified society. Savonarola was the striking figure who embodied this revolt and vision. The futility of his heroic gesture of reform appeared when his movement collapsed and he was burned at the stake and his ashes cast into the Arno. The third was the ecclesiastical revolt against an unspiritual ecclesiastical system accompanied by the vision of a pure and spiritual church. Wyclif and John Hus were the heroic forerunners, but here also the movement did not attain great proportions owing to the powers in opposition. It was reserved for Martin Luther who led the religious revolt to succeed where others had failed. The direct vision of God and justification by faith was the mainspring of Luther's great epoch-making protest.

There is no time to trace the Protestant movement except in a very general way. It broke up into denominations of various types. I name a few of these. There is the episcopal type in which life and activity turn upon questions of authority and government. There is the creedal type in which activity is largely concentrated, upon conformity to creeds. There is also the sacramental type in which undue emphasis is given to the ordinances or sacraments as a means of salvation. There is also the rationalistic type in which all Christian doctrine is reduced to the terms and norms of the natural reason of man.

Now the Baptist type is now and has been since the Anabaptist days of pre-Reformation times, different from any of the above types. It has sought to embody and express the principle of divine life in the soul and the direct relation of man to God in all the relationships of life. It is a type which the world needs to-day, a synthesis of all that is good and Christian in other types.

To describe that need: What the world needs is not an intellectual revolt that swings away from Christ and the Christian foundations. It is not a moralism which can map out programs but cannot supply power to carry them out. It is not a dissolution of church polity into a nondescript vagueness and indefiniteness without coherence or power to impress the world. It is not a religious life that eliminates sin and the need for atonement and justification. It is not a doctrine of authority that follows Newman to the papacy on the one hand, or on the other dethrones Christ as Lord of life and glory, and abandons the New Testament as an agglomeration of myth and fable.

The modern world of common life and the modern world of culture eagerly await a type of Christianity that fully expresses the life that is in Christ. Baptists are not burdened with ecclesiastical forms beyond the minimum of a simple New Testament polity. They are under no necessity to prove a historic episcopate or apostolic succession. They have no citadel of sacramental grace to guard and defend. They have no authoritative creeds save the New Testament and should not waste time over creedal questions. They have no confusing mixture of personal faith and proxy faith in their message. They have no complex and involved system of orders in the ministry and hence are free from many vexing and annoying sacerdotal questions.

The supreme challenge of the modern world to Christianity is to *moral* and *spiritual* efficiency. The questions it asks are such as these: Can you produce the highest type of character? Can you exhibit social efficiency in removing entrenched evils and promoting the general welfare? Can you supply the *spiritual life* necessary to reorganize society in harmony with the Kingdom of God? Can you become the medium of a missionary zeal and passion and self-sacrifice adequate to the task of evangelizing the world?

Now the Baptist life in the world's life is confronted to-day with tests of many kinds. It will be well to consider some of these tests.

First, I name the test of internal Baptist unity and co-operation. We now number around twelve million members. We are scattered through about fifty countries. We can demonstrate spiritual unity or we can become as many conflicting parties as there are groups. We have no centralized authority. We are wholly dependent on two things: good sense and God's grace. Our democracy and autonomy expose us to great dangers, and present great opportunities. We can commit great folly or cultivate great wisdom. Wise men and fools are normal fruits on the Baptist tree. Our freedom is a freedom for folly to run its course and for wisdom to guide towards the great ends. Among Baptists every agency and instrumentality may become a weapon of destruction, or an influence for Kingdom building. The pulpit, the platform, the teacher's chair, the book, the pamphlet, the newspaper—these may be used by folly or wisdom, by the carnal or the spiritual mind. Baptist life produces the prophet who is a divine voice calling men to higher things; or it may produce the man who is an echo, or the echo of an echo of an echo. The finest product of the Baptist spirit is the man who recognizes agreements, rejoices in the great common ends of the Kingdom, co-operates for greater effectiveness, employs charity and restraint in judging the brethren.

The non-Baptist part of Christendom has long been skeptical as to the possibility of a permanent and effective Baptist unity. The ecclesiastical guerilla, the theological bushwhacker, has liberty to run his course. The reckless accuser and maligner of his brethren on the one side and the radical overturner of truth and doctrine find their opportunity in our Baptist democracy. The problem for us is whether our life in Christ is strong enough and constructive enough to survive.

The Baptist World Alliance is a brave gesture of Baptists to prove to mankind that we are not a miscellaneous group of sects, some under Paul, some under Apollos, and some under Cephas, but rather that we are one group under Jesus Christ, supremely loyal to him and his revealed word.

A second test of Baptist life in the world's life is its message on Christian unity. This is becoming a burning question among some of the denominations. The recent deliverance emanating from Rome on Christian unity should not have occasioned surprise. It was an expression of the inevitable logic of the papal system. In the quest for unity some have treated other considerations lightly. But Christian unity must be viewed not as the sole or chief element in Christian life. It must be duly combined with other elements.

Now Baptist life regards unity in its larger context and not in isolation. We find in the New Testament that at least two other elements are bound up with unity. These are liberty and loyalty. The Baptist formula for Christian unity is: unity plus loyalty plus liberty. Paul writes to the Ephesians his earnest desire that they keep the unity of the Spirit in the bond of peace. He says: "There is one body and one spirit even as ye were called in one hope of your calling"—and that is unity. Then he says: "One Lord, one faith, one baptism"—all that is the loyalty. Again he adds: "One God and Father of all who is above all, and through all and in all"—and that is the liberty. (Eph. 4:3-6) This then is Paul's great conception of Christian unity: The unity of the Spirit in the bond of peace—in loyalty to the one Lord, one faith, and one baptism—and in the liberty of an ample life under the eye and in the strength of the one God and Father of all, who is "above all, and through all and in all".

These three principles according to our Baptist view mutually condition and define each other. We do not seek unity at the expense of liberty. Hence we oppose great ecclesiastical systems under episcopal authorities. We do not seek liberty at the expense of unity. Hence we oppose irresponsible individualism which would convert the denomination into a free lance club with every man doing and believing that which is right in his own eyes. We seek rather the Pauline standpoint and make loyalty the centre of liberty and unity. Loyalty to the one Lord makes the unity Christo-centric. Loyalty to the one faith makes it coherent and self-consistent. Loyalty to the one baptism gives it an impressive and convincing outward symbol.

From the Baptist standpoint liberty by itself is an abstraction, and unity by itself is an abstraction. You can put into either or both of them any meaning you wish. But when you deal with Christian unity and Christian liberty you at once introduce a larger principle of which these are parts, viz., loyalty. Loyalty to Christ is Christianity. It is regulative of all the Christian life in all relationships.

It follows that for the Baptist only those forms of Christian activity in which the voluntary principle finds play can adequately express unity. Co-operation for common ends without compromise on points of divergence expresses the ideal. It follows also for the Baptist that only those forms of unity in which the principle of loyalty finds play can express the New Testament ideal.

Another and third test of our Baptist life in the world's life is in the sphere of the state. Our plea has been that self-determination in the church is the mother of self-determination in the state. The right to vote in matters, civic and political, is the analogue of the right to vote in matters spiritual.

But there are many critics of democracy arising. We are now told that the democratic idea is a great fallacy; that *vox populi* is not necessarily *vox dei*. The anti-slavery conviction was first not the voice of the people but of the prophet; the missionary vision was not the vision of the mass but of the seer, like a Carey or a Judson, that only slowly the masses catch the vision.

But democracy is not put to confusion by these objections. Its reply is convincing. We must admit that democracy in church and state moves slowly because it is spiritual and has a long way to go. It describes a circle so vast that any particular arc of the circle looks like a straight line. Oligarchy and autocracy are more direct and apparently more efficient. But evils easily become entrenched and unchangable under autocracy and oligarchy. Under democracy no evil can become stereotyped. Things are in flux. Conscience can rebel. Leadership can start a revolt. The people can be aroused. A new movement can be inaugurated. Nothing obnoxious to the moral sense can become permanent. It is true that the lower elements in human nature are released in democracy; but so also are the higher spiritual elements.

There are, we may say then, three great advantages of spiritual democracy in the modern world. One I have just mentioned. Evils do not become permanently entrenched. They can be corrected. A second advantage is that democracy in church life is a splendid instrument of missionary propaganda. You can only use Baptist churches for spiritual ends. You cannot mobilize them for political purposes. The Soviet Government in Russia has made this discovery. Hence the marvelous success of the Baptist movement in Russia. A third great advantage of spiritual democracy in the modern world is that it must necessarily stress regeneration. A democratic church must needs be spiritual. The new heart is its specialty. And the new heart is the supreme postulate of world-peace. Baptists have a great contribution to make to internationalism in that their fundamental propaganda looks to the creation of a new attitude between men of different nations. World peace is predicated upon the peace of God that passeth all understanding, and this is the great objective of Baptist missions.

In a recent article on the subject of World Peace the writer analyzed various proposals for abolishing war. Reducing armaments, he said, would not abolish war, because nations could manufacture arms very quickly if war should break out. The proposal to humanize war by abolishing gas and the submarine, he said, was unworkable because war is not a friendly game, and it cannot be humanized. Man's natural savagery reaffirms itself when war begins. Again he said the ideals of brotherhood among all nations and the application of ethical principles to international relations have failed because men are not willing to apply these ideals. He closed his article with a pessimistic note and affirmed that only one thing could cure the world of the malady of war and that is a new heart, but, said he, there is no means of imparting a new heart and hence we cannot hope to abolish war.

In reading the article one could but wonder if the writer had ever heard the Gospel of the new birth. Surely this is a great contribution to internationalism—the remaking of the human heart in the image of Christ. This is the fundamental cure for war and the greatest contribution to the state it is possible for Christianity to make. Our Baptist faith with its spiritual foundations and its central appeal to the conscience and will and mind of man is the greatest hope of the world. The greatest ambassadors between the nations to-day, the greatest diplomatists are the foreign missionaries. They are mediators teaching the nations mutual understanding, respect and love.

That was a striking tribute paid by a non-Baptist traveler in Europe to our Baptist movement there. He said: "There are two great forces contending for the spiritual life of modern Europe. One says 'No baptism without salvation,' the other says 'No salvation without Baptism.' That means a spiritual versus an ecclesiastical Christianity.

Another and fourth test of our Baptist life is in the economic sphere of human relations. Democracy is not a leveler except in the divine sense. It does not affirm equality of ability among men but insists upon equality of rights. It does not disregard differences of talent but pleads for equality of opportunity. It recognizes the difference between the clodhopper and the genius, but stands for the rights of the clodhopper with the same intensity as for those of the genius. It recognizes differences in the glory of human personality. There is one glory of the sun and another of the moon and another of the stars, and one star differs from another star in glory. All this it recognizes but it also recognizes that every personality has one chief glory—it is made in the image of God. Measured from the ground up men vary in physical, mental and moral stature, but measured from the heavens down they are equidistant from God. Spiritual democracy seeks to keep the space upward between God and man free from obstructions. Hence autocracies and aristocracies and oligarchies had to go. In the parable of the pounds Jesus forever asserts the sovereign authority of God in bestowing rewards. In the parable of the talents he affirms the inequalities of men in the eternal kingdom of God.

These then are the ideals and standards which we must apply in the economic relations of society: not socialism with its arbitrary and enforced equality; not the anarchy of an exaggerated individualism, but rather the recognition of the value and dignity of all personality and the maintenance of all the basic and divinely given human rights in a social order which seeks to do justly and love mercy and walk humbly with God.

A final test of Baptist life in the world's life is in its intellectual ideals. The scientific spirit is passionate devotion to reality; and that is the Baptist spirit. The scientific spirit is the hatred of shams and makebelieves and that is the Baptist spirit. The scientific spirit is acceptance of God's revelation of Himself in nature as well as his revelation of himself in the Bible, and that is the Baptist spirit. The scientific spirit is humility in the presence of any great manifestation of God in nature or in grace, and that is the Baptist spirit. The scientific spirit is loyalty to fact and that is the Baptist spirit—loyalty to all facts—the facts of nature and the facts of grace; the facts of the cosmos and the supreme fact of Christ.

The Baptist spirit must be large enough to absorb all true culture. It must be loyal enough to conserve every element of life in the Gospel of Christ.

The task of Christianity is always the same. It must be able to dominate civilization or it will be dominated by it. The rod of Aaron and Moses swallowed up the rods of the Egyptian soothsayers. This was necessary else it would itself have been swallowed up.

Fierce attacks are now being made upon our principle of individualism and freedom. We are accused of advocating a destructive principle in modern life.

In order to make clear how urgent and vital is this issue in the intellectual life of our age I cite a bit of recent Catholic logic. Mr. T. F. MacManus in the May *Atlantic Monthly* says: "There are only two systems of religious thought in the western world to-day. The authoritarian or Catholic, and the sectarian which is Protestant." He affirms that the basic sectarian or Protestant principle is the principle of private judgment, or individualism in religion, or as expressed by the Baptists the direct relation of the soul to God, the right of every man to worship God or not to worship Him according to the dictates of his own conscience. Mr. MacManus states the contrast thus: "The Catholic principle is, of course, the principle of truth conveyed by Christ through his church; the Protestant theory, the theory of truth conveyed to the individual by interior illumination, of whose authority he and he alone shall be the judge."

Now this Catholic writer with all vehemence and Catholic honesty makes the following affirmations of the Protestant principle of individualism and of private judgment in religion.

First—It is a negative and not a positive principle. It is the mother of all the isms and ologies of modern times.

Second—It is a "dissolvent and a separative principle—automatically and irresistibly and invincibly so."

Third—The sects anathematize all authority and say full steam ahead to the intellect. The individual is assured that he is his own judge, jury, pope, and God.

Fourth—You can sum up Protestantism in statements like these: "It makes no difference what a man believes"; and "one man's guess is as good as another's."

Fifth—Sectarian congregations have left sectarian churches because there was nothing left to hold them. Their churches are empty because their creeds are empty.

Finally—Protestant individualism is bearing fruit in flapperism, eugenics, contraception, companionate marriage, divorce and progressive polygamy, murder, socialism, anarchy, war and general ruin. Mr. Mac-Manus says: "If ever there was ritual without reason, or mummery without meaning, it is the varied and various forms of brick, mortar and millinery in which private judgment has decked itself out since its first clamorous appearance several centuries ago."

Having unmasked the great Protestant and Baptist principle of private judgment and individualism and shown it to be the horned and cloven-footed and sinister Mephistopheles of modern times sowing the seeds of destruction in church and state, Mr. MacManus arrives at the inevitable conclusion that the only safety of man and civilization is obedience to God—that is to say, to God's vice-regent on earth the Pope of Rome, the church, the priesthood. Translated into plain English it means: cease to think except the one thought of submission; cease to believe except as your beliefs are prescribed by ecclesiastical authority; cease to act in religion except as your actions are directed by a superior.

Mr. MacManus invites the world back to the good old days before Savonarola's ashes were cast into the Arno, and before the little Monk from Wittenberg climbing the *scala sancta* in Rome on his knees heard the epoch-making and immortal words of Paul and Habakuk ringing through his soul: "the just shall live by faith." He invites us back to the golden age of Mother Church, when the snows of Canossa were cold and kings were docile, when the Dominicans (called dogs of the Lord) knew their stuff, when Copernicus and Galileo with their pestiferous practice of private judgment and individualism were properly held in leash. Yes, he would have us return to that springtime of human hope so closely associated with the historic word St. Bartholomew and the historic and glorious name of Torquemada, and with that fairest blossom of human hope and Catholic dogma known as the Inquisition, whose normal functioning brought glory to Mother Church by chasing heretics up to heaven through martyr flames or down to hell through dungeon darkness as the case might be.

Now Mr. MacManus commits various fallacies in his Philippic against individualism and Protestantism. The Baptist has little trouble in answering him.

Our Catholic friend fails to distinguish rights from beliefs. We have ever stood for the rights, civic, intellectual, political and religious of the rationalist as well as the Christian. But that is a far cry from accepting the beliefs of the rationalist.

Individualism is a dangerous principle but so is every other great principle of enlightenment and progress. As held by evangelical Christians it assumes that God made man in his own image on the one hand, and on the other that He made nature and Christianity. The mind of man, therefore, can find truth if left free to seek it. The alternative is to permit man to attain full growth under a system which allows him to think for himself, with the Bible as his guide, or to remain intellectually and spiritually a moron under a system of compulsion and repression.

God reveals himself and his revelations become man's discoveries. The Reformation along with the Anabaptist movement which preceded it was the rediscovery of God in Christ. "Justification by faith" was the formula which expressed the spiritual meaning of that discovery. The equal right of all men to direct approach to God was the necessary assumption back of the discovery. The Scriptures as the authentic and authoritative record of Christ and his salvation were the sourcebook which led to the discovery. The Holy Spirit regenerating the soul of man and illuminating his intellect in accordance with the facts and teachings of the New Testament was the safeguard of the individual in his progressive interpretation of the meaning of the great discovery. Loyalty to Christ and submission to his will in all things are the guaranty against rationalistic license in thought and the pledge of righteousness in life and character.

Our Catholic friend omits from his description of Protestantism the authoritative Scriptures, the regenerating and illuminating Spirit of God, the transforming experience of God's redeeming grace in the soul, and the supreme Lordship and Saviourhood of Jesus Christ. For the authoritative New Testament he substitutes the Church; for the Holy Spirit he substitutes the sacraments; for the transforming inner experience he substitutes an outward conformity to ritualistic observances; and for the Lordship of Christ he substitutes the earthly vice-regent, the pope.

The right of private judgment is a dangerous word, but it is a winged and emancipating word. It is the sole guaranty that man will pass out of the childhood to the manhood stage of religion. It is the key that Hubmeier and Bunyan used to unlock the door of the dungeon wherein man's intellect had been so long imprisoned. It was the hammer with which Roger Williams broke the chain which united church and state. It was the word which inspired the heroic courage of Oncken, and the stubborn, passive, resistance of a Clifford. The right of private judgment, kindled the vision of world evangelization to the faith of William Carey and transformed western Christianity. The right of private judgment: yes, a dangerous word, but a word which started man on new voyage of spiritual discovery, a word which gave his spirit wings to soar among the angels in its flight upward to God.

The right of private judgment, a mighty word, unsealing the fountains of power in the nature of man, and bearing fruit in countless numbers of towering personalities, precipitating many a heroic struggle for the rights of man, producing the Puritan and Pilgrim migrations, creating modern democracies and crushing ancient tyrannies.

It is true it produced the sects of Protestantism. But these, after all, are not comets or wandering stars without central control, plunging blindly through space. Jesus Christ is their centre and sun. They are separated planets some nearer to and some farther from the centre. But their loyalty to Christ balances their right of private judgment and is the guaranty that the faith of the New Testament shall not perish from the earth.

Baptists believe that they have stripped away the adventitious elements clinging to most Protestant bodies as a heritage from medieval

Catholicism; that they retain and promulgate Christianity in its New Testament simplicity, with its universal elements, and with its spiritual appeal—and as such adapted to the intellectual and spiritual needs of the world for all time.

We, like all others, however, have had our faults. There are dangers and pitfalls peculiar to our genius.

We have not always been controlled by our ideals and affinities so much as by our antipathies and oppositions, not by our likes, but by our dislikes. A man's enemy may dominate his life by imposing upon him the law of his conduct. A man who orders all his actions to circumvent his foe is the worst kind of a slave of that foe.

A man is transformed by the thing he comtemplates. "Vice is a monster of such frightful mien—that to be hated needs but to be seen, when seen full oft, familiar with her face—we first endure, then pity, then embrace."

This also is true:

> "Virtue is an angel of such gracious mien
> That to be loved needs but to be seen
> When seen full oft, familiar with her face,
> We first admire then welcome then embrace."

Baptists should be a race of lovers not a race of fighters. Our work is constructive not destructive. We need the mood of all the great builders because our task is essentially a constructive one. We need the imagination of the architect because we are building a human temple with living men as stones. We need the passion of the great poet because divine fire alone can fuse human spirits into the unity and glory of the image of God. We need the patience of the great painter and sculptor, because the human material on which we labor is refractory and yields but slowly. We need the inspiration of the great composer because we live essentially in a world of spiritual harmonies, and it is only as we are swayed by the eternal music that is sounding itself forever through the heart of God that we can do his work in the world. We need the sense of proportion of the landscape gardener and his skill in combining the features of a landscape into harmonious unity because we must take human nature as it is in all ranks and conditions and combine it into spiritual harmony. We need the constructive genius of the great statesman because we are a vast people ourselves and deal with vast problems. We need education and culture because our method of winning men is the appeal to reason and conscience. We need skill to touch human motives and the springs of human action because we can only appeal to men through the highest there is in them. We cannot compel men by authority or attract them by external pomp and grandeur. We have but one way of making men and that is the lure of the eternal, the fadeless splendor of righteousness, the matchless potency of love and the undying power of religion itself.

Our Relation to Other Protestants
F. W. Patterson

I regard this morning session of the Congress of the Baptist World Alliance as of singular importance. Organized religion tends always to be influenced by the character of the political and industrial organization of its day. In industry, this is the day of "big business," of mergers and of colossal organizations, and organized religion has become infected. From some sources come overtures that look ultimately to the union of all churches, while from others comes the suggestion that a merger of at least the major Protestant bodies would greatly advance the kingdom of God. In some countries—Canada is a conspicuous example—notable movements looking to the union of all Protestant bodies have already taken place. Many who suggest these mergers give their suggestion the effect of a demand, and assume that the organic union of all Protestant churches is the ecclesiastical *summum bonum,* and the choice of a separate ministry the great ecclesiastical immorality, the supreme disqualification for any ministry at all.

In such a setting we meet to-day. The fact that we meet as a Baptist World Alliance assumes that we believe that we are justified, for the present at least, in continuing a separate existence. Yet the session of this morning implies that in choosing to preserve our denominational entity we do not wish to withdraw ourselves from the main trends of Protestantism. We cannot live to ourselves alone, unmindful of the opinions and unrelated to the tasks of others. The task assigned me today is that of stating wherein we are at one with the great body of Protestants, and wherein we find it necessary to function separately. I take it that with such a setting and with such a task, I am to speak not as an individual expressing an individual opinion, but as a representative; for the twenty-five minutes allotted to me, the voice of the Baptist world; my task to get beneath the differences that are supervicial to the unities that are fundamental; to select from the several voices of the Baptist world the common notes that make the Baptist world voice.

Two sentences contain the pith of all that I might say. First: Baptists generally are not antagonistic to other Protestants, nor in their major aims in competition with them. Second: In the present state of Protestantism, Baptists are justified in maintaining a separate existence. All else that I have to say merely amplifies these two positions.

First—Baptists generally are not antagonistic to other Protestants, nor in their major aims in competition with theirs: Such a statement should not be necessary. The things that Baptists have in common with other Protestants are much more important than the things in which they differ from them. If we think of other Protestants in terms of origins, Baptists spring from the same general stock; if we think of them in terms of truth, Baptists confess joyfully that they hold great areas of truth in common; they are nourished by the same Scriptures; they believe in the same God and in His grace; they worship in the same spirit; they recognize equally the fact of sin, the necessity of redemption, the initiative of God in the work of redemption, and the sufficiency of Jesus Christ as the way to God. If we think of them in terms of objectives, our general aims and our major emphasis are the same. We know that Baptists have no monopoly of Christianity and that it is more important that men be Christian than that they be Baptist. The general aim of Baptists, as of other Protestants, is to extend and to establish the reign of God in the lives of men.

That I may make my meaning clearer, let me state my position somewhat differently. Imagine, if it is possible, two alternatives placed before this Congress. On the one hand, we are permitted to remove from the thinking of men all things that Baptists have in common with other Protestants and save for the world the distinctive tenets of Baptists. On the other hand, we are permitted to remove from the world the things for which Baptists today are distinctive and to save for the world the things that Baptists have in common with other Protestants. There can be no compromise; these are the only alternatives. The choice rests with us. Fortunately, such an alternative cannot arise, but it will aid our perspective if we face its possibility. Our action could scarcely be called a choice; at least it would be without hesitation. The common heritage of Protestantism must be preserved for the world, even though the distinctive heritage of Baptists be lost.

This oneness with other Protestants expresses itself in many ways. Our libraries contain the same titles; we confess our debt to the same expositors and critical scholars; we sing the same hymns; use the same vocabulary; speak from the same platforms; support the same causes; in great areas of our work our interests are one. And if this is true, the competition of enmity between Baptists and other Protestants is unthinkable. In the teaching of Jesus, enmity is reserved for sin and does not extend even to the sinner. To be at enmity with those whom we recognize as fellow Christians, and with whom we have so much in common, is a denial of the Gospel we profess.

Second—In the present state of world Protestantism, Baptists can do no other than continue their separate existence: It is probable that to some Baptists, as well as to non-Baptists, this will seem inconsistent with my earlier statement. I do not think that it is. My two positions are inconsistent only if the unities that I have affirmed are the whole of Christianity. It is the Baptist belief that they are not the whole of Christianity; or that if in any general terms they are, the faithfulness with which the implications are worked out is only less important than the truth itself. I have already stated that in their general aims Baptists are not in competition with other Protestants. This does not mean that there is no competition. Whenever and in just the degree that interpretations differ, competition is inevitable. Any given point of view is always in competition with a differing point of view, nor is such competition evil. It is evil only when any one point of view is held in pride, and the lust of victory displaces the love of truth. It is through conflict that truth is reached. The truths that any of us hold today have not won their place without struggle. If there is no conflict, there is no criticism, and truth that has not been criticized is truth that has not been vindicated. Truth is always larger than our conception of it. The interpretation of the individual must be subjected to the criticism of the group, and the interpretation of the group to the criticism of other groups. The disagreement of prejudice can serve only to perpetuate both the prejudice and the disagreement, but the disagreement of the inquiring is a necessary step toward the unanimity of truth. The existence within Protestantism of several groups holding the same general truths, but with differing emphases, has enriched Protestant thought and life to a much greater extent than would have been possible had there been only one Protestant group, even though that group had been a Baptist group. For in the conflict of opinions the truth that has emerged has been not quite the point of view that entered the struggle. In viewing the course of Protestantism, one can trace the changes in Baptist thinking through the criticism of others, as well as the changes in the thinking of other Protestants through the criticism of Baptists.

It is, of course, true that the organic union of Protestant churches ought not to hinder freedom of criticism. That in actual practice it would hinder it, I am sure. Even in smaller groups one sees the tendency to fix statements of truth by a majority vote, and when that danger exists it must be avoided at all costs. Two or more groups, working side by side, acknowledging a common heritage, yet each with a distinct emphasis, may be nearer the mind of Christ than one large group, in which differing emphases are either suppressed or neglected.

Neither can I bring myself to take seriously the plea that Protestants must effect an organic union if they are to compete successfully with Roman Catholicism. This plea assumes, falsely, that in the progress of the Kingdom of God the magnitude of the church is important. There are places where majorities, or the groups that can command majorities, count,—at the polls, in lobbies of parliaments,—in brief, wherever force, or the show of force, is a weapon. But when what the majorities, as such, can do has been done, the Kingdom of God will not have advanced one iota. In the things of the spirit, the victory must rest with quality and not with quantity. Majorities may be, and often are, singularly impotent. For neither a majority nor a minority as such, but spiritual vitality advances the kingdom that is within. The weakness of any large organization is not that it is large, but that, being large, it tends to rely on the forces that only a large organization can command. The periods during which the church has been persecuted because relatively small have usually been the periods of its greatest prosperity. The fear I have is that the church is already too large, that not all of its growth is the "increase of God," and that the great need of the church today is not that it be larger, but that it be better.

All this, of course, may be true and Baptists still be without justification for a separate existence. The statements I have made are general and may, or may not, be pertinent in the present discussion. That the early separatism of Baptists was justified will be freely admitted. Their contribution to the life of the church as a whole is generally, though sometimes reluctantly, recognized. But the situation has changed. The range of unities has broadened, the influence of Protestant bodies upon each other has been such that in basic faith they are more nearly one then ever before. No church wishes to make the mistake of many political parties, which come into existence to defend vital issues and later create issues to justify their existence. Are there yet issues that justify our existence, or are we merely deluding ourselves?

The Protestantism of Baptists is not primary; it is but the obverse side of great affirmations. The Baptist protest is two-fold. It is, first, a protest against the restriction of grace to mechanical channels, and the admission to the church of those whose fitness is their baptism administered by proper authorities. This protest grew out of their faith that the church was a spiritual organism and that only those who chose the Christ life should be its members. The second was a protest against the authority of crowns, of councils, and of creeds, and grew out of the belief that authority in matters of religion rests ultimately with the redeemed individual. Nor is this inconsistent with the recognition of Scripture as a sufficient authority in faith and practice. Nothing can become an external authority for one until it has received the visé of the authority within. These two affirmations, the authority of the individual and the spirituality of the church, may be called the Baptist principles; for out of these all else that is vital grows. These principles are of the essence of the religion of Jesus. The church must be founded on personal religion, and personal religion must be based on personal freedom.

In defining our relations to other Protestants, one cannot forget that we are meeting today not as Baptists of Canada, of the United States, or of Great Britain, but as representatives of Baptists throughout the world.

The relations we are considering in this address are not merely to Protestants with whom we have most in common, but to Protestants of all varieties of belief, and to Protestants everywhere. Of these, a very large number hold still to sacerdotalism. Believing equally with ourselves in the grace of God as the ground of human redemption, they destroy the majesty of their faith by restricting the channels within which that grace must flow. To state our principles as I have done is to suggest at once our relations to Protestants of this faith. Against all such restriction of the grace of God, the separate existence of Baptists must continue to protest.

But not all organized Protestantism is sacerdotal. What is to be our relation to Protestants who, equally with ourselves, deny sacerdotalism? Here one can speak only in the most general terms. There is not the time, neither is this the place to discuss the several varieties of Protestants. This, however, must be said. Baptists must reaffirm for themselves the spirituality of the church. Holding in principle to a regenerated church membership, in practice they find it easy to be false to their principle. As it becomes easy to unite with the church, the church itself tends to become less Christian. With such a difficulty within their own membership, Baptists must examine carefully every merger of which they are asked to become a part. The larger the organization and the more it secures an unofficial establishment, the more nearly the membership of the church tends to coincide with citizenship. From any merger that tends to make the church less of a spiritual organism, by opening its membership to those who have not chosen the Christ life, Baptists must withhold their support.

Let it be granted at once that there are movements looking toward union that cannot be criticised on these grounds. What is to be our relation to these? Again I must remind you that we are meeting as a Baptist World Alliance. During the years since the organization of the Alliance, Baptists throughout the world have achieved a sense of unity before unknown. During that same period, our members have greatly increased. That increase has been especially notable in continental Europe. In many of the countries in which Baptists have grown most rapidly, they have met bitter opposition and faced severe persecution. Today they need not only the financial help of Baptists in more favorably circumstanced parts of the world, but the help which comes from a common name, a common organization, and participation in a common task. We have only to recall what the Baptist World Alliance, through its President and Secretary, has meant to the Baptists of Roumania, to understand what it may mean to those unfortunately situated anywhere. It is almost certain that no larger merger into which Baptists could enter either would or could give the needed help in the hour of stress. In many of these communities Baptists are almost the only representatives of evangelical truth. It is, therefore, not less in the interests of the Kingdom of God on a world scale than in the interests of world Baptists that Baptists today continue their separate existence.

This, then, is our position. We have malice toward none; we have charity toward all; we hold equally with others the vision of a united church. We are suspicious only of any movement which thinks more of organized union than of the unity of the spirit. We regard the progress of the Kingdom of God as of greater moment than the progress of any church, even though it be our own. We welcome every advance of every group that means the advance of the Kingdom; with every such movement we gladly cooperate. We do feel, however, that we know our own business and the scale of the stage on which we must play our part, better than others who know little or nothing of the Baptist world outside their local communities. For the present, at least, we believe that we can best serve Him whose we are not by merging in a larger union, but by becoming better Baptists than we have ever been before.

5
Berlin
1934

Introduction

Destined to meet in Berlin in 1933, the BWA postponed its meeting until 1934. Meeting in that year provided Baptists the opportunity to commemorate three centennials: the death of William Carey, the birth of Charles Haddon Spurgeon, and the organization of the first Baptist church in Germany under the leadership of Johann Gerhard Oncken.

The BWA made much of those three names in Berlin in 1934. But the name of primary concern was not that of Carey or of Spurgeon or of Oncken. It was Hitler. In an atmosphere taut with anxiety, Baptists gave witness to the ideas of a free church in a free state and the lordship of Christ. The delegates passed significant resolutions on "Racialism" and "Church and State." Almost all of the addresses and reports of 1934 alluded, usually indirectly, to the political situation in Germany.

No presidential address was given in Berlin. John MacNeil, pastor of Walmer Road Baptist Church in Toronto, had been elected BWA president in 1928. Because of illness, he was unable to attend the Berlin meeting. The two addresses selected to mirror the Berlin conference are of different types. The first is the report of J. H. Rushbrooke, the general secretary of the BWA. His address—"The Baptist People and The World Alliance"—described the character and accomplishments of the BWA. Rushbrooke's reference to Oncken in the last paragraph was far more than a dull report or a historical illustration. Rushbrooke was speaking to the present situation. Thus, he closed with a question from Scripture: "If God be for us, who can be against us?"

Mr. Corwin S. Shank, an American layman and past president of the Northern Baptist Convention, US, spoke on the subject, "A World in Commotion." With a layman-like plainness and an Amos-

like tone, he forthrightly denounced race-prejudice and war. Mr.
Shank was, if anything, relevant. He asked—*in Berlin!*—"Shall the
Jew, the Gentile, the Aryan, the Caucasian, the Latin, the Celtic,
or any other, assert special claims on account of these racial differences?" And as for war, Shank called it "the curse of the world, the
blight of humanity and the world's mightiest ally of hell." Printed
here is an abbreviated version of Shank's address.

The Baptist People and the World Alliance
J. H. Rushbrooke

We are profoundly thankful that this Baptist World Congress is meeting
in Berlin.

Precisely twenty years ago, on August 4th, 1914, Britain and Germany
entered upon war. The devastating world-wide conflict shattered our
plans for holding a Congress in this city in 1916. August fourth has now
for twenty years remained an anniversary of sad and tragic memory; 1934
will, I venture to believe, see the day in some measure redeemed, so that,
at least for Baptists, and I would fain hope for multitudes outside our
communion, the fourth of August shall henceforth stand out as a day when
in Christian love and unity men and women of many races and tongues
and nations came together in Berlin to open a conference rich in potentialities of understanding and enduring friendship, emphasising from first
to last "one God and Father of all," and radiating throughout the earth
the spirit of the Prince of Peace. God Himself grant that this day become
a red letter day in our annals!

My task is, as your General Secretary, to offer a report. What has the
Alliance accomplished since the last World Congress? What are the outstanding achievements of the six years between "Toronto" and "Berlin"?

I.

Let us at the outset focus our thought upon the character of our Alliance. Its functions according to its constitution are "more fully to show
the essential oneness of Baptist people in the Lord Jesus Christ, to impart
inspiration to the brotherhood, and to promote the spirit of fellowship,
service and co-operation among them." Nothing more simple can be
imagined, and nothing more simply Christian. There is no authoritarian
note, no interference with the self-direction under God of our people or
our Churches, no attempt at unification or domination by legal prescrip-
tion or external constraint. Our Alliance is—if you will—undramatic: a
sensation-hunting press would not as a rule find its doings "good copy."

As Baptists we rely on purely spiritual forces: the redeeming grace of God in our Lord Jesus Christ, the power of His Spirit and His Word. In fellowship with Him we seek to strengthen one another in the faith, to the end that we may in all parts of the earth render our full meed of service for His Kingdom. Our unity is solely and essentially religious. As a religious communion, we hold no brief for any political party or for any national or economic programme. We are conscious of a loyalty that transcends all these and we bring all to the test of that higher loyalty. We limit our fellowship by no frontiers of race or speech or colour: we have not so learned Christ. We are patriots indeed, loving our own country, wherever it be; and when we claim, as through all our history we have always claimed, freedom from control by State or magistrate, we do so not only because as Christians we are bound to resist any invasion of "the Crown Rights of the Redeemer," but also because as patriots we know that the finest service we can render to country consists in the free expression of our deepest evangelical-ethical convictions. A fettered church can never uplift a people. The history of Russia has written that lesson in letters of fire and blood for all the world to read!

Brethren, the more I reflect upon the subject, the more I marvel at the unity of our Baptist communion. It has no parallel on earth. Ask what holds us together. Why from all parts of the world, from China to Chile, from Norway to New Zealand, have our people welcomed our World Alliance and voluntarily and eagerly joined it? We easily understand the unity of Methodists. Their splendid evangelical communities own a common origin in a great founder. We understand Roman Catholic unity, with its visible bonds of canon law, and a sacerdotal order culminating in the centralised authority of the Papacy. We understand the unity of the Anglican body or the Eastern Orthodox Church, resting on an episcopacy claiming "apostolical succession." But what of ours? In many parts of the world Baptist communities have arisen without their members even knowing that there were anywhere others like them—born of the study of the New Testament under the guidance of the interpreting Spirit. Our origins are sporadic and most varied: yet when we discover each other, we find ourselves one. I do not question—nay, I acknowledge with thankful praise to God—the reality of Christian experience beyond our borders; but this I maintain: that there is nothing, and nothing has been since the earliest days of the preaching of the Gospel, comparable with this phenomenon of the conscious oneness of the Baptist people secured by no external machinery but by spiritual forces alone. "This is the Lord's doing, and it is marvellous in our eyes."

II.

Now what service has the World Alliance of Baptists, as a free voluntary association, been able to render to its constituent groups in over sixty countries? It stands as we have seen first and foremost to express and to deepen the common life. *Fraternity* and *inspiration* are its key-notes. Such words may mean little to those who are dazzled by the splendour or stunned by the weight of the merely visible and tangible, but they mean everything to men of clear vision. "Not by might nor by power, but by My Spirit." Because I believe in fraternity and inspiration, I cannot share the point of view of those who sometimes slight the value of our Congress. I know our people. Thanks to the generous confidence of my brethren in calling me to serve first as Baptist Commissioner for Europe and afterwards as Eastern Secretary and General Secretary of the World Alliance, the privilege of intercourse with men and women of the Baptist world has been granted me in unique degree. And I know this: the spirit of this Congress in Berlin will be felt in Argentina, in South Africa, in China and in New Zealand, in India and Burma and Australia, as well as in every part of Europe. We who come from Britain or from the United States, where conferences abound, where hundreds of thousands of fellow-believers satisfy our craving for comradeship, and where the home work is on a vast scale, can scarcely realise the glowing, quivering interest stirred by the brother who goes from this city to tell a small group, feeling its loneliness amid the darkness of paganism, or striving to hold aloft the banner of the Cross amid superstition and indifference and contempt, that he has companied with those who represent millions of fellow believers, and has heard stories that have brought home to him the world-wide range of his Christian fellowship. Our Congress means something very great to our weak and isolated groups: even an Elijah is cheered by learning of the seven thousand!

These treasures of inspiration and fraternity have been mediated to our people in large measure through the personalities that God has shaped for service in and through our Baptist communion. Not only at World Congresses but in regional conferences, and in the visitation of fields far away from the centres of our denominational life, the impact—dare I say?—of God has been realised through the leaders He has granted us. My colleagues in the Executive Committee would be at one with me in naming with special emphasis the president elected at Toronto, Principal John MacNeill. His illness deprives us of the opportunity of voicing in his presence our appreciation and gratitude, but we shall find means of assuring him that he has won an enduring place in our people's heart. He has given us of his best—a fine best. His time and energy have been unsparingly devoted to the work for which we chose him. We recall his journey round the world in the Northern Hemisphere, and the tributes to his genial and inspirational qualities which poured in from Japan and China, Burma and India. His fervent evangelical outlook, his cheery temperament, and the grace of his spirit, gained friends and left a legacy of good everywhere. Dr. MacNeill is brotherhood incarnate, and in the person of its president the world-fellowship which the Alliance cherishes has been symbolised and vitalised for thousands. Nor has his influence been limited to the Far East; in a dozen European lands he has heartened and strengthened his brethren; and the United States and his own beloved Canada add their tributes. We glorify God in him, realising that in such an organisation as ours, where legal authority and sacerdotal status play no part, the personality of a president is a decisive factor. May the Alliance be able always to discover and welcome divinely-equipped leadership!

In speaking of the president, I have noted that the Alliance has through him reached brethren in far-off regions which can be but sparsely represented at a World Congress. This side of our activities has developed during these six years on a wider scale than ever before. During Dr. Mullins' presidency he planned a voyage to Australia, but his medical advisors interposed their veto. It was thus reserved for me, with the consent and goodwill of my colleagues, to become a living link with Australia and New Zealand, and incidentally to touch South Africa. I will not enlarge on incidents of the journey—the civic receptions, the friendship extended to me as the representative of a great religious communion by Governors and Prime Ministers, the generous hospitality, the extraordinary effective planning. In one great city the radio was invoked, so that while I preached in one church the congregations in others participated in the service and the broadcast reached the whole Dominion. These were but incidents. The great matter was the contact in Christian fellowship with those occupying the far-distant outposts, bringing home to them the fact that they are not forgotten, but that the Alliance has a special concern for them, and I am profoundly thankful that the visit served to deepen Baptist world-consciousness among our brothers of the Antipodes. More than a dozen of them have come from the other side of the globe to be present here to-day.

During these six years we have touched every continent of the Southern Hemisphere. My contact with South Africa was all too brief, but the Alliance is indebted to Mr. Arthur Newton, a past-president of the British Baptist Union, who in the course of a journey undertaken for the sake of his health, became our messenger to the scattered churches of that Dominion. The outstanding event during our period was, however, the Latin-American Baptist Congress at Rio de Janeiro. South America has in the last generation shewn itself widely responsive to our evangelical message, and a great crowd of Spanish-speaking and Portuguese-speaking Baptists from various parts of that continent gathered in the splendid First Church at Rio under the presidency of the eloquent Brazilian pastor, Dr. F. F. Soren. (He has since died, and his passing represents a severe loss to his country.) The Alliance accepted the invitation to send its General Secretary, and also asked two others who intended to be present, Dr. George Truett, a member of the Executive, and Dr. T. B. Ray, to represent it. We were all three made honorary presidents of the Congress, whereupon Dr. Ray remarked, using an American phrase that reduced a competent interpreter to utter despair, "This Congress is *topheavy on presidents.*" No one not actually there could begin to measure the value of that assembly. I leave aside my own messages. The dominant figure was Dr. Truett, and how he represented us! Evening after evening came his evangelical appeal to crown the day, and even under the disadvantage of speaking through an interpreter his passion and power won men and women to decision for Christ. The Congress stands out in my memory as also a discipleship campaign. Brethren, there is more to say of South America— the hunger of the people for the Evangel impressed me not only in Brazil, but in Argentina and Uruguay. I recall a Sunday in Montevideo. It was at the end of the fifth and last service of the day! I had offered a simple exposition of a section of the first chapter of the Gospel by John; at the close at least a third of the hearers were on their feet as seekers after Christ. I recall other incidents of similar character though not quite on the same scale. Strange that in some older countries the wonder and glory and transforming power of the Word appear lost! I am haunted by a sentence in Seeley's *Ecce Homo* which I read in my youth, "The article of conversion is *articulus stantis aut cadentis ecclesiae*"—the article of a standing or falling church. Of all people Baptists should realise that. We are not genuinely evangelical if we are not effectively evangelistic!

III.

Brotherhood, inspiration, the Evangel of the grace of God—the Alliance represents these, and not merely as abstract ideas. In the name of brotherhood it has undertaken specific tasks.

It has been our duty, as in earlier years, to stand for the defence of religious freedom wherever and however assailed. Conditions in *Rumania,* so far as governmental action is concerned, are definitely better— though not by any means ideal. *Russia* has occasioned the deepest anxiety. Russian Baptists returned from the Toronto Congress of 1928 to find their government preparing measures of repression, and early in 1929 these took the form of law. You will hear during this Congress a statement of religious conditions in Soviet Russia, and we may therefore omit details. Your Executive Committee took the only possible action by adopting and publishing a world-wide appeal in these terms:—

"The Executive Committee of the Baptist World Alliance assembled in Detroit, U.S.A., on Friday, 17th May, 1929, appeals to Baptists of every race and tongue and to other lovers of religious freedom in all parts of the world, to offer continuous and united prayer for their fellow-believers in Russia, and for all others who in that land, in this twentieth century, are denied religious liberty and exposed to disabilities and persecution because of their loyalty to their conscience and their Lord."

Would that it were possible to suggest that this appeal is out of date! Unhappily it is not. So far as we are able to judge, sheer brutality has somewhat diminished, but I have as yet found no trace of any weakening of the purpose to eradicate religion. The Bible cannot be printed in Russia. No Sunday school or Bible class can be held. No public evangelistic effort is possible. Ministers are denied the ordinary rights of citizenship. Many of our Baptist people are in prison or in exile. During the discussions in Washington last November regarding the recognition of Soviet Russia by the United States, we forwarded a letter to President Roosevelt in which, after setting forth the facts, we added:—

"We trust that you may be able to secure some definite modification of the attitude hitherto prevailing. In expressing this hope we desire to reaffirm and to emphasize that, deeply as we are moved by the heavy burdens borne by members of our own faith and order, our plea is not for Baptists as such, but for the freedom of conscience and worship and preaching which is a human right."

In other directions we have been active on behalf of our Russian brethren. The Baptist World Alliance is not an administrative body, but we could not close our hearts and hands in the presence of their need. Your Executive has directed attention to the necessities of the refugees in Manchuria and North-Western China, circulating such information as was available, and supporting with all its influence the efforts to help these as well as the victims of the famine which raged last year in certain parts of the Soviet territory. In response to these efforts substantial sums have been specially contributed and transmitted from the United States and Britain. Scandinavia has also done much, and to the honour of the Baptists of Germany it should be recorded that they, in association with the Mennonites, have done still more.

Our brotherhood with the German Baptists has found practical expression in connection with the exclusion of their missionaries from the *Cameroons*. We joined them years ago in a successful appeal to the British Government to permit German missionaries to work in the section of the Cameroons which Britain administers, and we stand with them in their claim for similar treatment by the French Government in its administrative area. The claim has unhappily not been admitted by France, and we feel that our German brethren have legitimate grievances in respect of the exclusion of their missionaries from their former fields, and the alienation of their property to a non-Baptist society. That society has indeed consented to employ some non-German Baptist agents, but this does not annul the essential injustice of action motivated by nationalistic ideas and prejudices. The German claim is not abandoned, and the issue will not be settled until it is settled right.

IV.

I pass on to call attention to certain new forms of activity which the Alliance has initiated in the interests of Baptist efficiency for Kingdom service.

(1) The first of these, and perhaps the most important, has been the appointment of *Commissions* composed of representative men and women, as far as possible with special qualifications, to study outstanding ethical issues, and to submit to this Congress their reports and recommendations. It is to your Executive self-evident that if Jesus Christ be, as our faith acclaims Him, Lord of all, the understanding of His mind and will must furnish definite criteria for the attitude and action of His disciples amid the confusion of modern thought and life. We could not conceive that He would have nothing to say in the presence of widespread abandonment of moral standards, envy and strife between classes, fear and suspicion between nations, "the clash of colour," rivalry in armaments, and so forth. Five important subjects were therefore selected for study, viz.: Moral Standards, Temperance, Economics, Nationalism, and Racialism. Those Commissions were appointed more than three years ago, and 155 members from 45 countries consented to serve upon them. The Alliance is indebted to all, and in particular to those who served as chairmen, and cheerfully accepted the heavy burden of gathering and summarising information. It is not to be expected that the reports on such complex subjects will in every sentence and syllable command the approval of all the members of our communion, but it is expected and hoped that they will provide evidence of a common mind and outlook, so that they may be commended to our constituent bodies as guides to definite action and a starting point for further study. The Congress will, we trust, recognise the value and the promise of this new method of co-operative thinking and encourage its wider development.

(2) Another new line of service, which has already justified itself, concerns Baptist *literature*. We have issued a series of articles dealing with the lives of great Baptists. Our various countries have their own treasures of Christian heroism, and the purpose of the series is to ensure that as far as possible these special treasures shall become the property of our whole

communion. The subjects have been carefully selected by the Executive, and the Alliance is deeply indebted to the writers. They are in each case men invited as specially qualified, and they have willingly served "without fee or reward." I am happy to report that the articles have been widely welcomed by editors throughout the world; they have been translated and printed in many languages, and in several countries have been collected and issued in book form. This experiment was so far successful that a new series of articles has been planned and already partly written. It deals with Baptist missionary developments since 1792. Each writer has to deal not with mission societies but with countries or regions. We need to break through our insularity. England, for example, knows the Congo, and a section of India and China—in other words it knows the fields of its own Baptist Missionary Society—but it knows little of Burma, of the wonderful "Lone Star Mission" in South India, of Nigeria or South America or Japan. I modestly select English Baptists as an illustration of our ignorance—but don't lay to your souls the flattering unction that others are better informed than the English! But if this series receives as wide a welcome as the first, it will extend our knowledge of the work of God in the world through His Baptist people.

In connection with this question of Baptist literature, let me offer a casual illustration of the ways in which the Alliance seeks to help the brethren. A letter came from a certain European country stating that the writer could find no simple book dealing with the duties and responsibilities of Church membership, and suitable for placing in the hands of candidates for baptism. Enquiries revealed a similar lack in other countries. It happened that an excellent pamphlet by Mr. Gilbert Laws on the subject had found acceptance in England. He readily consented to excise or modify the few passages—half a dozen sentences or so—which had reference to distinctively English topics, and within a very few weeks his pamphlet had been issued in nine countries and in twelve languages.

V.

May I devote a brief section of my report to the work of the Committees during this period? The *Executive Committee* has held no less than seven full sessions, and it is but just to its members to acknowledge the keen attention which the great majority devote to their work. It must needs be that some living far away from the places of meeting cannot attend; but as a rule these have taken steps to name proxy-holders who can. You should also know this: nothing could be more harmonious than an Executive meeting of this Alliance. We know no sectional or personal divisions. Our concern is for the whole brotherhood. If any point of view ever receives preferential consideration, it is that of absent members. Because this spirit rules, the Committee has constituted the British members an

Administrative Sub-Committee with large powers, so that I might have the advantage of consulting a group which could be easily summoned and could authorise action. This sectional Sub-Committee, everyone recognises, has never been sectional in its outlook or decisions; and nothing it has done during these six years has failed to receive unanimous endorsement at the next full meeting of the Executive.

A word should be devoted to the *Youth Committee* under the chairmanship of Dr. T. G. Dunning. He and Dr. Frank Leavell and their colleagues have given new reality and warmth to the international fellowship of the young people of our communion. A separate report of their conference in Prague, and the intervisitation that has marked the years, will be presented at their own meeting next week. But all that makes for the health of young Baptist life concerns the Alliance as a whole, and you would wish to congratulate the Committee on its energy and its success. Some service, especially for peace, has also been undertaken by the *women*, and it has revealed a weakness in our organisation. More and better work could have been done, in the opinion of many, if there had been a standing committee to lead as the Youth Committee leads; and at this Congress your Executive has already given notice of a constitutional amendment to ensure in future a sufficient number of women members to make a special committee possible. Spirit is more than organisation, but we wish to make our organisation capable of giving full expression to the spirit of our people.

<h2 style="text-align:center">VI.</h2>

A well-known passage in *Ecclesiasticus*—not a canonical book, but very fine nevertheless—contains the words:—

> "Let us now praise famous men,
> And our fathers that begat us.
> The Lord manifested in them great glory. . . .
> Such as have brought tidings in prophecies:
> Leaders of the people by their counsels,
> And by their understanding men of learning for the people."

How the language fits men who have been called from us during these years! *Edgar Young Mullins*: we named him at Toronto the Baptist *par excellence*. As thinker, educationist, author, administrator, he held a unique position among us, and the great presidential address at Toronto read in his absence (for already the sickness held him from which he rallied awhile but did not recover) remains as a legacy of inspiration and challenge—supreme even among the utterances of a man of rare intellect and penetrating spiritual insight. He belongs to history. *Charles Alvin Brooks:* even after years I can scarce trust myself to speak of him, the best of friends and comrades, a man I loved and love. Europe owed him much. Never can I forget that adventurous journey he and I undertook in 1920. He claimed that he saved my life on one exciting occasion, and I think the claim was justified. He served on the Executive but a short time; and then, just as his American brethren had called him to high and responsible service, His God called him to higher. "I know transplanted human worth will bloom to profit, otherwise." *C. H. Parrish:* winsome, vigorous, loveable: his long service for the spiritual uplift of his fellow negroes and on our Committee is unforgotten. *W. J. McGlothlin:* erudite, genial, brotherly, whose tragic passing cast its shadow upon the Washington Convention, and who lives in the admiration and gratitude of Southern Baptists, but not of them alone. He, too, was a member of our Committee. *William Young Fullerton* was not; nevertheless in countless ways, never troubling about recognition, he served this Alliance with pen and tongue. Paul Besson (or as South America calls him *Don Pablo*) a romantic figure, knight-errant of the Gospel, crusader for religious liberty in the land of his adoption—a man in whom were united an amazing scholarship, an arresting audacity, and a profound Christian humility: our Baptist communion has in all its story no more fascinating hero than Don Pablo of Argentina. To all these we apply the words of Ecclesiasticus, "The Lord manifested in them great glory"; and our Baptist life is enlarged by what they through His grace have contributed.

These heroes have passed on to join the company that includes those outstanding men whose centenaries we celebrate this year—Carey, Spurgeon, Oncken. "These all died in faith"; and the word confronts us "God having appointed some better thing concerning us, that apart from us they should not be made perfect." How searching, challenging, that word! They fail, unless their spirit lives in us and we carry on their work. Building sepulchres for the prophets, chanting the praises of the fathers—it is all meaningless unless their faith, their venture, their patience, their courage animate us to render service in our day as they wrought in theirs. Are we facing our task as they faced theirs? Have we the vitalising energy of great convictions and a great experience? Have we the same hold on the Living God? The world, the flesh, and the devil—unbelief and lust, greed and hate—shriek against us. "Who is sufficient for these things"? In the land of Oncken you his countrymen, and we all with you, will catch anew the vision that Oncken had. "You will find, Herr Senator," said Oncken, "that all your labour and effort to suppress us by force will be in vain." "Be it so" was the menacing answer, "as long as I can move my little finger it shall be raised against you." And Oncken retorted: "Herr Senator, I believe that you cannot see what I see: I see not a little finger, but a great Arm—the Arm of God. So long as that Arm can move, you will not bring me to silence." "If God be for us, who can be against us?"

"With force of arms we nothing can,
Full soon were we down-ridden;
But for us fights the proper Man,
Whom God Himself hath bidden.
Ask ye who is this same?
Christ Jesus is His Name,
He, and no other one,
Shall conquer in the battle."

A World in Commotion
Corwin S. Shank

There are certain outstanding causes which chiefly contribute to national disorder, economic loss, moral debauchery and human misery. I shall not attempt specifically to refer to more than two of these. The first I shall mention is race prejudice. The nations are no longer separated as they once were. Modern inventions have brought the teeming populations of remote regions into close contact with the active world, so that we may, in a new sense, acknowledge all nations and all peoples as our neighbours. The great trans-oceanic liners have woven a web around the globe. The air is no longer an unexplored region reserved as the exclusive domain of birds, but out of the ether come from every land the ships of the air that faster than the flight of the eagle convey across sea and land messages of one nation to another. Man's last accomplishment to link the peoples of the world has harnessed the vibrant things of space, and with one flash those in "palace, tavern or cot," may listen to the music, the news of the earth, and to everything which is transmissible by sound from the remotest corners of Christendom. The world is now one great neighbourhood lending a new meaning to the Master's great analysis of "Who is our neighbour?" "There is neither East nor West, Border, nor Breed nor Birth—when two strong men stand face to face, though they come from the ends of the earth."

In this question of race prejudice is tied up elements affecting the peace and harmony of the world. Shall the white race be pitted against the yellow? Shall the Jew, the Gentile, the Aryan, the Caucasian, the Latin, the Celtic, or any other, assert special claims on account of these racial differences? This question is urgent just now as the teeming millions of the Orient are pressing their claims upon the rest of the world. Who can say that in connection with the recent conflict in Asia there did not enter into the action of the League of Nations the element of race prejudice in the manner in which the dispute over Manchuria was handled? Can we regard the withdrawal from the League of certain European and Asiatic nations as wholly free from considerations of race? Just as we have a propaganda among the white people of the world against the yellow, so there is among the yellow peoples a propaganda against the whites. A crystallization of racial consciousness and strength is being steadily urged.

There is only one course by which we may ultimately hope to break down this prejudice and make a real world brotherhood, and that is for the Christian churches to develop an atmosphere of brotherhood and so overcome the selfishness and greed lying at the base of racial estrangements.

Christian brotherhood has stood not ineffectively for a moral leadership, in that it has sought to impress upon the world an idealism founded in the principles of religious liberty and brotherhood. As an evidence of the fruitage of that atmosphere of Christian brotherhood enveloping the world, we have had some outstanding examples of the way in which this finest of all things in human life has broken down selfishness and has ignored racial differences which have caused so much distress. In times of great national calamity, when earthquakes have wrecked island empires, or disease or famine has stalked forth as a grim ravaging spectre, there has arisen from Occident and Orient alike a chorus of sympathy. Race differences were forgotten. While this great human need existed among whatever people, race or colour, there was no faltering throughout the world in bearing the burdens of mercy that humanity might be relieved.

Is it not strange that people will give on this impulse of brotherly love when human beings are in distress, and yet for some trivial matter, and perhaps without any valid excuse, indulge in wars and cause the earth to run red with human blood?

Beyond question, peace between races must go hand in hand with peace between nations. The white race cannot reckon without the yellow, or the yellow without the white. If peace is to be preserved, the brotherhood of man must be as much a reality as the Fatherhood of God among all races, classes and conditions.

Methinks I see a day when the nations of the world will come trembling up to the Throne. Not in tribal bands, not in squadrons of colour, but in one vast throng will they come from the ends of the earth, and each will find in his heart the same song, a chorus of the redeemed.

I invite your attention to a second great problem that the church must face—the curse of the world, the blight of humanity and the world's mightiest ally of hell—war.

Since 1914 the world has learned as never before what war really is. The millions who lie beneath the sod, their resting-place simply marked or even unmarked, as well as those who are going through life crippled and maimed, are mute evidences as to what has been and may be done to our brother man by this relic of barbarism.

To-day there is no nation that is not in the throes of an economic hurricane, due directly to the world war. We know as well as we know anything that none is better off because of the war, but that every nation is suffering from the holocaust.

With these conditions the church must grapple, and it must declare itself as to what course it will pursue in the future with reference to this demon war.

We all recognise that the moral fruits of war are jealousy, hatred, and the breaking down of the moral fibre in the individual as well as in the nation. Where is the man who will rise to-day to say that one good thing comes from war? Did not Christ come to strike the deathblow at everything for which war stands, and does not Christianity seek to establish principles which in every detail are against the teachings of war?

In all systems of Christian morals, jealousy, hate and envy are the enemies at which Christ strikes. It therefore becomes incumbent upon all Christian bodies to work systematically for the spread of the principles of brotherhood throughout the world in order that war, the arch-enemy of mankind, shall be forever outlawed.

There is much said these days about the economic conditions of the world being the moving causes of unrest and distrust between nations. Napoleon, the world's greatest soldier, said: "The world is governed by two powers—the sword and the spirit—but in the end the spirit will always triumph." This was a statement made a century ago, and it is as true to-day as then.

There is little room to question that those who are to-day foremost in the materialistic movements throughout the world have attained their power because they are teaching the adoration of the sword and not of the spirit. I am persuaded that at heart the nations do not seek war; that they do not want war; but they make it, nevertheless, by loudly acclaiming personal and national powers, rather than emphasizing the spirit of that great Advocate of peace Who in all His teaching sought to lay down principles that would bring peace to this earth.

From the time when Christ walked the earth and declared the great doctrine of Peace on Earth, Good Will Towards Men, down to this present hour, there has been only one source of strength to combat the power of the sword, and that is the power of the spirit. In all organized fields of activity the churches are the only bodies which have achieved a sound grasp of this great fundamental world problem and have organizations that enable them to cast an atmosphere over the whole world. The church has been the creator of the international soul.

What the world needs is religion. What it must have is religion. As Roger Babson says:—

"What does permanently change the desires of men and women? Only one thing—namely, Religion. What is Religion? It can not be explained any more than electricity, but, like electricity, we know it is all powerful. The Christian religion is the acceptance of God as one's Master and source of strength as revealed through Jesus. This strength is secured through prayer. Religion expresses itself through those fundamentals of prosperity —a desire to be honest, just, kind, pure, thrifty, industrious, and to render true service. A religious man will worship God and knowingly harm no one. He will do unto others as he would have others treat him. When people become actuated with these desires, it is very evident that all the social, industrial and international problems will quickly solve themselves."

These are plain, homely words from a great economist and business man. Listen to his words again:—

"I feel especially keen in regard to this, as the great need of the day is a national revival of righteousness. The future of our country depends, not on any system of government, but upon the religion and philosophy actuating the men operating our Government. Hence the great need of to-day is a national revival of righteousness under the leadership of those who have integrity, courage and vision."

Here is the challenge of the church. No other organization is set up in a manner that will produce a world atmosphere, and bringing to the world peace among men must comprehend within its plan mankind as a whole and the establishment in the hearts of men of the principles for which Christ lived and died.

With the church's missionary organization, she has reached out into the remotest parts of the earth and has secured a world-view of affairs. The church is the only unselfish organization which has risen above the miasmic fogs of nationalism and has gotten its head into the sunshine of the heavens so that it can look out upon the world and establish an international viewpoint. The church also knows as no other organization does the disintegrating forces of hate, jealousy, and the lust of power. It is the only body of people in the world whose underlying principles are practical ideals urging them onward without regard to personal and private ends to a consideration of what is best for the whole human race.

The church alone can bring about a satisfactory solution of these great world problems; not by meddling with political machinery, but producing a new spirit among men that will permeate the existing order and make it the vehicle of justice and the expression of Christian ideals of neighbourliness and brotherhood. It should have blazoned upon its banner "Above all nations is humanity."

The church is not without a magnificent record of accomplishment. Wherever human beings have been bound down by slavery the church has struck at their shackles until they were broken. It has softened the harshness of feudalism; it has struck at the opium traffic of the world, and is still striking. It has raised womanhood to new high levels. It is an active solvent for the eradication of wrong and the establishment of good. It is daily changing men's hearts and creating new lives.

These achievements and results have been accomplished by creating an atmosphere in which men think and act, and by moulding men into practical harmony with the principles that Christ taught and—most potent of all—changing the attitude of men one towards another.

If we could but keep in mind the fact that war does not spring out of forms of government, but out of the minds of men, then the great mission of the church in dealing with the minds of men would be more concrete and it seems this is an essential.

I would recommend that this Congress take immediate steps to assume its full share in impressing upon the world that it stands for peace and international justice based upon the brotherhood of the Christ of Galilee. I realize that this means the uprooting of the seeds of hate and of jealousy which have grown and borne fruit for centuries in many of the war-torn nations of the world, but the atmosphere of the gospel is like the radiant sunshine which brings healing in its wings.

Let us here declare ourselves and then go to our respective countries and work with an energy never before equalled in creating an atmosphere for peace, and making prominent in the world the Christian's declaration that war is the enemy of both God and man and out of harmony with His great plans in the world.

6
Atlanta
1939

Introduction

Baptists gathered in the sweltering July heat of Atlanta, Georgia, for the sixth Baptist World Congress. This was the first time the meeting had been held in Southern Baptist territory, and it proved to be the largest of all previous gatherings of the BWA. Over 12,000 "messengers" registered, but more than 100,000 others participated in the proceedings.

The Atlanta Congress, in its addresses and resolutions, reflected international tensions and anxieties. In his presidential address, George W. Truett described the situation as "one of the most ominous and epochal hours in the life of the world." "Wars and rumors of wars" circulated among the peoples of the world. Freedom, both civil and religious, was having a hard time in various parts of the world.

In the face of such cosmic darkness, Truett spoke on "The Baptist Message and Mission for The World Today." Ernest Payne, writing after the Congress, hailed the address as "a masterly exposition of Baptist principles by one of the greatest orators and preachers of our time." Truett used the first part of his address to summarize "the Baptist message." Here he underscored traditional Baptist emphases, such as biblical authority, the competency of the individual, religious liberty, the spirituality of the church, and the Baptist attitude toward Christian unity. The last subject was of particular importance in Atlanta because of the Oxford and Edinburgh Conference and other developments in ecumenical Christianity.

In the last half of his address, Truett spoke of "the mission" of Baptists in the contemporary world. He described the Baptist task as "nothing less than the evangelization of the whole world, and to bring it into obedience to Christ." Calling fellow Baptists out of defeatism, he pointed them toward the ideals of courage and faith.

An excellent report had been given on Tuesday morning by N. J. Nordström on the subject of "War and Peace." On Friday evening, the closing session of the Congress, Dr. S. W. Hughes, former pastor of Westbourne Park in London, delivered a challenging address on "World Peace." Hughes's sermon, presented in the form of a threefold creed, needs to be kept before Baptists and the world.

The Baptist Message and Mission for the World Today
George W. Truett

As Baptists from around the encircling globe are gathered in the beautiful, forward-looking and nobly hospitable city of Atlanta, in the Sixth Session of the Baptist World Congress, surely gratitude deep and joyful is in all our hearts, when we recall the grace of God bestowed upon our world-wide Baptist fellowship, during the thirty-four years of the life of the Baptist World Alliance. We are here from five continents, and from some sixty different nations. These messengers of good will are here from the Far East—from India and Burma, and China and Japan; from Australia and New Zealand; from Africa and South America; from practically all the countries of Europe, except Russia, and even that great land will be represented by some of her exiled sons. We are here from Canada and Alaska, and Central America and Cuba, and from the Islands of the Seas. We are here from the United States, North, South, East and West.

One may well wonder whether there has ever assembled on this Continent a more significant religious gathering than is this Congress. The Baptist communion is the largest Free Church communion in the world, numbering between twelve and thirteen million adult members, not including Russia and some other sections where recent statistics are lacking. The Baptist family is by far the largest non-Catholic communion in the United States, her churches numbering more than ten million members. Included in this large company are between three and four million Negro Baptists, whose remarkable growth in numbers and in glorious achievements, let me say to our fellow Baptists from other lands, will forever stand out as epic chapters, in the religious life of America.

All these Baptists here assembled, and the millions of Baptists represented by these messengers, we would fervently salute with Paul's benediction: "Grace be unto you, and peace, from God our Father, and from the Lord Jesus Christ. I thank my God always on your behalf, for the grace of God which is given you by Jesus Christ." Nor would we stop with our salutations to our fellow Baptists, but we would also say with Paul, to our fellow Christians of every name and land: "Grace be with all them who love the Lord Jesus Christ in sincerity."

It is especially gratifying to us all that so many missionaries, from lands near and far, are here with us in this Congress. They are our most honored messengers. The largest and best contribution made to the missionary cause is the missionary. More important than all our gifts in money, important as these are, are the lives of the missionaries. The paramount benefactors of the world today are not those who add to life's quantity, but those who add to its quality. Well does our Master say: "A man's life consisteth not in the abundance of the things which he possesseth." What money gift to missions could compare with the life of the missionary, William Carey? Or with the lives of Adoniram Judson, and Luther Rice, and Matthew T. Yates, and Lottie Moon, and Henrietta Hall Shuck, and Robert Morrison, and David Livingstone, and John G. Paton, and John E. Clough, together with an unnumbered host of faithful men and women whose missionary lives have markedly changed the world? Carey translated the whole Bible into six different languages, and the New Testament into twenty different dialects. The capable, faithful Christian missionary is the chief ambassador, the best interpreter, the most faithful mediator in all the world. We stand in most grateful salute, upon every thought of our valiant missionaries and their immeasurably blessed work!

I would also speak a very personal word concerning one who is here with us today, even our own beloved World Secretary, Dr. J. H. Rushbrooke. Through the years of intimate association and conference and travel with him, he has continually loomed larger in Spiritual wisdom and strength, and in epoch-making serviceableness. He is the best informed man about Baptist affairs in all the world today. The indebtedness of our Baptist world family to this humble Christian brother, and this incomparable Baptist leader, can never be fully realized by us while we are here in the flesh. His record is on high, and glorious shall be his reward from Him Whom he lives to serve. He is one of God's chiefest gifts to our Baptist people, in all their long and eventful history. May God spare him to us yet many years, and crown all these years with ever-increasing happiness and usefulness!

It is no small matter that these thousands of Baptists have journeyed from near and far, to this World Congress. You have come together in one of the most ominous and epochal hours in the life of the world. Stupendous influences and forces are shaking the world to its very foundations. The deadly menace of materialism casts its baleful shadow throughout all realms, and among all peoples. The astounding fact of ghastly persecutions, both racial and religious, continues to challenge the whole world with horror, and to make a blot that is an unspeakable disgrace to civilization. Fear seems to have the pass-key to whole nations, as well as to myriads of individuals, whether in palace or cottage. Vast changes are rapidly sweeping the world as swirling ocean currents sweep the seas. These changes are economic and financial, political and governmental, educational and social, moral and religious. The world is still in the dreadful aftermath of the most ghastly and widely desolating war in all the history of mankind. The instability of reconstruction continues to plague the nations, both large and small. Misunderstandings, both national and international, seem relentless in their persistence. Wars and rumors of wars even now are casting their dark shadows across the earth. All these conditions poignantly remind us how desperately we need help above ourselves.

On every hand, the acutely searching question is heard: Have Christians an adequate remedy for the poignantly troubled world situation of today? Is there a Door of Hope in the valley of Achor? Is there any helper anywhere who is able to heal the awful hurts of our wounded, sinning, suffering world? Happy am I to believe that this assembled Congress, with united and unfaltering conviction would answer: "Yes," to such question. We would fervently sing with the poet:

> "We know of lands that are sunk in shame,
>   Of hearts that faint and tire;
> And we know of a Name, a Name, a Name
>   That can set such lands on fire."

And there is only one Name that can do it. "Thou shalt call His Name Jesus, for He shall save His people from their sins." An ancient prophet foretold His coming in these words: "For unto us a child is born, unto us a son is given; and the government shall be upon His shoulder; and His name shall be called Wonderful, Counsellor, the Mighty God, the Everlasting Father, the Prince of Peace."

Here then is the one all-sufficient Mediator between God and man, between man and man, and between nation and nation. He is the Mighty Daysman, the Great Reconciler, the Center of Unity. When men really love Him, they will love one another. He is the outstanding miracle of the ages. The search-light of criticism has been focused upon Him, both by friends and by foes, for nearly two thousand years, and yet it has failed, through all the centuries, to find in Him one suggestion of sin, one ill-advised word, one selfish deed. He was born in the first century, yet He belongs to all centuries. He was born a Jew, yet He belongs to all races. He was born in Bethlehem, yet He belongs to all countries. His challenging call is alike to Saxon, and Teuton, and Mongolian, and Slav, and Latin, to come penitently to Him for His forgiving grace, and His empowering help. Oh! who would not wish to follow in Christ's train; through all the swift-changing years of time, and then, beyond, throughout the ceaseless cycles of eternity?

The question arises: What is the purpose of this Baptist World Congress? What brings together this vast company of Baptists? The general answer is that we come on a mission of fraternity and inspiration. The more definite answer is that we come to get and to give renewed emphasis to "THE BAPTIST MESSAGE and MISSION for the WORLD TODAY."

This Congress does well to have as its Motto Text, Paul's positive pronouncement: "For other foundation can no man lay than that is laid, which is Jesus Christ." The first question in the building of any structure relates to its foundation. One is a foolish builder if he fails to look carefully after the soundness and safety of the foundation of his building. There must be a foundation for a building, for a vocation, for a nation, for a life. The abiding strength and real value of any structure will depend ultimately upon its foundations. If the structure be built upon the sand, it is doomed to defeat when comes the storm. Even so, a religious faith must see well to its foundations, or it will fall. Any and every religious denomination should be able and ready to give a clear reason, or reasons, for its distinctive faith. I would here frankly say that for Baptists there is one authoritative and final source of religious truth, and that source is the Bible. Our contention is that God's Will for mankind is fully expressed in the Bible, and to that Will we are bound to conform, in all matters relating to doctrine, polity, ordinances, worship and Christian living. How shall we find out Christ's Will for us? He has revealed it in His Holy Word. The Bible, and the Bible alone, is the rule of faith and practice for Baptists. To them the one standard by which all creeds and conduct and character must be tested, is the Word of God. They ask only one question concerning all religious faith and practice, and that question is, "What Saith the Word of God?" Not traditions, nor customs, nor councils, nor confessions, nor ecclesiastical formularies, however venerable and pretentious, guide Baptists, but simply and solely the will of Christ as they find it revealed in the New Testament. Christ is our one foundation, and we are to build alone upon Him. He is our Prophet, Priest and King, our one authoritative Teacher, our atoning, adequate Savior, our Divine Lord and King. His word is our Court of last appeal, and His Command is to be faithfully obeyed, whatever may be the cost. The mighty preacher, the late Dr. B. H. Carroll, has thus stated it for us: "The New Testament is the law of Christianity. All the New Testament is the law of Christianity. The New Testament is all the law of Christianity. The New Testament always will be all the law of Christianity." Baptists hold that this law of Christianity is the unchangeable and only law of Christ's reign, and that whatever is not found in this law cannot be bound on the consciences of men; and that this law is a sacred deposit, an inviolable trust, which Christ's friends are ever faithfully to guard and perpetuate, wherever it may lead, and whatever may be the cost of such trusteeship.

Just here it is seen that the Baptist message and the Roman Catholic message are the very antipodes of each other. The Roman Catholic message is sacerdotal, sacramentarian and ecclesiastical. In its scheme of salvation it magnifies the church, the priest and the sacraments. The Baptist message is non-sacerdotal, non-sacramentarian, and non-ecclesiastical. Its teaching is that the one High Priest for sinful humanity has entered into the holy place for all, that the veil is forever rent in twain, that the mercy seat is uncovered and open to all, and that the humblest soul in all the world, if he be truly penitent, may enter with all boldness and cast himself upon Christ. Baptists are in conscience compelled to reject and oppose sacerdotalism that puts a priest between a soul and Christ; and sacramentarianism that makes external ordinances in themselves, vehicles of grace; and ecclesiasticism that puts a church between a sinner and salvation. We are, in all kindly candor, compelled to say that the Catholic doctrines of baptismal regeneration and transubstantiation are to the Baptist mind fundamentally subversive of the Spiritual realities of the Gospel of Christ. Likewise, the Catholic conception of the church, thrusting all its complex and cumbrous machinery between the soul and God, prescribing beliefs, claiming to exercise the power of the keys, and to control the channels of grace—all such lording it over the consciences of men, is to the Baptist mind an insufferable tyranny in the realm of the soul, and tends to frustrate the grace of God, to destroy freedom of conscience, and terribly to hinder the coming of the Kingdom of God. Still further must Baptists say frankly but kindly that they find no authority in the New Testament for one man as the infallible head of an ecclesiastical organization. Peter evidently did not know that he was a Pope, nor did his fellow apostles know it. He was a fallible, married man; he did not appoint the successor to Judas; he associated with his fellow Christians. It will be recalled that Paul withstood Peter to his face. History will not let us forget that papal aggression began with Leo, about the middle of the fifth century, and culminated with Hildebrand, about the middle of the eleventh century, and reached its astounding climax at the Vatican Council, in 1870, by the formal declaration of papal infallibility. That was one of the astonishing events in all history, when the Vatican Council, by majority vote, decreed the dogma of papal infallibility. It is not to be wondered at that the excitement was at white heat, during the discussion of such dogma, and especially when the final vote was announced. You will recall that in the midst of all the turmoil and tenseness of that excited assemblage, Cardinal Manning stood on an elevated platform, holding in his hand the paper just passed, declaring for the infallibility of the Pope, and shouted these words: "Let all the world go to bits, and we will reconstruct it on this paper." A Baptist smiles at such an announcement, but not in derision and scorn. Although the Baptist is the very antithesis of his Catholic neighbor, in Biblical conceptions and contentions, yet the Baptist will wholeheartedly insist that his Catholic neighbor must not be prevented from having his candles, and incense, and sanctus bell, and rosary, and whatever else he wishes in the expression of his worship and faith. A Baptist must, in conscience, at all times, and everywhere, plead for absolute religious liberty for his Catholic neighbor, for his Jewish neighbor, and for everybody else. But what is the Baptist answer to the contention of his Catholic neighbor for papal infallibility? Holding aloft a little book, the name of which is the New Testament, the Baptist shouts this cry: "Let all the world go to bits, and we will reconstruct it on the New Testament."

It matters vitally what we believe. Ideas rule the world. The world's conduct is moulded by its beliefs. A religious denomination is moulded by its ruling principles, just as is a nation, and as is an individual. The late President Mullins has left on record one sentence that may well characterize the historic significance of Baptists. That sentence affirms the competency of the individual, under God, in matters of religion. That principle is the keystone truth of the Baptists. By this principle is meant, not a competency of the individual in the sense of human self-sufficiency, but a competency, under God. Religion is a matter of personal relationship between the soul and God, and nothing extraneous may properly intrude here—no ecclesiastical nor civil order, no church, nor ordinance, nor sacrament, no preacher, nor priest, may dare to stand between the individual soul and Christ. Out of this cardinal, bed-rock principle, all our Baptist principles emerge.

When we turn to the New Testament, which is the law and guidebook for Christ's people, we find that supreme emphasis is everywhere put upon the principle of individualism. The individual is segregated from family, from church, from state, from society, from dearest earthly friends and institutions, and brought into direct, personal dealings with God. Everyone must give account of himself to God. There can be no sponsors or deputies or proxies in such vital matter. Each one must repent for himself, and believe for himself, and be baptized for himself, and answer to God for himself, both in time and in eternity. Quaint John Bunyan was true to the New Testament teachings, when in his Pilgrim's Progress he made the entrance into the narrow way to heaven, a wicket gate so small that only one could go in at a time. In the Kingdom of God the individual is always the unit. The clarion call of John the Baptist is to the individual: "Think not to say within yourselves, we have Abraham to our father, for

I say unto you that God is able of these stones to raise up children unto Abraham. And now also the axe is laid upon the root of the trees; therefore, every tree that bringeth not forth good fruit is hewn down and cast into the fire." One man can no more repent and believe and obey Christ for another, than he can take another's place at God's judgment bar. Neither persons nor institutions, however dear and powerful, may dare to come between the individual soul and God. "There is one mediator between God and men, the man Christ Jesus." Let both the state and the church, let any institution, however dear, and any person, however near, stand aside, and let the individual soul have his own direct and personal access to God. One is our pontiff, and His name is Jesus. The undelegated sovereignty of Christ makes it forever impossible for His saving grace to be manipulated by any system of human mediation, whatsoever.

It follows, therefore, logically and inevitably, that every man has the right to worship God according to the dictates of his own conscience; and that no man, nor set of men, no government, religious or civil, has the right to dictate how a person may worship God, and to punish him if he does not worship that way. The right of private judgment is the crown jewel of humanity. And for any person or institution to dare to come between the soul and God is a blasphemous impertinence and a defamation of the crown rights of the Son of God. Baptists regard as an enormity any attempt to constrain men by penalty or patronage, to this or that form of religious belief. What a frightful chapter has been written, the world around, by disregard of this lofty principle of freedom of conscience, and its inevitable corollary, the separation of church and state! John Bunyan was kept in jail for twelve long years, because he utterly rejected the claim of the state to forbid his preaching the Gospel of Christ. Yonder in Massachusetts, Henry Dunster, the first President of Harvard, and one of its chiefest helpers, was removed from the presidency, because he objected to infant baptism. Roger Williams was banished, John Clarke was put in prison, and Obadiah Holmes was publicly whipped on Boston Common; and all this, because they refused to stultify their consciences. In Connecticut, the lands of our Baptist people were confiscated and their goods sold, to build a meetinghouse and support a preacher of another denomination. In old Virginia, the battle for religious and civil liberty was long and grandly waged, and the final triumph recorded there was such as to write imperishable glory upon the name of Virginia forever. Fines and imprisonments and persecutions were everywhere in evidence in Virginia, for conscience' sake. On and on our Baptist forbears waged their unyielding battle for religious liberty, in Virginia, in the Carolinas, in Georgia, in Rhode Island, and Connecticut, and Massachusetts, and wherever else they lived and labored. They dared to be odd, to stand alone, to refuse to conform, though it cost them suffering and even life itself.

They pleaded, and suffered, and kept on with their protests and remon-
strances and memorials, until, thank God, forever, their contention was
won, in these United States, and written into our country's Constitution,
that church and state must, in this land, be forever separate and free, and
that neither must ever trespass upon the distinctive functions of the
other. Historic justice compels me to say that this was preeminently a
Baptist achievement. Let me hasten to add that this achievement was not
because Baptists were inherently better than their neighbors—we would
make no such arrogant claim—but because of their unwavering loyalty to
the God-given principle of freedom of conscience. The impartial historian
will ever agree with Mr. Bancroft, our American historian, when he says:
"Freedom of conscience, unlimited freedom of mind, was from the first
the trophy of the Baptists." And such historian will also agree with the
noble champion of human rights, John Locke, who said: "The Baptists
were the first propounders of absolute liberty, just and true liberty, equal
and impartial liberty." And still again, will he agree with the eminent
Judge Story, long a member of our Nation's Supreme Court, when he says:
"In the code of laws established by the Baptists in Rhode Island, we read
for the first time since Christianity ascended the throne of the Caesars,
the declaration that conscience should be free, and that men should not
be punished for worshipping God in the way they were persuaded that
He requires."

Whitelaw Reid says that the greatest fact of modern history was the rise
of the American nation. We must demur to such statement, and insist,
instead, that the greatest fact of modern history was the discovery of the
idea of liberty, religious and civil, and that such discovery was made
preeminently by the Baptists. Religious liberty is the nursing mother of
all liberty. Without it all other forms of liberty must soon wither and die.
The Baptists grasped this conception of liberty in its full-orbed glory, from
the very beginning. Their contention has been, is now, and must ever be,
that it is the God-given and indefeasible right of every human being, to
worship God or not, according to the dictates of his conscience; and, as
long as he does not infringe upon the rights of others, he is to be held
accountable to God alone, for all his religious beliefs and practices. And
Baptists make this contention, not only for themselves, but as well, for all
others—for Protestants of all denominations, for Romanists, for Jews, for
Quakers, for Turks, for Pagans, for all men everywhere. Their contention
is not for mere toleration, but for absolute liberty. There is a wide difference between toleration and liberty. Toleration implies that somebody
falsely claims the right to tolerate. Toleration is a concession, while liberty
is a right. Toleration is a matter of expediency; while liberty is a matter
of principle. Toleration is a gift from man, while liberty is a gift from God.
It is, therefore, the consistent, insistent and persistent contention of our

Baptist people, always and everywhere, that religion must be forever voluntary and uncoerced, and that it is not the prerogative of any power, whether civil or ecclesiastical, to compel men to conform to any religious creed or form of worship, or to pay taxes for the support of a religious organization to which they do not belong, and in whose creed they do not believe. God desires free worshippers, and no others.

In view of their essential principles, it is easy to understand why Baptists believe that every State Church is a spiritual tyranny. In the very nature of the case, there can be no proper union of church and state, because their nature and functions are utterly different. Jesus stated the principle in the two sayings, "My Kingdom is not of this world," and "Render unto Caesar the things that are Caesar's, and unto God the things that are God's." When, therefore, the state seeks to play mentor to the church, or the church to the state, a Pandora's box of evils will be loosed upon the people.

> "Let Caesar's dues be paid
> To Caesar and his throne;
> But consciences and souls were made
> To be the Lord's alone."

In their adherence to the union of church and state, Luther and Calvin and Zwingli and other great reformers suffered the Reformation to pass into eclipse, in a distressingly large measure. That one utterance of Jesus, "Render unto Caesar the things that are Caesar's and unto God the things that are God's," marked the divorcement of church and state, once and for all. It marked a new era for the creeds and deeds of men. It was the sunrise gun of a new day, the echoes of which are to go on, and on, until the doctrine of "A Free Church in a Free State," shall have absolute supremacy, in every land, whether great or small, around the encircling globe.

Concerning the church, Baptists hold that it is a Divine institution, not evolved from the changing conditions of society, but expressing the mind of Christ; that it is an enduring institution, adapted to all times and climes; that it is the custodian of the truth, to hold and teach it to the end of time, and to all peoples. They hold that a church of Jesus Christ is a spiritual institution, and that it is a pure democracy, without disbarment of franchise to any member, on the ground of nationality, race, class or sex. There are two ordinances of the church,—Baptism and the Lord's Supper, neither as a means of salvation, but both figurative and commemorative. It is a vital Baptist principle that spiritual birth must precede church membership and these two ordinances.

Baptists hold the immemorial position that all true believers in Christ as their personal Savior, are saved, having been born again; and this without the intervention of preacher, priest, ordinance, sacrament, or church. Therefore, we profoundly rejoice in our spiritual union with all who love the Lord Jesus Christ in sincerity and truth. We cherish them as our brothers in the saving grace of Christ, and heirs with us of life and immortality. We love their fellowship, and maintain that the spiritual union of all true believers in Christ is now, and will ever be a blessed reality. This spiritual union does not depend on organizations, or forms, or ritual. It is deeper, higher, broader and more stable than any and all organizations. Baptists joyfully cherish all these believers in Christ, as their brothers in the common salvation, whether they be found in a Protestant communion, or in a Catholic communion, or in any other communion, or in no communion.

Surely, surely, all right-thinking Christians, whatever their name and creed, must cherish in their hearts a deep and abiding Christian love for all their fellow-believers in Christ; and must most gratefully rejoice in all that they are doing for the salvation of the lost of earth; and for every token of honor that they bring to Him Who is Lord over all and blessed forevermore. This joyful and understanding fellowship of Christ's people is to be cherished and magnified in every wise and worthy way. Well does John Calvin remind us that disagreement among Christians may proceed without any violation of charity, and that there is no spiritual unity except in Christ, and no charity of which He is not the bond. Wisely and faithfully does Calvin go on to say that the chief point in preserving charity, is to maintain faith, sacred and entire. One thing must be clear to us all—there can be no real unity at the expense of the truth. Any unity, except in the truth, would not only be fatal, but it would also be treachery to Christ. It behooves all Christians faithfully to inquire how they may come closer together. Shall they do so by reducing their beliefs to the minimum? Any union which is not based on the unreserved acceptance of the Lordship of Christ, falsifies itself, and should be promptly rejected by all serious minded men. That would indeed be very shallow and unworthy reasoning which advocates union by compromise, in the realm of spiritual truth. Its voice is the voice of Jacob, but its hands are the hands of Esau.

Our Baptist message to our brethren of other communions may be stated in these three words—Truth, Freedom, Unity. And these words stand in the order named—Truth, Freedom, Unity. Our first concern must ever be for truth. "Ye shall know the truth, and the truth shall make you free." Any other union is fictitious and must end in disaster. Let us ever hold fast to our one source of authority in spiritual matters. It is not in a man, nor in a church, nor in personal desires and expediency. In the days of the ancient Judges, "Every man did that which was right in his own eyes." Jesus' word is, "If ye love me, ye will keep my commandments." The only possible road to real Christian union is by the way of the unreserved acceptance of the Lordship of Christ, as revealed in the Holy Scriptures. "One is your Master, even Christ, and all ye are brethren." The abiding word for us all is: "Whatsoever He saith unto you, do it."

The fact of our joyful Christian fellowship with Christ's people—which fact is ever to be wisely magnified by us all, does not mean that we are to play fast and loose with our Christian convictions. Indeed, the momentous days which are now upon us call mightily for renewed clarity of thought, and for deepening of convictions concerning the message and mission of all Christ's people. It is conviction that convinces. "There's untold power in him who knows a thing is of God's own willing, though doubts may shroud in cloud the transient hour." "We cannot but speak the things which we have seen and heard." "If the foundations be destroyed, what can the righteous do?" "For if the trumpet give an uncertain sound, who shall prepare himself to the battle?" The place of the Christian pulpit and the Christian teacher is no proper place for a religious stammerer. We need a reincarnation of the John Bunyan spirit, throughout all the Christian world today. He was long kept in jail, because of his fidelity to his Christian convictions. When he was offered his freedom, if he would put his conscience in shackles, he made the sublime reply: "I will stay in prison till the moss grows on my eyebrows, rather than make a slaughterhouse of my conscience, or a butchery of my principles." That is the spirit for all God's people today.

Let us hark back again to the great doctrine of Religious Liberty, and its inevitable corollary, the Separation of Church and State. I speak now this special word to our Baptist people of our United States of America. While we are lamenting the loss of religious liberty and other civil rights, in different sections of the world, it behooves us to open our eyes to insidious encroachments here in our own land. With a great price, our fathers purchased this great freedom which we now enjoy. Let us see to it that we do not forget it, nor allow anybody else to forget it. Over a great bridge is a tablet which reads: "This is what the bridge cost." Then follows the list of the names of the workmen who lost their lives in the building of the bridge. We have no complete list of the many who suffered in this land that we might have the priceless boon of religious and political liberty. Their epoch-making service must not be forgotten. "Eternal vigilance is the price of liberty." In illustration of the subtle, but real encroachments upon liberty in America, call to mind the recent agitation in connection with the National Congress, to include church employees in Federal Security pensions. To be sure, such proposal was defeated by church pressure, but let the ominous fact be remembered that it was also church pressure that introduced the question into Congress. Take again, the fact of the allocation of public funds to sectarian purposes. That question has long and often been in the public mind, in one form and another. Bills are proposed, in various states, again and again, for taxes to be appropriated for sectarian schools. If haply any of our Baptist people have, in an hour of weakness, been in any way enthralled by this encroachment, let them speedily repent of such inconsistent course, and go and sin no more! Nothing in all the world is worth doing wrong for! Right at this point all our people need to be wide awake to danger, and faithful to principle, or results will badly plague us, later along. Once more, the frank declaration is here made that any trend or suggestion of the possible establishment of diplomatic relations between the United States and the Vatican would call forth an immediate and unyielding protest from uncounted millions of our American people. Our doctrine of religious liberty in America is for all our people alike. The Pope is simply the honored head of the Roman Catholic Church, and the plea that his dominion over a few acres of ground, called the Vatican City, gives him the status of a temporal Sovereign, is essentially unreal. He has, in fact, no better title to receive governmental recognition from the United States than has the Archbishop of Canterbury, or the Moderator of the Presbyterian General Assembly of the United States, or the Presiding Bishop of the United Methodist Church of this country. We call God to witness that we do not wish to be petty and inconsistent and un-Christian in our frank reference to this matter. But we do wish to be consistent and faithful to priceless principles, profoundly believing that these principles are of indispensable value, alike to Baptists, to Protestants of every name, to Catholics, to Jews, to Quakers, to everybody in our land.

If, forsooth, the charge is sometimes made that our Baptist people are "exclusive" and "intolerant," and "illiberal," let the answer be modestly repeated that, for the very religious liberty which our cherished brethren of all communions enjoy, they are, most of all, indebted to the Baptists. Surely this charge of intolerance and exclusiveness and illiberality is made without considered thought. Are our Baptist people exclusive and intolerant and illiberal, when the very foundation of their church polity is liberty, not only for themselves, but alike for everybody else? In all their unwavering advocacy of soul-freedom, in its completest measure, and of the destiny-determining principle of the Separation of Church and State, our Baptist people do not have a fleck or stain upon the fair page of their history.

What of our Baptist Message and Mission for the world of today? Is our message any longer needed, and will we be true to our heaven-appointed mission? It is an hour when we should look both backward and forward. The present is inexorably bound with both the past and the future. A mighty heritage now is ours, because of the great names and deeds of our Baptist forbears. There is John Bunyan, the immortal allegorist; and John

Howard, the noble philanthropist; and John Foster, the brilliant essayist, and John Clifford, the mighty defender of men's rights; and Alexander MacLaren, the peerless Bible expositor; and Charles Haddon Spurgeon, the most glorious Gospel preacher, perhaps, since Paul. And there are our world-famed missionaries, the story of whose great deeds must forever thrill our hearts. And there were our great teachers like Boyce and Broaddus and Mullins and Strong and Robertson. There was Roger Williams, the outstanding apostle of religious liberty, for America and for the whole world. And there were great editorial voices sounded out in behalf of our Baptist World fellowship, like Prestridge and Pitt and others. There were B. H. Carroll, the Pauline preacher, and J. B. Gambrell, the sane philosopher, and R. C. Buckner, the wonderful friend of orphan children. There was John Hope, whose name and noble service enhance the glory of the fair City of Atlanta and the whole country. And there was Booker T. Washington, the world famed teacher and leader in the uplift of his whole race. We call to mind all these noble dead, and many others of our immortal forbears, our hearts paraphrase the cry of Wordsworth: "Milton! thou shouldst be living at this hour—England hath need of thee."

We must not, dare not be indifferent to the heritage of mighty names and vital principles that have come down to us. We must vindicate our faith and heritage by our deeds. Over the doorway of the old Moorish palace, the Alhambra, carved in stone on one side was a book, and on the other, reaching out to clasp the book was a hand. There was a legend that when the hand clasped the book, the Alhambra would fall. That old Moorish palace is a fitting symbol of that Kingdom of evil which is prevalent throughout the earth, and for whose complete downfall and destruction Christ's soldiers go forth to war. Every faithful sermon is a cannon shot in this war. Every worthy Christian life is a steady bombardment against all evil. When will Satan's stronghold fall and the victory of Christ's soldiers be complete? When the hand worthily clasps the book, the Alhambra of Evil will fall. The hand is the hand of duty, the book is the book of doctrine, and when duty and doctrine clasp each other in fulness of Divine meaning and power, the reign of iniquity will crumble to ruin and utter defeat. "Lead on, O King Eternal, the day of march has come!"

This incomparably fateful hour in the life of the world calls for the dedication of our all for the furtherance of Christ's Kingdom throughout every nook and corner of this earth. Our task is nothing less than the evangelization of the whole world, and to bring it into obedience to Christ. Christianity cannot yield its claim to supremacy, everywhere, nor will it consent to enroll Christ in any Patheon, anywhere. Christ must be Lord of all, or He will not be Lord at all. There are not two Saviors but one, and hence Christ's holy religion must be exclusive and adapted to all mankind. Paul states this vast truth in his sermon to the philosophers at Athens: "God hath made of one blood all nations of men for to dwell on all the face of the earth, and hath determined the times before appointed, and the bounds of their habitations, that they should seek the Lord, if haply they might feel after Him and find Him." A universal religion is required by the unity of the race. Christ's religion is necessarily intolerant of all pagan faiths, as truth is necessarily intolerant of falsehood and of error. There is no permanent standing room on this planet for the religion of Jesus Christ, and any alternative. It is an inevitable conflict to the finish, between Christianity and every high thing that exalteth itself, or opposeth himself, to God and His Christ. We must secure the acceptance of Christianity everywhere, if we are to preserve it anywhere. The self-preservation of Christianity is conditioned upon its universal sovereignty. It must win everywhere or run up the flag of surrender and defeat. There can be no concordats or compromises in this eternally important matter. "He must reign until He hath put all enemies under His feet." We are in no losing battle when we follow Christ.

> "He has sounded forth the trumpet that shall never call retreat;
> He is sifting out the hearts of men before the Judgment Seat;
> O, be swift my soul to answer Him, be jubilant my feet,
> Our God is marching on."

Every Christian is to take Christ's world view of the Christian task. Three workmen on a cathedral were asked what they were doing. One said, "I am working for three dollars a day." The second said: "I am cutting this stone to make it fit into its place in the wall." The third said: "I am doing my best to help build that noble cathedral." There were three motives stated—wages, duty, vision. Every Christian is to say with the immortal Wesley: "I look upon the world as my parish"; and "The best of all is, God is with us." Balboa who first discovered the Pacific Ocean, stepped out into its briny waters, and planting there the Spanish flag, claimed that vast body of water, with all the lands it touched, for Ferdinand and Isabella, his King and Queen. With far larger confidence and courage we are to go forth to win this whole world for our Lord and His Christ.

To such end, we must major on Evangelism. That is the first note in the marching orders of our risen Savior and Lord. Evangelism is the missionary spirit in action. It is the forerunner and builder of churches. It is essential to all Christian expansion, and must give its benign influence to all sound teaching in the churches. Dr. Duff well said: "The church that ceases to be evangelistic will soon cease to be evangelical." In the New Testament, everything goes out from the churches and draws back into the churches. Whatever good may be done by methods and institutions apart from the churches, let us remember that Christ has put His honor in the churches, and it needs to be urged with all emphasis, that the hope of the people for a sound gospel, both for today and tomorrow, centers in the churches of the living God. "The Church of the living God, the pillar and ground of the truth." And the first and supreme business of every church is to win souls to the salvation and service of Christ. This work is not secondary and incidental, but it is primary and supreme. "As my Father hath sent me, even so send I you." "The Son of man is come to seek and to save that which was lost." If the seeking note for the salvation and training of souls be absent from a church, how much difference would there be between such church and an ethical club? All the estates of a church are to go afield, and stay afield, in this Christly work of winning souls to Christ. And all who are won to Christ should follow Him in baptism; and these should all be faithfully taught and enlisted in the doing of all things Christ asks of His people. The preacher, the parent, the teacher, the laymen, the women, the eager young people, are all to be mobilized for this matchless crusade.

Certain fundamentals must be regarded if the soul winner is to win. First of all, there must be a deep realization of human need. God's people are often at ease in Zion, because they do not realize the depth and peril of humanity's need. The supreme tragedy of the world is sin. The whole earth is groaning under its curse. Sin turns the joys of life into the ashes of despair. Sin reigns alike in the hovels of the poor and in the palaces of the rich. Sin is the great separating force of life, even as love is its binding force. Sin divides families and communities and nations. Worst of all, sin separates man from God. The darkest hour this world has ever seen was when God hid His face from the dying Savior, and the saddest cry that earth has ever heard was that Savior's cry: "My God! My God! why hast Thou forsaken me?" Oh! that God's people might worthily realize that all about us are lost souls, hurrying on without hope and without God in the world!

But it is not enough for us to be given the vision of a lost world—we must also know of an adequate remedy for such lost world. Just here we come upon the most enchanting theme in the universe. It is the Gospel story of how a sinner may be saved. "There is none other name under heaven, given among men, whereby we must be saved." This gospel is the one, all-sufficient hope for mankind. It is the hope for the individual, and it is the hope for society. It changes the social order by first changing the social unit. Grace is as real as sin, and grace is far more powerful than sin. "Where sin abounded, grace did much more abound." Wherever the vital facts of Christ's death and resurrection are faithfully proclaimed, Christ verifies His promise: "And I, if I be lifted up from the earth will draw all men unto Me." This very hour, Christ is saving Korean demon worshippers, and South Sea Cannibals, and African Hottentots, and Indian Pariahs, and Confucian Scholars, and Brahmin Priests, and men of every type and temperament under heaven.

> "I ask them whence their victory came?
> They with united breath,
> Ascribe their victory to the Lamb,
> Their triumph to His death."

Let me hasten to say that our indispensable need, in the winning of souls is to have the power of God with us. Certain it is that without that supernatural power for which the early disciples tarried at Jerusalem, we might as well surrender the whole Christian propaganda. We would be left helpless in the presence of problems that not only perplex but utterly baffle us. There stands the glorious pledge of Christ to His people: "Ye shall receive power after that the Holy Ghost is come upon you." And, again, He says to His people: "Lo, I am with you always." Granted this Divine guidance and power, difficulties melt away as fogs before the rising sun. Take a hasty glance at the Acts of the Apostles. The whole book is one triumphant song. Not a minor chord, not a discouraged preacher, not a fainting church, not one note of unfaith and fear can anywhere be found. What if they were thrown into prison? They had One who could use an earthquake as a key to open every dungeon on earth. What if there were mountains of difficulties to be faced? There was One with them who could pluck up the mountains and cast them into the sea. Oh! Let us be done with "limiting God"! He is the Almighty God, and our sure and adequate help is in Him. Let us be done with limiting God!

> "Give us a watchword for the hour,
> A thrilling word, a word of power;
> A battle cry, a flaming breath.
> That calls to conquest or to death;
> A word to rouse the church from rest,
> To heed its Master's high behest;
> The call is given, Ye hosts arise;
> Our watchword is Evangelize!
> "The glad Evangel now proclaim,
> Through all the earth in Jesus' name;
> This word is ringing through the skies,
> Evangelize! Evangelize!
> To dying men, a fallen race,
> Make known the gift of Gospel Grace;
> The world that now in darkness lies,
> Evangelize! Evangelize!"

The story is told that Julia Ward Howe once wrote to an eminent Senator, in behalf of a man who was suffering a great injustice. The Senator replied that he was so much taken up with plans for the benefit of the race that he had no time for individuals. She returned to the Senator this answer: "When last heard from, our Maker had not reached this altitude." God is great enough to specialize. One by one, was Jesus' method, as indicated in His parables and miracles. It was not a lost flock, but one lost sheep that drew the Shepherd into the night and storm. It was not over a Pentecost, but over one repenting sinner that the angels sang. It was not a lost race, but a lost son that kept the father waiting at the gate. Jesus never raised an army from the dead. He stood at the bier and said: "Young man, arise!" He stood at the graveside and said: "Lazarus, come forth." In our Lord's sermons we find vast truths of His holy religion uttered, not to a great congregation, but to an audience of one. To a nameless woman, He announced the great principle of spiritual worship. To a proud ruler He preached His wondrous sermon on the new birth.

Well may Jesus' disciples walk in His steps. Andrew, when he found Jesus, brought his brother Simon to Jesus. Phillip, when he found Jesus told Nathaniel. Peter went from Joppa to Caesarea to have a personal interview with Cornelius. Paul, earth's greatest preacher, was an indefatigable personal worker. See him as he appeals to the Governor of Cyprus, to Felix, to Festus, to Agrippa, to Onesimus the runaway slave. This appeal to the individual is the supreme secret of success. Every Christian of every age, condition and circumstance is to be an unceasing witness for Christ.

As we go on our world crusade, let all our Christian agencies be kept aflame with the passion of New Testament Evangelism. Let us call all the people back to the Bible, and end the famine that now obtains concerning it. Let plans be made that will regularly carry our religious papers into every home. Let all our training institutions dare to be aggressively and sanely Christian. Let us dare to live the glorious gospel we profess, and if need be let us gladly die for it!

Our declared principles inexorably commit us to a large program of service. The whole gospel for the whole world is our God-given program. The acid test of Jesus is: "By their fruits ye shall know them." The truth is not to be wrapped in a napkin for safe keeping—the truth is to be promulgated. "Why call ye Me Lord, Lord, and do not the things which I say?" Faith is more than a dogma, it is a passion, it lifts, it achieves, it arrives. Great believers are always great doers. Entrusted as we are with such a gospel, what ought we to be and do about it? If we are to be true to our Baptist Message and Mission, we must be missionary enthusiasts. It was no accident that William Carey became the founder of modern missions. His fundamental Baptist principle of obedience to Christ made him a missionary. And so with Judson and Luther Rice, and with all the valiant men and women who followed in their train. If these thousands and thousands of Baptist men and women, now gathered in this World Congress, have the true Baptist spirit, it will leave us no choice but to go and to give, and to live, and if need be to die, that the glorious gospel of Christ may be made known to every human being. There are enough friends of Christ in this Congress, who, if fully dedicated to Christ, could change the whole world. Gideon with three hundred men routed the hosts of darkness at Midian. John Wesley insisted that with one hundred fully dedicated men, he could soon turn the world upside down. This is an hour for the rededication of our all to Christ. "Paul and Barnabas hazarded their lives for the name of Jesus." What are we hazarding for Him? Will we pay the price to inform and to enlist our millions of un-trained, inactive Christians? God's ringing cry sounds louder and louder: "Awake, awake, put on thy strength O Zion." And again, His cry from old comes ringing in our ears: "My people are destroyed for lack of knowl-edge." It is high time for Baptists to take a great step forward. A lassitude seems to have settled upon many of Christ's people. Something grandly heroic and sacrificial needs now to be done to quicken the pulse-beat of our vast Baptist family, and start our people in every land on the upward march. Carlyle's final message is the message for us all: "Give yourself royally." Let us dare to tread the way of the Cross. Let us glorify coopera-tion and not abuse our liberty, remembering that love and not liberty is the last word in our Baptist vocabulary.

Always somewhere in the world it is midnight. Even so, it is also true that, as it is written on a sundial in Brighton, England: "It is always morning somewhere in the world." This is the word for us today. As we look at some sections of our world today, they are as unpromising as darkness and as ominous as the grave. Violence and tyranny seem to be invincible. Sin and moral chaos appear to rule with unrelenting fury. Just as surely, however, there are great sections of our world which are full of promise and radiant with hopeful outlook. These are the morning places, where the sun is shining and the denizens of darkness are driven to their lairs. Fear and terror are driven away by the coming of the morning. God is not dead, and rebellion against Him must go down before His Divine purpose and power. Every Babylon of iniquity will ultimately go down before Him. It is always morning somewhere, and by and by, it is going to be morning everywhere. The days of sin and suffering and sorrow cannot always last. "Weeping may endure for a night, but joy cometh in the morning." "He must reign till He hath put all enemies under His feet." One day, war will be put under His feet, forever—may God hasten that day! One day, intemperance in all its hydra-headed manifestations will be put under His feet, finally and forever. One day, death shall be under His feet, so that even the very prospect calls forth the victorious shout: "Thanks be unto God Who giveth us the victory through our Lord Jesus Christ." Let us be done with the spirit of unfaith and defeatism and fear, this day and beyond, forever! There is an ancient tradition of the Jews that in heaven there is music every morning. This is referred to in an old legend about Lucifer, Son of the Morning, who, for pride, was cast out of heaven. Some one asked him what he missed most of all that he had lost, and his reply was, "I miss most of all the sound of the trumpets in the morning." Is not that note—the joyous, challenging, triumphant note—the note most missed with Christ's people today?

As of old, the world was shaken at Pentecost, so will it be again. What would Jesus say to us if He were visibly present with us in this Congress today? We need not guess, we know what He would say. See Him and hear Him on Olivet: "All authority hath been given unto Me, in heaven and on earth. Go ye, therefore, and make disciples of all nations, baptizing them into the name of the Father, and of the Son, and of the Holy Spirit! teaching them to observe all things whatsoever I have commanded you: and lo, I am with you always, even unto the end of the world."

Let us go to our world mission, in no defeatist spirit but with all-conquering courage and faith. We are following a Leader who "will not fail nor be discouraged, till He hath set justice in the earth; and the isles shall wait for His law." "His dominion shall be from sea to sea, and from the river to the ends of the earth." Let us say with Dan Crawford: "Hats off to the past, coats off to the future." Let us say with Rupert Brooks: "Now God be thanked Who matched us with this hour." Will we be big enough to see our day? Will our leadership be worthy? Will we now as never before cast ourselves upon God? Let us take the long look. The short view is always inadequate. Christ's people are engaged, not simply in a battle, but in a campaign, the outcome of which campaign is certain to be victory for Him Whose right it is to reign, today, tomorrow, and beyond forevermore. "Jesus shall reign where'er the sun does his successive journeys run." He is steadily marching on to His coronation, when He shall be crowned with many crowns—the crowns of creation, of revelation, of history, of salvation, of all the crowns. Oh! who would not wish to link his all with this Eternal Savior and Lord? "Bring forth the royal diadem and crown Him Lord of all!"

> "Let every kindred, every tribe,
> On this terrestrial ball,
> To Him all majesty ascribe,
> And crown Him Lord of all!

"O that with yonder sacred throng,
We at His feet may fall,
We'll join the everlasting song
And crown Him Lord of all!"

World Peace
S. W. Hughes

Let us consider this urgent matter in terms of a three-fold creed:

1. We believe that the desire for World Peace is common to the vast majority of the 2,000 million inhabitants of the world.

2. We believe that this universal desire is an expression of the Will of God—therefore it will prevail.

3. We believe that Jesus Christ, "The Prince of Peace," can make mankind capable of achieving this world-hope.

I.

This Majority-Desire Must Become a Common Passion in the Faith That It Can Be Fulfilled. There *can* be fulfillment through faith, understanding, service and sacrifice. President Roosevelt has affirmed the solemn duties of leadership, and the common people must discipline their desire to dynamic power. The desire for Peace is as universal as the fear of War—and Peace must prevail. If, as an American Senator (Senator Borah) asserts: "Twelve men today could plunge the world into War without consulting a single citizen," there ought to be enough intelligence and moral fibre amongst 2,000 million inhabitants of this planet to avert such a hideous crime against God and Man. In such peril every citizen ought to be dedicated to Peace, Justice and Honour:

"Never one man achieves
The good for ages due,
One dreams his mighty dream
Ten thousand make it true.
"All men for every man—
A singing multitude—
Work out the shining plan
Achieve the eternal good."

We Need Faith and Understanding. Faith that God can lead believing people from a fear-ridden existence to a life of peace with international justice and honour. Terrific demands are made on the morale and brain of Man. He must understand the relationship between moral indifference and material chaos, between unrighteousness and war, and, above all, the awesome power for good which lies hidden in Man's God-given faculty for knowledge, industry, and service.

Abhorrence of War Is Not Enough. It must run deep to reasoned fear of secularism and irreligion. The study of post-war humanism has surely left us convinced that unrighteousness is man's undoing, that unbelief towards God leads to cynical undervaluation of man in power—politics. Human values fall when God is ignored. Science and education without reverence for God may bring cunning brutishness. The strategies of evil are worked through the debasement of keen intelligence. The implements of slaughter index amazing knowledge and skill.

The Duty of An Understanding Mind. Why have a few Ex-Soldier-Dictators held the world in thrall to their word? We know that God-fearing people would not long remain in pawn to their militarised power. In 1922, newspapers were misspelling Hitler's name, and dismissing his propaganda with contempt. In six years of his Chancellorship he has remoulded the life of Germany, and Nazism has profoundly affected the life of a Continent. Today, fear and rearmament are ironical tributes to his power.

(a) Will history relate his rise to power to the collapse of the German mark fifteen years ago?

(b) Did economic distress lead to the surrender of individual freedom to a Dictator's power so that he might rehabilitate their fallen civilization? In those days financial collapse meant that the savings of the Middle Class were wiped out. Salaries paid every three days were likely to lose a quarter and half of their value unless converted into food or commodities in the next thirty minutes.

(c) Do the early post-war relationships and treaties suggest that: "Reform delayed is revolution begun"?

(d) Is militarised Nationalism the answer to a common indifference towards international ideals that remain though the machinery of Federation may change? The dread is that Nations will fight if they do not federate—and federation for mutual good ought to be the immediate task of Leaders and People.

(e) Will America and Britain lead in uniting the fifteen Democracies in what is called by Clarence K. Streit—"Union Now"? A review of their powers: material, organic, and moral confirms the view that a pacific and progressive Fraternity of Nations is possible on the basis of which the potent powers of mankind would find their God-willed purposes. The dread alternatives are hatred, fear, and rearmament—which means the perversion of the labour of the common people for that which they abhor. If Axis-powers can unite, surely the Democracies can find a way of Federation. Meanwhile not one of them ought to perpetrate the grim irony of supplying war material with which to menace their own civilization.

Turning pruning-hooks into spears is galling work for man made in the image of God. Even employment therein cannot allay fears of inflation, and then, that falling mark and poverty again which have argued the dictators rise to power. The dictum about "fooling some of the people all the time, and all the people some of the time, but not all the people all the time" has relevance for this age which is being shocked into disillusionment. Today and a distant yesterday give guidance to common people.

Dictators Fear the Common People. They fear to trust them with the freedoms of true citizenship. In their ruthless censorship, they seem to disregard common intelligence and conscience, and then proceed to inflame ill-informed patriotism into warlike passions. The fear of freedom for the common people is an augury of declining dictatorship. There is no abiding sovereignty in scorn of Man's regal freedoms of thought, speech and conscience.

The Enemies of Christ Had Their Serious Foreboding When "They Feared the People." They crushed them for a time, and spat on Him, but the common people rallied after His Resurrection, and they speak God's assurance through all the Centuries, that He will make His believers to prevail. Pentecost, from whence the upward final march of Man began, was heralded by an ex-fisherman, and 3,000 ordinary people converted to Christ, began a work that soon eclipsed the paganism which, at first, outmatched them with its revolting brute-force. "Christianity overcame because the Christian beat the pagan in living, in dying, and in thinking— he outlived him, outdied him and outthought him" (The Record, U. F. C.). Let the common people hear Jesus gladly, and the world will hear less and less of craven people cowering beneath authority that never wins true loyalty.

II.

The Desire for World Peace Is An Expression of the Will of God. Neither tyranny nor indifference can cancel out the will of God. Man's true destiny is fixed in the changeless mind of God. What God the Father has willed, Man the "Brother" must fulfill. With sublime confidence God made the inspired heraldry of the Incarnation to proclaim "on earth, peace, goodwill towards men." It seemed grotesque: "a babe wrapped in swaddling clothes, lying in a manger," destined to meet the might of Rome, to transcend it in His Cross, then by His Resurrection power to begin to raise Man above everything against His holiness and love. The Incarnation means that God is on earth the Infinite pledge of "peace and goodwill toward men." "Every battle of the warrior is with confused noise and garments rolled in blood." The pacific issue of the Incarnation is as clear to the mind of God as it is essential to the life of Man.

All Evil Is In Conflict With God—That Is Its Doom. However long the process "God is our refuge and strength" because He is God. He maketh wars to cease to the ends of the earth and because "the earth is the Lord's" war is monstrous mockery here. The majesty of His Creatorship is upheld in His Fatherhood. To God the Father, all war is civil war, and it can become family-murder in a veritable paradise. As God becomes God to Man, war will become as alien to his thoughts as it is to the mind of God. The wages of irreligion is a solemn warning to Europe and the world. Because God has been deemed irrelevant to life, Mankind is competing with implements of death to battle for a fear-ridden existence. And still God "The All-Loving" and "The All-Terrible" too, does not yield His purpose. He can make believing Man capable of its fulfilment. This makes more terrible the teaching of people by their imperious Dictators to say: "Our wills are ours to make them thine." This debasement of Man's moral nature is surely reaching a critical phase, so much so, that a Dictator whose annexation-subtleties have increased his Nation by millions dare not let an Ex-Submarine Commander go free from his unjust incarceration to teach that:

> "Consciences and souls were made
> To be the Lord's alone."

There is moral prophecy in the drama set between Hitler and Niemöller. Concentration camps are within the circuit of God's judgments.

We Must Not Be Crisis-Driven From Faith in God. God is at work in the terrific paradox of rearmament and abhorrence of War. A common revulsion of feeling may become a revolution in thought and conduct. The breaking of the bow and cutting the spear asunder can be done for God by those who made them. If a few Ex-soldiers can enforce rearmament, God can move their disillusioned workers to rise up for justice, peace and disarmament. Experienced soldiers, whatever the zeal of young recruits, are passionately arguing for reason, arbitration and peace. "Our God is marching on." Meanwhile, His enemies are finding that victories may not mean victory. The enemies of God and Man will finally learn that nothing fails like their success.

III.

Jesus thrilled to stir men's hearts with the prayer: "Our Father, Thy Kingdom come, Thy will be done on earth as it is in Heaven." Such praying made His enemies wince. They became skilled in cruelty to prevent such praying. But a few kindred souls caught the gleam of the Saviour's mind and risked death to spread this revolutionary hope of a new world. How else can "Man" live except with the conviction that the

Will of God worked out on Earth gives befitting purpose to life, and immortal hope, too.

Belief in God and Man Through Jesus Christ Would Place Man in the Centre of the Universe. People were not created to be the slaves of externalism, human cogs in commercial machinery or cannon-fodder for wars which they do not instigate. Jesus would make Man conscious of his central purposeful place in a universe where he sees God making all things for him. Otherwise when the suppression of Man passes into depression, we can understand how volcanic forces may spread insomnia amongst Rulers who seem haunted by the people enslaved to their ingenious power. Nietzche is reported as saying that there has only been one Christian and He was crucified. Nietzche failed to see that Christ, by the Cross, created people who justified the unwitting compliment of having "turned the world upside down"—and such people can do it again.

We Believe That the Forces of Renewal and Hope in Christ Are Stronger Than the Forces of Evil and Reaction. Christ is not our problem. He is our Saviour. He is more than an interesting figure in history. As Sovereign Ruler of all Mankind, He is the interpreter of history and the Judge of all Mankind. People and Nations will live as befitteth moral and immortal beings when they believe of Christ: "For of Him and through Him and unto Him are all things." That's the faith that will bring peace in the human heart and in the soul of Mankind. Obvious conclusions must intensify our Christian witness.

(a) *World-Peace Must Be Sought for the Fulfilment of Christian Ideals.* Fear of War must be coupled with the fear of its causes and consequences. We have to fight against Insular patriotism. False imperialism with its military sovereignty. Secularised Education leading to paganised industry and commerce. Industry and skill must serve human need. Labour must be regarded as the instrument of God in answering Humanity's prayer for "daily bread"—bread for body, brain and spirit. It is scientifically computed that man could make the earth's wealth exceed his needs six times over, yet inventions become our fears and genius may become the genesis of slaughter. Man, in rearmament, is displaying ability and wealth equal to all his social needs.

(b) *The Realism of Jesus Must Become the Rationalism of Man:* Jesus reckons with human nature first and insists upon its reconciliation to God as the beginning and basis of human relationships. Now, Dictators are capturing Schools and Churches lest that be taught—but the sublime doctrine awaits Man's disillusionment and will accomplish it. Seeking first the Kingdom of God and His righteousness in His infallible assurance that all necessary things would be added to us. For trifling with that order, Man becomes subordinate to things. If God were first, Man would become regal.

(c) *Christ's World-conception of Man is the Only Thinkable Inter-Nationalism.* National Inter-relationships need dignifying by Christian honour and trust. Even biology argues the wickedness of racial hatreds. Mankind is varied by unchosen parentage. To make birth an argument for estrangement or persecution is sin against the Fatherhood of God and against human parentage. "God hath made of one blood all nations of men for to dwell on all the face of the Earth" (Acts 17:26).

Christ alone can blend National characteristics into human harmony. He did it in His discipleships. It was one of the marvels of Pentecost, and after a keen debate in the Early Church, the kinship of all Believers regardless of Race, Rank, or Colour, became a part of this wonderful Gospel. Nations are mutually dependent—Imports and Exports attest this. The growing demand for access to raw materials accords with God's intent. The Lord's prayer is an inspired sanction for this plea.

In things of the soul, a Baptist World Alliance can illustrate the powers that transcend all National barriers. London had a thrilling illustration of this idea when Toscanini (Italian) conducted Orchestral Expositions of Beethoven (German) before English audiences with all the world able to listen-in. Truly: "Mankind are one in spirit."

We believe that the one God and Father of all Mankind can make Mankind one through His Wisdom and Power. For universal Man Christ is the way of life. This claim is exclusive to Him. The Whole Church of Christ must witness in this victorious faith. The age demands our utmost for Christ. Humanity is lost and ruined without Him. But in His Sovereign Power, He can make all things new—and all Christians are ordained to be Co-workers together with Him.

Christianity Is the Only Answer to Man's Despair. The Christian Church can only retain its title as insight, unity, urgency, mark its witness for Christ. World-events move with critical speed. Unbelievers are making great haste. Nations are being changed with appalling disregard of Christian standards. It is generally assumed that the conflict is between the "isms" of Nazism, Bolshevism and Communism. On these contentious levels, there can be no peace. There is a deeper challenge which Christianity makes to every secular "ism." The real issues are between belief and unbelief, between righteousness and unrighteousness. The world's great heart is aching because its mind is confused through separating its "isms" from people, its problems from personality, and in its fears, it is saying of armaments: these are our refuge and strength. In the presence of such means of escape, we Christians are God's people of destiny. Before the Cross of Christ in a war-fretted world, we have come to a new Judgment Day, and, as we see our adorable Saviour despised and rejected of His enemies, are we willing and worthy to answer the challenge of those "two arms outstretched to save" all Mankind? God is saying: "BEHOLD,

NOW!" In the inspiration of His confidence, and knowing that no power in the conscription of Man by his imperious rulers, can finally outmatch the eternal forces with which Christ invests His consecrated followers, the Church of Christ can prove the deciding factor in leading this troubled world to

> "The day in whose clear-shining light
>   All wrong shall stand revealed,
> When justice shall be throned in might,
>   And every hurt be healed.
>
> "When knowledge, hand in hand with peace,
>   Shall walk the earth abroad,—
> The day of perfect righteousness,
>   The promised day of God."

Note

1. Ernest A. Payne, *Baptists Speak to the World* (London: The Carey Press, 1939), p. 11.

7
Copenhagen
1947

Introduction

At Atlanta in 1939, Baptists of the world had elected their retiring General Secretary, J. H. Rushbrooke, as the new president of the BWA. As was the case with Robert Stuart MacArthur, E. Y. Mullins, and MacNeill before, however, Rushbrooke did not get to deliver his presidential address before the Baptist world gathering in Copenhagen in 1947. Prior to his death in February 1947, Rushbrooke was very involved in planning the program for the Copenhagen meeting in July-August.

The theme of the 1947 Congress was "The World Responsibility of Baptists." A world war had left its heritage of hurt and hostility for the second time in the century. Baptists, therefore, spoke in Copenhagen with relevance regarding relief and reconciliation. Note the timeliness of a few of the topics: "The Limitations of Science" by E. C. Rust, "Christianising the Social Order" by D. R. Sharpe, "Baptists and the World Council of Churches" by Henry Cook, "The Colour Bar in the Light of the New Testament" by J. Pius Barbour, "The Baptist Contribution to World Peace" by Ernest Brown, "The United Nations from a Christian Viewpoint" by J. M. Dawson, and "The Baptist World Alliance and Relief" by W. O. Lewis.

The two addresses printed here are by Brooks Hays and Harold Cooke Phillips. Hays was, at the time, a member of the United States Congress. A prominent layman of the Southern Baptist Convention, Hays called upon Baptists of the world to recognize the role of government in relief efforts. He also alluded to the ecumenical task in post World War II world, arguing that Baptists "should firmly state our case . . . , but we must seek to establish the greatest possible degree of understanding and goodwill."

Harold Cooke Phillips, pastor of the First Baptist Church in

Cleveland, Ohio, was one of Baptists' most celebrated preachers. His Congress sermon in Copenhagen demonstrates this fact. It is replete with direct and indirect references to the state of the world in 1947. Preaching on the subject "Christ the Foundation," Phillips pointed to the flimsy foundations of the twentieth century world, "Two world wars in one generation, with their dreadful legacy of vast and desolate ruins, physical and spiritual, of un-imaginable human tragedy, suffering and woe, speak more loudly than words of the insecurity of our foundations."

Baptists and World Tasks
Brooks Hays

I am grateful for the high privilege of occupying one of the greatest forums of this post-war year 1947. I am pleased that the sessions are being held in Denmark, which, with its Scandinavian neighbours, has contribut-ed so much to the building of America. Many of us know something of the thrilling story of Denmark's agricultural progress. We appreciate particu-larly its spiritual implications, for underlying the great land reforms was the concept that "the earth is the Lord's." Nations, like individuals, must have ideals of stewardship. I wish there were time to say more on this subject, but since there is not I close the reference with a phrase some-times heard in my own land, "Denmark, the holy land of agriculture."

A thousand of us have come from America for these sessions. We want to understand you and your problems in Europe, and we want to be understood by you. We must have understanding if we make our fight together for a decent world.

A French lady once said to me, "You cannot understand us because you have not suffered." But she was mistaken. We have suffered, and some among us have suffered greatly. It is true also that some have been un-aware of the suffering of their neighbours—too concerned with the ab-sorbing interests of prosperous America. On the other hand, millions have endured grief and personal pain in the war, and there is a widespread consciousness in American churches of your privations and sacrifices. Great tribulations unite us.

Now we cannot meet the appeal of stricken Europe without using the processes of a Christian Government. Our Church resources are hope-lessly inadequate for such a task. One of the last actions of the Amer-ican Congress before its recent adjournment was the appropriation of $1,600,000,000 for Europe's aid. It was not a partisan move: it was sup-ported by both political parties. Many of us in the Congress believe that the parties must forget their differences in this monumental effort to save Western civilisation.

May I suggest a warning to my American listeners? It deals with Europe's first problem—that of food—and is in the nature of a paradox. Some of us crossed the Atlantic by luxury-liner—and certainly the "Queens" are well named; some by the last word in trans-ocean air transport. In either case, nothing that could be humanly controlled was spared that might make our voyage a pleasant one. Therein lies the paradox of my warning. There is danger, in this summer of 1947, that Americans abroad may be made too comfortable. We come from all parts of the United States. The moment we get home we will start talking about our trip. We will talk in our churches and Sunday school classes. We will talk to civic groups and to women's clubs, farm groups, and labour organisations. We will talk to neighbours over the back fence. What we say as first-hand witnesses of Western Europe this summer is going to have an impact on American thinking and the American policy that grows out of it. Because what we say matters so much it is important that we get our facts straight. One of the reasons for selecting Copenhagen as our meeting-place is that the food position of Denmark is unique in Western Europe. Denmark's highly productive agriculture is a source of admiration everywhere. And when the Nazi occupiers were crushed the tide of invasion that swept them back came over another shore. We have not forgotten the pictures of courageous Queen Wilhelmina visiting, in an Army duck, the Dutch farmers on to whose fields the retiring Nazis had loosed the destroying salt waters of the sea. Holland, too, was a productive agricultural area, and she has not recovered.

Then the Nemesis that the Germans brought upon themselves after wrecking Western Europe came from East and West into the agricultural areas of the Reich and not much is left there to-day.

And after the war came weather. Britain survived the blitz only to receive a second blow from the blizzard. One-and-a-half million sheep were frozen or drowned this past winter, and when the snow melted floods delayed spring planting. About a third of Britain's normal spring and summer food supply was lost.

This past year it has been hard for us at home—eating better than Americans have ever eaten—to grasp the fact of this ruin, and the malnutrition and discouragement that are its inevitable result. It is only human, I suppose, at the end of a war to want to push unpleasant facts out of sight.

But if we come over here this summer, eat as we have been eating at one of the few tables in Europe where food can be spread in relative plenty, and then go home and say those other facts do not exist, we shall have done a major disservice to our fellow-citizens in the Western World whose share of our war-time alliance was so much heavier than our own.

And we shall have done a disservice to the Christian community in whose name our voyage was undertaken.

It is obvious, from our discussions here, that we believe the world's current crises are a concern of organised religion. We believe that mankind has a destiny in this world as well as in another. Our beloved Dr. Truett used to say that one reason we know so little about the other world is that it was God's deliberate decision not to detract from the critical importance of this earthly existence.

We must take a look at the vast changes in the physical world and re-define our civic and educational purposes in the light of these changes.

Our primary interest, of course, deals with individual commitments and personal experience, but we must not retreat from the obligations which this commitment involves in the political realm. We must condition the minds of our people for sweeping adjustments which are now imperative.

I speak as an American, and as a Baptist layman, and, if I may use a word that is flavoured with some prejudice—a politician. Some of my first lessons in the functioning of democratic government were in a Baptist congregation, and my concept of democracy as a community of free men is associated with this experience. The commonwealth is one of the Christian's workshops.

We have experienced in our generation some of history's supreme tragedies in the seizure by perverse and evil men of the processes of State. Many have come, therefore, to look upon the State as essentially evil; but its good or its evil is rather the good or evil in us. Political patterns will always yield to human efforts—when vigorously exerted—to bring them into conformity with Christian principles. I speak primarily of America's responsibility because of our present position of leadership, and I want that leadership to have moral power. Whether we have it or not depends upon Christian forces primarily of our country, but to some extent of the world.

The Governments under which we all live are much involved in the great enterprise of extending liberty and perfecting the processes of law for its security in a peaceful world. The modern Christian State, though not the source of liberty, is nevertheless its guardian, and must be physically and morally strong.

Liberty is the heritage of millions, but for vast populations it remains only a hope and a pursuit. It is too often conceived of as exclusively a political matter. Historically its roots are in religion. It is not the gracious gift of the State, but the inherent right of men and women as God's creatures. Our most famous philosopher of the West, Thomas Jefferson, won its acceptance in America's constitutional law on this basis. God willed us to be free—in the highest sense; free to worship—or not to worship; to assemble; to utter our grievances; and to be unrestrained by any political power in the exercise of basic human rights. To the sovereignty of the human soul every power of the State must yield. What a world this would be if all its rulers would accept these simple Christian truths!

We cannot yield on this point. No considerations of diplomacy will keep us from saying to the temporal powers that religious liberty is our right. We will continue to claim it, and we will not be deceived by pretensions that it exists if it does not. At the same time, we do not identify our faith with governmental or economic patterns. There can be fellowship and harmony between us and those who oppose our preferred political forms no matter how violent the differences provided the sanctity of the individual conscience is recognised. We should always be found opposing any policy that limits the scope of conscience or expression of opinion. A good test of the existence of liberty is whether there is the right to criticise the Governments under which we live. Our anxiety that gates now closed might be opened for the promotion of our work throughout the world must not force us to a compromise that sacrifices our principles.

No Government that cherishes individual freedom has anything to fear from Baptists. Our Church bodies have not thrust themselves between the individual and the State. Our spokesmen have protested threatened invasions of our prerogatives, but we have left to the State the adjudication of conflicts and have avoided arbitrary positions as a group. The taxing of our wealth, the policing of our activities, the exercise of the State's prerogative of making secure its citizens in their lives and property, will always have our loyal support, for the State must reserve its right to the final word in borderland issues. This requires a bold faith on our part. Standing for ecclesiastical decentralisation, we have no power to match even the weakest Government. Where we have had a chance to try out the idea, however, our faith that popular Governments, under the nourishment of Christian teaching, would deal honourably and justly with its constituency has been fulfilled.

Christian leadership in America is presently involved in the making of extremely difficult decisions. In the making of them wisdom, charity, and tough-mindedness are required. Here, for example, is the problem of using greater military force in our national policy. It is related to our international obligations. The United States will likely inaugurate some type of universal military training. It will be a departure from our policy of the past and, while this is not an appropriate time to discuss its merits or demerits, it does carry an assurance that our foreign policy commitments are not lightly held. Sound educational and moral principles must be projected into the new programme. Military strength must be maintained in a world that is still full of dangers. At the same time, we pray that America will not give offence to any other people or appear in any role except that of friend and co-worker with all who love freedom and justice. Our new power must never be used for aggrandisement.

Both in America, where Christians must lead the way for a wholesome internal policy, and in the work of world-reconstruction we must cultivate good inter-group relations. It must be done with precision tools, not a blunt instrument. We have much in common with all who seek to exalt religion in a world that is threatened by materialism. As we inevitably move into areas of disagreement we should firmly state our case, for truth is partisan, but we must seek to establish the greatest possible degree of understanding and goodwill.

Another controversy touching Church policy involves public education, which is an indispensable force in maintaining our free way of life. Recent events require us to assert again our devotion to the principle of separation of Church and State. These events also dramatise the failure of the public school system to lay strong foundations for Christian citizenship. A way must be found to use that system for fortifying Christian ideals as applied to civic life. Otherwise we shall continue to be plagued by a situation that legalises the teaching of an agnostic view of life and outlaws the teaching of a Christian view.

It presents a complex and delicate problem, but not one that is beyond solution, and the alternatives to finding that solution are unthinkable. The public schools owe a debt to Christianity that can be discharged only by the placing of a positive emphasis upon the basic assumptions of Christianity, leaving to the denominations the interpretation of their distinctive tenets and cultivation of the individual's religious life. If we are afraid to attempt the laying out of a policy that imparts through public education the idea that attitudes and actions must be Christian if freedom survives, then the forces of secularism will continue to claim their advantage.

I had planned to say something about the United Nations, but the subject was so adequately covered by Dr. Dawson on Thursday evening that I forgo any further reference to that all-important agency for peace. We would agree, I believe, that the great intangibles for which our churches stand should find expression in a well-organised and effective international structure.

Our problems are complex and baffling. Few of them can be resolved on the basis of political dogma. They involve human relations and yield only to the elements of compassion and constructive love taught us by the Bible.

We can replace war and exploitation with peace and human service if we move courageously into the political scene.

The business of politics is much more than manipulating mass sentiment for particular economic and social ends; it is one of the most satisfying expressions of faith in the efficacy of New Testament teachings.

Christt the Foundation
Harold Cooke Phillips

In Paul's First Letter to the Corinthians, the 3rd. chapter, at the 11th verse, we read: "For other foundation can no man lay than that which is laid, which is Christ Jesus. But if any man buildeth on the foundation gold, silver, costly stones, wood, hay, stubble; each man's work shall be made manifest: for the day shall declare it, because it is revealed in fire; and the fire itself shall prove each man's work of what sort it is."

These words have a peculiar relevance to our day and generation. They are a fitting commentary on our age. For the apostle is speaking here about foundations. They may be secure or insecure. We may build, he tells us, on the foundation God has laid in Christ, or on the materialistic values of our own creation—gold, costly stones, wood, hay, stubble. He goes on to suggest that, while both foundations may seem adequate for a while, there will come a day of reckoning, of judgment, in which the quality of our work will be revealed by fire.

This is why his words are a fitting commentary on our age. Our work has been tested. Its true nature has been revealed in fire which has destroyed so much of our substance, our treasure, our life. Two world wars in one generation, with their dreadful legacy of vast and desolate ruins, physical and spiritual, of unimaginable human tragedy, suffering and woe, speak more loudly than words of the insecurity of our foundations.

Let us, then, think to-day of Christ the foundation, and see how this day declares the truth of that statement. Let us consider four of the insights of Jesus, the truth of which this day has etched in bold relief against the context of life itself. For the truth of the Gospel does not depend simply on the context of a book; rather the Gospel stands verified in the larger context of life. These insights, verified by life, will illustrate what we mean when we speak of Christ the foundation.

For one thing, how this day is declaring the truth of Jesus' insight that the door to life is through spiritual reality! Jesus taught that man is essentially a child of God, made in His image, that he lives in a universe that is morally and spiritually sensitive, and that he cannot find life save as he reckons with the spiritual nature of reality. He taught that truth regarding individual life. "A man's life consisteth not in . . . things. . . ." "The life is more than meat. . . ." One may start off gaily and confidently like the prodigal, seeking life, but if one in his quest of life betrays the laws of God, he will not find life, but death.

He taught the same truth regarding society. Once as He and His disciples were walking through the city of Jerusalem, one of the disciples said to Him, "Look, teacher, what a size these stones and buildings are!" Jesus said to him, "You see these great buildings? Not a stone shall be left on another, without being torn down." Because, you see, the key to a city's life or, indeed, to the world's life is not to be found in its stones, or in its steel for that matter, or any material thing whatsoever. The key is spiritual, not material. "Seek ye first the Kingdom of God, and His righteousness; and all these things shall be added unto you." But when we reverse the process, put material considerations first, and to gain material ends betray spiritual values, the things are not added. They are subtracted, as this poverty-stricken world attests. In short, the Master taught that unless our material civilisation is undergirded by spiritual principles it is but a house built on sand. It will fall.

Twice in one generation it has fallen. For who can doubt that the ultimate cause of two world wars in one generation has been our wilful disregard and betrayal of the laws of God, the laws of righteousness and justice? Strange, is it not, that though we bow so obediently to the physical laws of God, we seem to think that in the moral realm we are in a fool's paradise where we can make our own laws? But what fools we are for so thinking! Every major crisis from the Flood until now has come from our betrayal of spiritual reality. The tragedies of life do not come because we lack intelligence but because we lack integrity.

Since this is so, it follows that the greatest peril of our age springs from its moral and spiritual illiteracy. Our greatest enemies are our moral idiots, who, unfortunately for mankind, so often occupy positions of power and leadership. These are the blind Samsons who send the temple of life crashing in ruins upon mankind. As Dr. Fosdick has written: "Unless we can learn the supremacy of spiritual forces the pall-bearers that have carried out other dead civilisations wait at our door." To learn that lesson, the truth of which this day declares, is what is meant by building on Christ the foundation.

Consider another insight of the Master. We refer to His emphasis upon community, fellowship, world brotherhood. Jesus was not the first thinker to envision the universal brotherhood of man. Before His coming other thinkers, of India, China, and Greece, had toyed with the idea. So had the Hebrew prophets. But with the coming of the Master these intermittent and fitful flashes disappeared in the full glow of the noonday sun. "I am the Light of the world," He said; and one of the truths He illumines is that we shall have to learn to live together if we are really going to live at all. It is not too much to say that perhaps the main reason why Jesus was

crucified was that He would not accept the particularisms of His generation, but embraced universality. He embraced universality when He
refused the title "Son of David" and chose instead the title "Son of man."
He embraced universality when He would not confine His programme to
the restoration of the kingdom of Israel, an essentially nationalistic kingdom, but proclaimed instead the Kingdom of God, a universal, frontier-
less kingdom to which men would come from the East, and from the
West, from the North, and from the South, and sit down with Abraham,
Isaac, and Jacob. "Whosoever shall do the will of my Father . . . the same
is my brother, and sister, and mother."

Jesus envisioned this spirit of fellowship among His own followers. He
prayed that they might be one—one flock, one shepherd. It was only thus,
He said, that the world could know. I am thrilled, as are you, at this great
gathering of Baptists the world around, assembled here at this World
Congress in Copenhagen. There is only one gathering that would thrill
me more, and that would be a gathering of Christians of all denominations
who bear the name of Christ. Baptists alone cannot save the world, and
Baptists will not save the world alone. Perhaps there is no greater sin in
Christendom than this, that we have permitted differences in ecclesiastical practice and procedure, which of and in themselves neither guarantee
nor even necessarily indicate Christian discipleship, to become an obsta-
cle to Christian fellowship. "Ye are all one in Christ Jesus." That is the one
and only New Testament test of fellowship—being in Christ, partakers of
His spirit.

But the Master was more daring than that. Not only did He envision
fellowship for His followers, but for all mankind. He made the audacious
claim that the entire human race was a family under the universal Fatherhood of a God who has made of one blood all men to dwell upon the face
of the earth. St. Paul took Him seriously. "There is neither Jew nor Greek
. . . for ye are all one in Christ Jesus." "He . . . hath broken down the middle
wall of partition between us." The missionary movement, perhaps the
most significant and promising enterprise on the face of the earth to-day,
bears living witness to Jesus' faith in the brotherhood of all men in God.
This plea of Jesus for world brotherhood may once have seemed to us
sentimental nonsense. Is not this day declaring it to be soberest common
sense? World brotherhood is no longer a luxury; it is the necessity for
human survival.

The story has it that someone said to a man from Texas: "I have heard
that the State of Texas is so large that all the people on earth could be
gotten into it standing up." "So they could," replied the other, "if they
were friends." That is precisely mankind's dilemma to-day. Science has
brought us together and we are not friends. The world has shrunk un-
believably under the magic touch of science: distances are no more. We

are literally rubbing elbows together. We have physical proximity, but we lack spiritual community. The world is a neighbourhood, but we lack the spirit of brotherhood.

Indeed, I think science has played a mean trick on us. Just now, when it has brought our backyards together, it has given us the deadliest of all weapons, the atomic bomb, which by the use of rocketplanes we can hurl at each other almost as readily as throwing bricks over the back fence. Science seems to be saying to us: "You will either learn to live together or you will not live at all!"

Jesus' plea for world friendship, therefore, is no longer optional. It is imperative. The great question for man to-day is just this: whether or not those who have been brought nigh by science can be brought nigh by the blood of Christ; whether we can discover the universal language of understanding, brotherhood, and goodwill which will drown out the miserable dialects of prejudice, greed, and pride. "One world or none": that is the choice before us. To accept that concept of Jesus and try to make it a reality—that is what is meant by building on Christ the foundation.

A third insight of the Master, the truth of which this day declares, is His emphasis upon inwardness; His insistence that the significant changes in life are never those that come from the outside in, but from the inside out. Upon the importance of inner change Jesus based His Gospel of repentance and His call for a new birth. It was this teaching that aroused the antagonism of the Pharisees whose religion had so largely degenerated into the meticulous performance of certain external rites. They were, Jesus said, like whited sepulchres, beautiful outward, but impure within. Upon the necessity and possibility of inner change He proclaimed His Gospel of the Kingdom of God. This Kingdom, the reign of righteousness and love, could not even be seen, let alone be entered, except by those who were converted. Thus the Master taught that the only door to a better world was through the inner transformation of human life. Only changed men can change the world.

How this day declares the truth of that insight! If we could only change the world by the manipulation of external forces, what a wonderful world we should have! But each attempt has ended in failure. Consider some of them.

Once we thought that science would give us a new world. This was the superstition we inherited from the 19th century optimists, who seemed to believe that as the light of scientific knowledge entered our heads the darkness of sin would be driven from our hearts. They were mistaken. So are we. Science has given us a different world, but in no sense is it new. Whereas once the robber would brain us with a club, now he riddles us with machine-gun bullets. Whereas once the evil man bent on an evil mission could get to his objective no faster than 15 miles an hour, now he can get there at 300 miles an hour. Whereas once in war you would not shoot until you could see the whites of their eyes, now the atomic bomb will flatten a city and destroy 100,000 souls in less time than it takes to tell it. But there is nothing new about this. This is just "worse and more of it." Mr. Winston Churchill may not have been far wrong when he said "the Stone Age may return on the gleaming wings of science." If it does, it will not be the fault of science, which is wholly neutral, but of man. When shall we learn that it is not science that determines what man will do, but man who determines what science does?

Again, we thought that economics would give us a new world. Karl Marx believed that, could we but dethrone the capitalist and enthrone the proletariat, the equivalent of the Kingdom of God would come. Communism gives us a different world, but it is not new. Communism has some commendable and laudable insights, but as it operates by and large in the world to-day there is nothing new about it. It is as new as arrogance, stubbornness, stupidity, and greed. Communism is as new as brutality, treachery, and tyranny. Communism is as new, in short, as human sin—and there is nothing new about that.

We thought that politics would give us a new world. When the League of Nations was formed, Lord Robert Cecil's brother said to him, "Will your League work?" And Lord Robert replied, "Hugh, does a spade work?" The League of Nations or the United Nations is but a tool, and while we cannot build a new world any more than a new house without tools, if we have nothing but tools we shall build neither. If the United Nations works it will be because men make it work, and if it does not work it will be because men keep it from working. This day declares the bankruptcy of secular statesmanship. Christianity, therefore, is vastly more realistic than secularism. It insists that man has to rebuild himself, or rather that God has to rebuild him, before he can rebuild his world. "Work out your own salvation with fear and trembling. For it is God which worketh in you. . . ." Until man himself is re-created nothing that man creates holds promise of his salvation. To believe, as did the Master, that the key to a better world lies in the necessity and possibility of the inner transformation of life by God's redeeming grace—that is what it means to build on Christ the foundation.

We mention one more insight of the Master, the truth of which this day declares: His concept of the nature and use of power. The problem of power is one of the major ones confronting modern man. This very age that has brought unparalleled power has created unparalleled peril. Jesus came into a world in which to be great was to be powerful, and to be powerful was to be tyrannical. Nietzsche, with his monstrous doctrine of the superman, made the tyrannical use of power the chief end of man.

The aim of man, according to him, is to be strong, and the role of the strong is to oppress the weak.

This has been by and large the ruling philosophy of the world, and how this day declares its inadequacy! If history proves anything it shows that no nation is so insecure as when it stakes its life upon the aggressive use of power. Before our very eyes we have seen this pagan philosophy of power not only bring destruction to the three nations that most brazenly espoused it, but death and unspeakable tragedy to the world. This day declares that it is not by might nor by force, but only by a new spirit that security is found. "The princes of the Gentiles exercise dominion over them, and they that are great exercise authority upon them. But it shall not be so among you: but whosoever shall be great among you, let him be your minister. And whosoever will be chief among you, let him be your servant. Even as the Son of man came not to be ministered unto, but to minister, and to give his life a ransom for many."

The very announcement of Jesus' birth symbolised this new concept of power: "Behold, I bring you good tidings of great joy, which shall be to all people. For unto you is born this day in the city of David a Saviour, which is Christ the Lord." A Saviour who is a Lord. How strange to apply the words "Saviour" and "Lord" to the same person! A saviour is like a servant, a lord is like a master. A saviour serves us, a lord rules us. But that is the mystery of God's revelation—the Lordship of Saviourhood, the greatness of humility, a new concept of power; one that reveals itself not in domination, but in service, God born in a stable, a Saviour who is a Lord.

In the Book of Revelation the name of the man who sat on the horse is called "the Word of God." To put the word of God in the seat of power: where else is there salvation for man? It was Nietzsche who said that the ideal man would be Caesar with the soul of Christ. That is an impossible combination, for if Caesar had the soul of Christ he would not be Caesar. He would be restrained by the thought that humility and service are the marks that Christ puts on power when it is informed by His spirit. To believe that and try to live it out is what it means to build on Christ the foundation.

Here, then, are four of the insights of our Gospel, the truth of which this tragic and tortured day of ours declares. If and when we find our way out, that way will be along this road that Christ has pioneered. First, that the door to life is through spiritual reality; second, that because man is essentially spiritual, a child of God, he can only find life in community, in fellowship with his brother man; third, that the way to this new world of fellowship is through the inner transformation of life; and fourth, that one mark of this transformed man will be his new concept of power.

As we contemplate these objectives, so great but seemingly so remote, well might we ask with the apostle, "And who is sufficient for these things?" And like him we must answer, "Our sufficiency is of God." How this day declares that truth! For the paradox of life to-day is this, that this very age which proclaims man's unprecedented greatness in the material world reveals his spiritual poverty and befuddlement. Yet it is our very insufficiency, would we but admit it, that is our most assured ground of hope.

We are being told that there is no defence against the atomic bomb. That is the verdict of the natural man, but it is not true. There *is* one defence, but it does not lie in the field of physics, but of ethics. Our one defence is moral and spiritual regeneration: a world founded on the principles of Christ the foundation and informed by His spirit. This is the Gospel of God, the Gospel of salvation, and therefore, of hope.

Can the Christian Church, by God's help, adequately declare this Gospel before it is too late? Will the world believe this Gospel before it is too late? God grant it may be so!

8
Cleveland, Ohio
1950

Introduction

"We are meeting here in the Eighth Congress of the Baptist World Alliance at a time when conditions in the world are bent on putting another straining test on our oneness and our fellowship," preached C. Oscar Johnson in his 1950 presidential address. Johnson, pastor of the Third Baptist Church in Saint Louis, Missouri, had been elected BWA president at Copenhagen in 1947. When he gaveled the Cleveland assembly to order in 1950, he was keenly aware of the centrifugal forces pulling at the harmony of the world as well as the Baptist World Alliance.

Chastened by two world wars, a repulsive racism, and a jingoistic nationalism, Baptists, like other Christians of the world, had lost the capacity to be sentimentally optimistic about the human condition. Other wars were threatening. Racism refused to die among Baptists as in the world. Nationalism and competing political ideologies were still very much alive at mid-century.

Even efforts toward unity produced disunity. Attitudes toward the United Nations as well as the World Council of Churches verify the fact. The latter movement, ecumenical Christianity, had become a subject of some controversy within the BWA. So Oscar Johnson was right. World conditions *were* putting another "straining test" on the oneness and fellowship of the Baptist World Alliance.

Both Gardner Taylor and C. Oscar Johnson spoke to the issue of the darkness of division and the need for unity in the mid-twentieth-century world. According to the official proceedings of the Cleveland Congress, the address of Johnson—"Our World Fellowship Through the Light of the Gospel of Christ"—elicited "thunderous and spontaneous applause."[1]

Gardner Taylor, pastor of the Concord Baptist Church, Brooklyn, New York, preached a sermon on Sunday morning in the Cleveland Public Auditorium. Entitled, "They Shall Ask the Way," Taylor's sermon "was heard in breathless attention."[2] This may be the most moving, inspiring and challenging sermon ever printed in a report of the Baptist World Alliance. Calling for unity in Christ, Taylor said, "Enough men and women committed to a oneness in Christ can break the evil spell of our recurring slaughters, pull down flags of national pride and raise the blood-stained banner of Calvary's kingdom in their stead."

Our World Fellowship Through the Light of the Gospel of Christ
C. Oscar Johnson

Forty and five years ago this month a group of Baptist leaders met in the city of London. They had come from many different nations and backgrounds but essentially they were one. Their purpose in meeting was to set up an organization which would promote this oneness and give inspiration to our Baptist family so widely scattered over the earth.

Those early leaders were wise in their purpose and plan. From the beginning it was made clear that fellowship and inspiration should be the main purpose behind the organization while showing our essential oneness in Jesus Christ. Seven times the Congress has met in six different countries. Twice the regularity of our meeting schedule has been interrupted by black and awful wars. In these national conflicts we found ourselves pitted against each other but through all of it we found our essential oneness in Christ continued, and the bond of fellowship in him has remained unbroken.

We are meeting here in the Eighth Congress of the Baptist World Alliance at a time when conditions in the world are bent on putting another straining test on our oneness and our fellowship. It is highly important that we who meet here shall acknowledge our debt sincerely to all those who so faithfully laid the foundation for our continuing fellowship, and at exceeding cost have built thereon. Six good and true men have served as President and three faithful men have served as General Secretary. Many noble men and women have served on the Executive and they and others have brought inspiring messages to the sessions of the Congress.

War clouds again hang over the world with foreboding awe . . . once again it may be ours to prove that our fellowship cannot be bombed and an Iron Curtain can never permanently separate us. Wisely has your committee chosen the theme text for this Congress. "The Light Shineth in the Darkness." Various facets of this gem of truth will be presented in vivid brilliance here. I shall be content to leave that to those chosen ones to bring to you the shafts of light to thrust back the darkness.

The President's address has dealt with many important subjects in the past. Each has been handled by a master, not only of assemblies but of the revealed truth of God. Some have been theological, some have been doctrinal, some historical, but even here we saw our essential oneness in Christ. Inasmuch as our fellowship has been tested in recent years by a world war and that a new and more severe test seems near at hand, it seemed good to me to speak to you on the subject of "Our Fellowship Through the Light of the Gospel."

Fellowship is a word which may be used in several connections. There is a fellowship of darkness. Those who insist on living in darkness have a kind of fellowship with each other, a fellowship among thieves, a fellowship of fools. This seems almost like profaning so fine a word by dragging it down to such low levels. Today we see it draped about by new and strange banners seeking new adherents to a fellowship which promises light, but ends in extreme darkness. In the forefront of this long array at the present time is the proffered fellowship of communism of which someone said a month ago, "Communism is not a philosophy, but really organized conspiracy." Most of us here have watched this cloud start when it seemed little larger than a man's hand. Today it has spread and become dense and dark at the center. We are seeing the forked lightning of its increasing fury followed by the rumbling thunder of its enveloping program.

This is not a beautiful picture but it furnishes a suitable backdrop against which the Light of the Gospel of Jesus Christ may be seen in greater glory and beauty. Our fellowship is familiar with scenes like that, for the Gospel of Christ is our light and the heart of that is darkness and storm and lightning and earthquake for the Son of God is dying to make possible our lasting fellowship in him.

Against this cloud of Communistic conspiracy it is ours to shine. The blackness makes our lights the brighter, but let us not forget that the darkness is not all confined to Communistic-dominated countries. There are sadly neglected areas in all our lands which present a dark picture needing light. In this very nation wherein we are meeting there are two sister evils which threaten the light that is in us, commercialism and materialism. They are dangerous because they attack from within. They steal away the oil from the lamps. They divert its flow to the flame. They dilute and adulterate the pure oil which gives true light.

From these two come strife between men and women, labor and management, white and colored races. From these also come wars and conflicts. The darkness deepens and from the faint rays of light still shining we see little children lying helpless on piles of rubble, gaunt men and women drag themselves painfully in search of food, food! Old men sit and starve; young men shrug their shoulders in a gesture of futility, a fellowship of misery, hunger, suffering, death.

It is time now that we ask ourselves what is this fellowship of which we are justly proud and which we seek so earnestly to preserve. It is, of course, primarily a Christian fellowship. Back of that, however, stands our belief in a God, a God of power and justice and righteousness to be sure, but also a God of love, mercy, peace and good will. He is the unknown God of the Athenians, whom Paul declared unto them. He is the God whom we love and embrace and seek to serve. The God whom communism bans from national and as far as possible from personal life. He is the God of the Hebrew children in their test of flames. The God of Daniel in the presence of lions. The God of Elijah beset by designing Ahab and Jezebel. We believe he is the same today whatever the crisis may be. Our God is "Our Father who art in heaven." Our fellowship becomes intimate and precious in knowing God as our Father. We here are from many lands and races but our fellowship is found to rest upon the Fatherhood of God revealed in Jesus Christ. He said, "I am the Light of the World." Later he said, "You are the Light of the World." Our "God is light and in him is no darkness." Our gospel is the light that "shineth in the darkness."

We have fellowship here in the light of that gospel. Our fellowship centers also around Jesus Christ. Our essential oneness is in him. The question of Caesarea Philippi still calls from each of us an answer, "Who do you say that I am?" It is the individual's right answer to this question that makes our world fellowship possible and enduring.

We recognize no other authority than his, no other guiding light, no other Lord, no other trusted and dependable leader. His right to this position has always been challenged. Just after his baptism at the very beginning of his ministry Satan tested him for days and then as always he proved his worthiness to be our incomparable leader. He began at once to build a fellowship out of a few selected friends through whom he would set going a program of world fellowship. This fellowship has grown until we see here today only small groups of millions who have been brought into it.

The record of how he sought to impart to those twelve friends the real meaning and purpose of the fellowship is a thrilling story of patient instruction and discussion. They never came into its full significance while he lived. It took what seemed to be a great crisis, not to say tragedy, to reveal to them that this fellowship was deeper even than life itself. They learned that "God commends his love toward us in that while we were yet sinners Christ died for us."

The light of this gospel has always been thrown against a black cloud of sin and suffering. On the cross the flame appeared to flicker and to go out. But a brighter day was ahead for them and the world. It was not many days after that that the slightly enlarged number in the fellowship took stock of themselves, after much prayer, and at the end of ten days a great event occurred; a Spirit, the Holy Spirit, came upon and filled them all. Immediately the fellowship that was to circle the earth was launched.

For nearly two thousand years now we know the story of the growth of this fellowship around the world. Opposition from without has hindered its progress. Worse still, divisions and indifference within have done more harm. In all lands today calls of Christian fellowship exist in spite of extreme suffering and persecution. Candles of light still glow in the darkness with assurance that darkness cannot put it out.

The designation of our particular fellowship group is Baptist. Our history has been one of peculiar experiences. Sometimes only a small minority, persecuted even by others who also claimed to be in the fellowship. All of this has worked out for us a greater solidarity and kept us united in our great body of truth, faith and practice while fully recognizing the rights of every individual and the autonomy of every local Baptist church. Many of our brethren of other groups have marveled at our ability to have and maintain such unity in the midst of such seeming diversity.

The Baptist World Alliance has recognized this from the beginning and we are committed to keep sacred this trust committed to us through all the centuries. We seek fellowship with all people on the basis set forth in the New Testament, our rule of faith and practice. In this sense we are foes of communism, but not of communists. We must seek them for our fellowship on the basis of the Light of the Gospel. Our fellowship has been enriched greatly by those who have come into it from all lands, languages and races.

A world fellowship surely is meant for all the people of the world. Baptists are so constituted as to make them well qualified to spread this light to all nations and peoples.

What of our continuing fellowship? This question emerges naturally out of our present day world. Some bodies in our fellowship have established connections with other groups of Christians not of our Baptist family. These efforts at wider co-operation have in some unions and conventions been desirable for common interests and ends. Others in our family have not so united for good and sufficient reasons to them. These convictions must be respected and safeguarded for all time. This has been the genius of our Baptist heritage from the beginning. We must not allow these positions of our constituent bodies to mar or in any way to disrupt our fellowship in this great Alliance of fellow Baptists. So long as we hold together on our great doctrines as set forth in the New Testament, we will hold together at the center and at the same time recognize the rights of some to follow the leading of the spirit in their particular union or convention. We must never allow our unity in Christ to be disturbed by such actions by constituent bodies who in their judgment and under the leadership of the Holy Spirit take such action as for them seems best so long as we remain steadfast in the basic principles of our Baptist position and practice.

Our Baptist fellowship must continue and increase under God's leadership. Our greatest contribution to any world-wide fellowship among all Christians would be to make our Baptist fellowship the strongest possible. To that end let us highly resolve to strengthen the ties that bind us together around the world while joining in spirit with all Christ's followers we can, that the light of his gospel may continue to shine in a dark and disunited world.

What more can we say? If God be for us, who, then, can be against us? I am persuaded that nothing can separate us from his love and I pray that nothing shall separate us from each other. Trials and tribulations have served to bring us even closer together. The soil of persecution and suffering has always been fertile ground for our Baptist faith. Our message of individual freedom and worth has found ready response among the oppressed and downtrodden.

What about this fellowship in the days ahead? Even now the lightning streaks across black clouds hanging ominously over much of the world. We are not thinking of dispelling the storm clouds by release of physical force. We insist on doing it by light, the light of His gospel which is a gospel of peace to all the world. If we will follow Christ as our leader with His spirit in our hearts we can win without a bomb or a gun. We stand today as always upon a solid rock while all around us are swirling tides of isms holding out false hopes to sinking humanity. These man-made houses are built upon the shifting sands of material force, godless philosophies and are futile against the down-beating storms which must come.

Baptists of the world, we must guard against schism in our ranks. Our united contribution must be made in a world so filled with darkness, tension and sin.

Our world fellowship will be extended as always through our continued peristent efforts in evangelism. It is our primary business to win men to Christ, to make disciples, thus to bring light to shine in the darkness in every land. We have from the beginning been commissioned to preach the gospel to the poor. We are in good succession in this for it was the final answer Jesus gave to John's inquiry as to who he was. Many things were being done, blind saw, lame walked, dead were raised, but the climax of his answer was, "And the poor have the gospel preached unto them." Baptists have for the most part been satisfied with their mission to all men, especially to the poor. God has a great many poor children whom he loves. The fields, indeed, are white. Gathering this harvest should keep us both busy and united. If the necessary energy is used in this direction little time will be left to stir up dissension or division among the brethren.

Our schedule calls for our next meeting to be held, preferably in London, to celebrate a half century of our history. No one among us is wise enough to know whether such plans may be carried out. At least twice in the forty-five years of our existence our meetings have been delayed because of serious and awful conflicts between the nations of the world. Even as we meet here headlines of the papers tell of rolling tanks, flying bombers, marching men, casualty lists, and increasing fear. It is the more important, therefore, that we who are privileged to be in attendance at this Eighth Congress shall highly resolve that we will be even more alert to the command of our Lord to "Let our light shine before men."

These clouds are but temporary clouds that may hide the light for a time, but they cannot put it out. With that assurance we can heartily sing:

> "We are not divided, all one body we;
> One in hope and doctrine, one in charity."

In the light of our present world situation, then, as well as in the light of the gospel which we bear, what shall be our attitude and position, both as regards ourselves and those others of the world for whom the light is intended? Paul in his writings to the Ephesians has a very appropriate word to say which seems worth giving you just in this connection. He tells us, "Henceforth, you must grow strong, through union with the Lord and through his mighty strength. You must put on God's armor, so as to be able to stand up against the devil's stratagems. For we have to struggle, not with enemies of flesh and blood, but with the hierarchies, the authorities, the master spirits of this dark world, the spirit forces of evil on high. So you must take God's armor, so that when the evil day comes, you will be able to make a stand, and when it is all over to hold your ground. Stand your ground then with the belt of truth, around your waist, and put on uprightness, as your coat of mail, and on your feet put the readiness, the good news of peace brings, besides all these take faith for your shield, for with it you will be able to put out all the flaming missiles of the evil one, and take salvation for your helm, and for your sword the spirit which is the voice of God."

We see here clearly delineated the position that a follower of Christ and a believer in His gospel must always firmly take. There is only one way that we can justify this gathering as well as the many local congregations which we represent. We are a "born again people." We have been made alive unto God. We have taken up a spiritual warfare against the forces of darkness and evil. The coat of mail and the equipment which Paul outlines for those early Christians is still appropriate for us.

The Christian's gospel is a gospel of love. We must, therefore, love those who are our enemies. We must love them in spite of provocation, which they may hurl at us. We must love them in the name of Christ, not for what they are, but what they may become through faith in him. We must love them in sincerity so that they will know that the contest in which we are presently engaged through force is not the real expression of what those of us who are Christ's followers want.

Not only must we outlove those who are against us. We must also live firmly and strongly our profession. The equipment given here is truth and love, the gospel, salvation, and such things. This equipment should enable us to stand our ground. We are not to compromise or receded in our loyalty to this faith. As Baptists through the centuries, we have undergone much persecution. The black clouds have hung over us again and again. Many of our predecessors have been put in prison. They have been driven underground. They have been put to death, but we must stand our ground for the truth, for the freedom of the individual against the hierarchies in government and church. We must stand our ground against all opposition to the worth of an individual and the right of access of every person to the God who created him.

It requires boldness to do this. We are not using man-made weapons of force and destruction. We are rather engaged in a spiritual conquest which will ultimately overcome, but while the advance is being made much patience, sacrifice, and high devotion to his cause is required. No gathering such as this can be stronger than its constituent bodies and no union or convention or association or church can be stronger than its individual members.

It comes back, then, to this very definite and personal challenge that any follower of Christ anywhere must live up to the maximum of his purpose and his profession. The world is far more concerned about our demonstration of that spirit than they are about our pronunciation of phrases, however significant they may sound. It is a demonstration such as Christ himself gave, in the supreme sacrifice on the cross for the sins of mankind. We must, therefore, go back to our various localities and with renewed purpose and dedication give ourselves utterly to this business of living the Christian life.

Only as we do that can this Baptist fellowship shed light on a world that is so desperately in need of it, only as we exemplify this light within us can people really see that it is real, and not simply a story out of a fairy-tale book. With this firmly fixed in our minds and hearts it is ours under God to here dedicate ourselves in order that we may let all the world see from their cloud-ridden areas that there is light, a glowing and steady light in the gospel which we preach. This light is the Light of the world. We are the light of the world through Him, and together we must carry this light, so that those who walk in darkness may not fall into the abyss.

My fellow Baptists, I here and now summon you to a high resolve on your own individual part that it shall be your aim to completely dedicate yourself to the high calling which we have in Christ Jesus. We are in the world, but we are not of the world. We are to be lights in the world. We are to steadily take our positions against all spiritual wickedness in high places, and hold our ground being assured that ultimate victory is ours. In these high and noble ideals I am sure that we are here united. It will be our aim and I am sure our desire to carry this spirit of unity back to every area that we can touch for the cause of our Lord.

The whole cause which Christ Himself came to establish had some very dark hours in the beginning. One of those, darkest of all, was in the Garden of Gethsemane; it seemed there that the light that was to shine forever was about to go out. We will never know all that went on in that garden. We know enough of it to know that the One who knelt there in prayer was setting a pattern for all who follow after Him, and that is, that no high and holy ideal can be realized without the willingness to deny oneself and make the supreme sacrifice of all that one has for that ideal.

We are thankful today that our Lord did not stop in the garden, but that gaining strength from his surrender in the memorable statement, "Not my will, but thine be done" He went on to the consummation of His purpose on a cross, and it was from that cross that the light began to glow like a lighthouse set high on a hill that the people in all the dark areas may see the light and rejoice. And to make it more easy, that light has been transplanted into the lives of millions of His followers in order that those who are blinded may see, close at hand, what the light is like and find the path that leads at last to God.

Here we are met. Soon the days will be done, and we will go our many scattered ways, but may we not earnestly pray that none of us shall go back to his home except with a higher purpose to follow Christ wherever he leads, whatever the cost. And as we do that we may be assured that our Lord, our King, our Eternal Leader is leading on.

"Lead on, O King Eternal, The day of march has come;
Henceforth in fields of conquest Thy tents shall be our home,
Through days of preparation Thy grace has made us strong,
And now, O King Eternal, We lift our battle song."

They Shall Ask the Way
Gardner Taylor

There is a question on the lips of our times, a poignant, desperate, haunting question. A question which arises because our old confidence is gone. We were sure yesterday that we had the future neatly folded, wrapped and ready for delivery. Utopia was in our hands—our chromium-plated, push-button conveniences told us so. A swaggering age was ready to wave a jaunty "Farewell" to God, for we had outgrown him—our streamlined gadgets were the credentials of our adulthood, our by-pass of the old verities. We were quite certain that any further truck with God would be on our own terms—all in the frame of our new Science.

"Glory to man in the highest. For man is the master of all things." We granted, with a bit of impatience, that everything was not completely perfected: here and there could be seen man's brutality to man. Education was the answer to such brutality, and since we were not the victims, the length of time it would take was not so critical a matter. In the meantime, those who were suffering the indignities ought to be patient. However, we forgot that history and history's God would not wait on our disposition. Education was the answer, until along came the Nazi horror, established in the best-educated land on earth. Along it came, breathing its threatenings, opening its gas chambers, multiplying the horrors of its concentration camps, venting demonic violence on the basis of race, which was but the elaboration of what other parts of the world had done—some not too far from this pleasant lakefront. An uncertainty leapt to the countenance of our generation.

With a shrug of our shoulder, in the days of our self-confidence, our age confessed that in a world of plenty there were millions who went to bed each night without sufficient food, shivered in the blasts of winter without sufficient clothing, crowded in hovels and ghettoes without sufficient shelter. Such conditions men dismissed with catch-phrases—the enlightened self-interest of free enterprise would take care of all that. Only it didn't.

With an arrogant twist of the head, a confident age agreed that there were sections of the world where people were denied access to public places, equal wages and self-government in lands where their fathers had lived for centuries. After all, they were backward peoples who probably did not want anything better. They were the "White man's burden." The mutterings have mounted to thunder in Asia and Africa, and storm clouds hang over lands long smouldering in virtual bondage. The thunders from the East have put a question on the lips of our generation. Our streamlined gadgets, graphs, charts, and scientific knowledge before which we genuflected in worship as to a new god somehow lack the answer to our haunting uncertainties.

We knew that churches divided along the lines of race, class and section were mockeries—but were sure that a more feverish campaign for numbers, a new educational building, larger budgets and well-worded resolutions when we sat in solemn conclave, would more than atone for what we lacked of the inclusive spirit of Christ. The only trouble is that the world scorns our preaching of Christ, in whom is neither east nor west, when we give such poor witness to him in our actions. There is a question on the lips of our generation!

Our gadgets have turned now into threats, our push-buttons now contain cosmic death. The voice of judgment is raised to tones of thunder in our day. Over us the clouds of war hang low: our confidence is shattered. Men ask a repentant church to show the way to the world's great dreams of peace and harmony.

In their question is our opportunity. Our situation calls to mind the words set in the fiftieth chapter of the Book of Jeremiah at the fifth verse, "They shall inquire the way to Zion with their faces thitherward." These words come at the close of a bewildering experience of slavery, hard by the low canals and willow trees in Babylon. For years Zion, City of God set on a hill, beautiful for situation, has been to these poor exiles but a dream, a hope long deferred. But now the long night of captivity is past; the purpling dawn of a people's hope brightens the horizon. The children of captivity are free to go home. History's God has given to them a new national opportunity. Alas! the road across the desert is unknown to them; there are no waymarkers on their journey, but their hopes and hearts are turned toward the city of their dreams. If they can find their way, they will come to its heights, walk its ways which have been hallowed by prophets' tread, and build again on Mt. Zion a sanctuary for their dearest hopes. Thus the word, "They shall inquire the way to Zion with their faces turned thitherward." From the New Testament, as though the question were raised to cosmic proportions, there is bold answer in the fourteenth chapter of John and the sixth verse, "I am the Way."

On the lips of our generation, weary and sick, overtaken by uncertainty, desperate, afraid, lonely and sick, there is the same question. Our age is asking the way: everywhere there is recognition that we are lost.

War after war has been fought with the hope that it was the last one. Alas! the crimson harvest of each succeeding conflict has seemed to bear the seed of the next. Some deep awareness tells us that human life is too precious in the gaze of God to be wasted in the sudden destruction of battlefields, and as targets for bombsights. War is immoral, some deep instinct makes us know. It is not our destined way. We inquire the way to that height where they shall not hurt or kill in all his holy hill. Our faces are turned in the direction of peace; our hearts yearn for it. We ask the way to Zion.

Our question is made the more desperate because we are faced with the old mandate of God underscored with atomic power. "This do and thou shalt live. This do and thou shalt surely die." Holding in our hands the cosmic flame, we inquire for the cosmic wisdom to use it right. But how? Larger armies have not protected us against war, greater navies are no guarantee against bloodshed. The centuries speak with one voice at that point. From sea to shining sea—men inquire the way to Zion.

We who name the name of Jesus as Lord proclaim that in his spirit is the way to the world's long-hoped-for Zion of peace. He has plumbed the depths of our universe and come aloft bearing in his spirit the way to peace, the only way honored by the very structure of our universe. It was his faith that a band of committed men and women, partakers of his spirit and consecrated to his will, would be a saving leaven in the world loaf. At a certain point in his ministry, he waited for the return of his disciples he had sent out. When they reported to him their success, his word was "I saw Satan fall from heaven like lightning"—as if their experiences ratified a deep conviction of his. Men aflame with his purposes can storm the ramparts of this world's disharmonies, can bring a new earth wherein dwelleth righteousness and peace. Our world's greatest need is men and women in every land, of every kindred and of greatest need is men and women in every language committed to our oneness in Christ, that is deeper than any national difference—our common faith leaping iron curtains, bridging oceans, uniting continents, abolishing borders, bringing to pass that anguished prayer fashioned in his spirit "Holy Father, keep through thine own name those whom thou hast given me, that they may be one, even as we are." Enough men and women committed to a oneness in Christ can break the evil spell of our recurring slaughters, pull down flags of national pride and raise the blood-stained banner of Calvary's Kingdom in their stead. "I am the way" is his unequivocal word flung back to our desperate questioning. Deeper than all differences of nation or language or culture is our oneness in Christ who hath broken down the middle wall of partition. Committed Christians of every language, of every kindred, of every tribe shall make the earth hear echo of heaven's theme:

> "Jesus shall reign where'er the sun
> Does His successive journeys run,
> His Kingdom stretch from shore to shore
> Till moons shall wax and wane no more.
> People and realms of every tongue
> Dwell on His love with sweetest song
> And infant voices shall proclaim
> Their early blessings on His name."

We are beginning to recognize that the problem of race sorely vexes our Christian witness as it does our world's peace. There was a day when men boldly proclaimed the superiority of race, even supported it by spurious interpretation of Scripture, a reflection on the integrity of God and the Justice of the Eternal. The day is far spent when men can believe that souls can be evangelized with a Bible in one hand and a whip in the other. Brave voices in Christ are standing up everywhere to declare such doctrines contrary to the spirit of him who made a mercy seat on the ledge of a well in Samaria, and who gave his pronouncement on the oneness of humanity in a parable about a dangerous curve on the road that led from Jerusalem to Jericho. There was a time when men sought to by-pass the ultimatum of the gospel for one humanity by a frenzied emphasis on individual salvation, thus bringing a shadow on that fundamental truth. Surely, the claim of God is laid in sovereign demand at each human heart. A man and his God are the crucial figures in the drama of redemption—but the stage for that tender drama is history, a social contact. Surely, the brave shepherd goes a-questing through the night for one sheep—but goes that he may lay it across his shoulder and come home—to put it back in the fold. No doctrine of race can be made to fit the frame of the gospel of Christ. We shall be Christian at the point of race, or forced to confess we are not Christian at all. We cannot be strong on faith and weak on work without being contradictory. How tragic that within the body of Christ there is such mutual enmity and suspicion. Churches all black are no less racial sins than churches all white. I blush still at memory of the words of a friend who a few days ago said in my hearing, "There is more segregation at eleven o'clock on Sunday morning when we stand to sing, "In Christ There Is No East nor West," than at any time in the week in the market place, sports arena, or stadium or gaming casino."

We are realizing that ill will begets ill will. Antipathy is not one-sided. Majorities and minorities share the same hatred which is death to both. The same poison is discovered at the bottom of the heap which is so evident at the top.

Thank God for courageous voices in the most difficult places inquiring the way to Zion from this captivity of racial hatred. Thank God for a growing awareness that we are all one race—the human race. In the midst of our asking the way, we hear a voice, stronger than the iron mountains, more winsome than the sound of many waters, "I am the way."

The glory of the early church, feeling the fresh breezes of his spirit, was in the abolition of the problem of race. Here men of diverse backgrounds, proud friends and kinsmen of the Caesars, and humble denizens of the back alleys of the cities of the empire, found in Christ a common gathering place which raised them to the level of a new, blessed, releasing relationship. Perhaps some poor slave in Philippi picked up a letter one night to read it to a gathering of the disinherited of the city.

By the flickering light of a humble room he came to the close of the letter, sealed in an affection of brotherhood. These were the words that humble assembly heard, "All the saints salute you, chiefly they that are of Caesar's household." They found their answer to the problem of race in him who says, "I am the way." In the beleagured catacombs, in a humble upper room, during the treasured hour around a table of the Lord, the early Christians wiped away their early differences of race, awed a world with their devotion to all men, snapped the fascination which old Rome held over them, drew gasps of wonder from their generation, raised the banner of a new kingdom and made the name of Christ a household word in homes around the Mediterranean.

The world looked at them, as it can look at us, asking the way. "What makes you so happy?" said a cynical age to them. They answered saying, "We have come unto life. There is a new dimension to our existence. We were dead behind our crisis-event. Our signal that we have passed from death unto life is, 'We love the brethren.' Love has given us new life, immune to even the harvest of death."

His way of a new brotherhood deeper than race is the only way. In a daring parable he sketched the conditions of admission to see the King Eternal. The lines we make he abolishes, the conditions we raise, he wiped out. How shall we see the King? Deeds of kindness, thoughtless incidents of brotherhood are our passports, so said Jesus. A cup of cold water to a thirsting friend, never mind who he is; a visit to a lonely place, never mind who is there. "Inasmuch as ye did it unto one of the least of these—come ye blessed of my Father, inherit the kingdom prepared for you."

Do we ask the way to Zion? We hear the question framed in the crash of empires, the deep uncertainty which has gripped our times. Agonized, the years of our days seem to wait for some answer. Around us is a world desperate for a new world wherein dwelleth righteousness and peace. "They shall ask the way to Zion with their faces turned thitherward."

Do we ask the way to Zion? Across the centuries his clear voice declares "I am the way"—a family in God, a brotherhood originating in me, a comradeship beginning at Calvary, a community in love, a colony of heaven in earth, a blessed fellowship, closed ranks of a marching army moving to the music of God's stirring act in Christ—"I am the way."

Are we sure our universe will support our way? Are the tides of eternity on our side? Is there some sovereign who guarantees our way is right? In other words, is our gospel underwritten by the ultimate nature of our universe? Can we be sure?

Quickly we move to an event inserted by God's love in the centuries.

God has set authentic evidence for the validity of our way in history. He has given sign and token that he will at all hazards stand fast by our way, will not forsake our way, will not abandon it, though the iniquities of hell spill over the earth. At the place of a skull he left the signature of his power on the side of our way. Dramatic words accompany the event. The sun, as hell and earth do their worst, fades in mourning folds of embarrassment as our Way is tested before the blasphemous eyes of irreverent men. The earth quivers on its axis, as if shocked by the severity of the test to which our Way is subjected. There is a hint that the music of the spheres is suddenly silent in the strain of the test to which our Way is put. For a brief, blinding moment our Way seems abandoned. A black, bleak cry shudders up from the hill, "My God, My God, Why?" Thanks be to God! the last cry is that heaven will not forsake our Way. Up through the pain a cry of tender vindication shatters the darkness. As He reaches for the scepter, we hear a cry that God is holding on, validating our Way. Hands, he says, strong like the fashioners of creations, reach down to vindicate Him by holding Him fast! Hands, great like those that have measured the waters in their hollows, firm like those that give power to the faint, reach down—the cry of validation of our Way is like some anthem as the morning breaks, "Into thy hands, I give my spirit."

Notes

1. *Baptist World Alliance: Eighth Congress, Cleveland, Ohio, July 22-27, 1950* (Philadelphia: The Judson Press, 1950), p. 71.
2. Ibid., p. 50.

9
London
1955

Introduction

In 1955 members of the Baptist World Alliance met in London to celebrate fifty years of BWA history. The theme of the Golden Jubilee Congress was appropriate: "Jesus Christ, the same yesterday, today and forever." Including the 1955 meeting, the BWA had met in nine world Congresses in six different countries: England, the United States, Sweden, Canada, Germany, and Denmark. Baptist giants had served as BWA presidents: Maclaren, Clifford, MacArthur, Mullins, MacNeill, Truett, Rushbrooke, Johnson, and Lord. Three men had served as general secretary of the Alliance: J. H. Rushbrooke of England, Walter O. Lewis of the USA and Arnold T. Ohrn of Norway.

During the five decades from 1905-1955, the BWA had firmly established itself in the worldwide Baptist communion. While never speaking for Baptists of the world in an authoritative way, the BWA certainly had described *to* the world basic Baptist convictions. In addition to providing a loose unity for the immense diversity of world Baptist life, the BWA had also been active in the life of the world. It had agitated, often with success, for religious liberty; it had pled for world peace, though often in vain; it had provided relief for the refugees of war; and it had placed the weight of its influence against racism and totalitarianism.

The Golden Jubilee Congress provided an excellent opportunity for remembering BWA history and reformulating Baptist ideals. F. Townley Lord remembered! His presidential address was entitled, "The Baptist World Alliance in Retrospect and Prospect." This, however, was no mere history lesson. He looked forward as well as backward, and he warned, "there can be no resting on our laurels."

Herbert Gezork, president of Andover-Newton Theological

Seminary in Massachusetts, restated four Baptist distinctives for the world of 1955. In "Our Baptist Faith in the World Today," Gezork reminded his hearers that Baptists had no monopoly on the gospel. He believed, however, that Baptists had "certain great and vital truths" which deserved a witness. He affirmed anew the authority of scripture but warned against a stagnant and sterile interpretation of the Bible. He affirmed anew the church as "a gathered fellowship of committed believers" but warned against low-demand discipleship. He affirmed anew the freedom of conscience and warned that "the most terrifying fact of our time ... is the totalitarian state." He affirmed anew that evangelism was the responsibility of every Christian and warned against the professionalization and partialization of evangelism.

The Baptist World Alliance in Retrospect and Prospect
F. Townley Lord

I have arrived at this Jubilee Congress with satisfaction and relief. Those who know the history of the Baptist World Alliance are aware that the office of President appears to carry with it certain risks! The first President, Dr. John Clifford, was able to deliver his presidential address in Philadelphia and lived to the grand old age of eighty-seven. His successor, Dr. R. S. MacArthur, died on the eve of the Stockholm Congress. The third President, Dr. E. Y. Mullins, was prevented by illness from attending the Toronto Congress. The fourth President, Dr. John MacNeill, was ill when the Berlin Congress was held. Happily the fifth President, Dr. G. W. Truett, was able to deliver his address at the Atlanta Congress, but his successor, Dr. J. H. Rushbrooke, died before the Copenhagen Congress. Fortunately the seventh President, Dr. C. Oscar Johnson, was able to preside with his customary grace and power over the Congress in Cleveland. So the casualties among the Presidents have been considerable, only three out of seven having been able in person to give an account of their stewardship at the Congress following their election. You will understand, therefore, why to-day I feel like singing the hymn with which our Methodist friends always open their Conferences in this country:

> "And are we yet alive
> And see each other's face?
> Glory and praise to Jesus give
> For His redeeming grace."

I

Fifty years ago to-day, on July 17th, 1905, the Baptist World Alliance was born. Six days before, under the presidency of Dr. Alexander Maclaren, whose *Expositions of Holy Scriptures* were linked with Spurgeon's *Metropolitan Tabernacle Pulpit* as the greatest feat of sermon-making in our time, the Baptists of the world had assembled for their first World Congress. The opening meeting in the Exeter Hall, which some of you remember, began with the singing by 3,000 delegates of the hymn:

> "From distant climes, from every land,
> Behold us, Lord, before Thee stand."

The day before the Alliance was born there had been a great open-air meeting in Hyde Park, with Dr. Clifford in the chair. He had drawn attention to the fact that the sun was shining—an event in our climate sufficiently notable to warrant comment. The sunshine, said Dr. Clifford, was a prophecy of our Baptist future. Among the speakers was Miss Nannie Burroughs whose subject was "The Triumph o Truth." On Monday, July 17th, the delegates crowded the Exeter Hall to hear addresses on the contribution of our Colleges and Seminaries, and then to witness the unveiling of the Spurgeon statue which stood upon the platform. True to our traditions, the meeting then took a collection, and then Dr. Crandall read the report of the Committee which had been set up to consider future Congresses. This report proposed that a Baptist World Alliance be formed. Dr. Clifford moved its adoption; it was seconded in several places and received with enthusiasm. From the chair Dr. Maclaren declared, "I feel like singing the Doxology in my heart at seeing the day when Baptists resolve on a world-wide Alliance."

The great audience that day did indeed sing the Doxology; now, fifty years after, we can voice our thanksgivings to God with a fervour and intensity greater than that of our fathers. Fifty years ago the eyes of our Baptist leaders were turned to the future, but they could not see what that future might bring. They could not know that within the lifetime of many then present in the Exeter Hall catastrophe would fall upon mankind, bringing suffering and tragedy before unknown. They could not then see that two devastating world wars would sunder the members of the newly-formed world organization. They could not then know that dark tragedy would stalk the world, that from the anguished hearts of millions groans and cries would arise, that millions more would rot in concentration camps or wander, homeless and stateless, across the face of Europe.

They could not know. But we have known; and yet with all this unprecedented confusion and turmoil behind us, we are able to declare that the fellowship which began fifty years ago has more than survived the storm and stress of five decades. By the grace of God it has grown, from some six millions to more than twenty millions. Its roots have become deeper, its range wider, its hands stronger in the clasp of fellowship and the gesture of compassion; until to-day, our Alliance stands in its greatest strength and its most effective comradeship. If our fathers sang the Doxology, we need a Hallelujah Chorus and more to do justice to the gratitude we feel for so wonderful a blessing.

Before I vacate this office, which in your great kindness you entrusted to me five years ago, I should like to pay grateful tribute to my predecessors who have provided a tradition of consecration and loyalty rarely equalled and never excelled. Our first President, John Clifford, shone in nineteenth-century Baptist life in this country with a brilliance all his own. There were times in his old age when, a slight, bowed figure, he would worship in the church of which I was then the young minister. So humble was he, and so self-effacing, that it was difficult to see in his modest bearing one who was an ancient apostle in a modern man, a champion of the oppressed whose eloquence could rouse great audiences to cheering enthusiasm, and who could be described by Lord Balfour as "Oliver Cromwell's successor." Robert Stuart MacArthur, the second of our Presidents, for forty years pastor of Calvary Baptist Church, New York, was more than a gifted preacher. He enjoyed the confidence of more than one President of the United States and valiantly carried the challenge of the Gospel into public affairs. E. Y. Mullins came to the Presidency at the height of his influence in Louisville Seminary where for twenty-eight years he combined administrative gifts and high cultural standards. His books, notably his *Christianity in its Doctrinal Expression,* had almost as great an influence here as in America. W. O. Carver did not exaggerate when he described his chief as the leading Baptist theologian of his time. We gratefully agree that Dr. Mullin's *Axioms of Religion* were both a "charter of Baptist Orthodoxy and a chart of Baptist progress." John McNeill, for so many years pastor of Walmer Road, Toronto, brought to the Presidency the heart of a pastor and the warmth of a friend. He addressed the first Congress fifty years ago, and during his presidency I had the joy of welcoming him to my own pulpit in Bloomsbury, where we learned the secret of his deep influence among the Baptists of Canada. It was in this very Hall that some of us came to know George W. Truett. To this day his name is magic in Dallas where the First Baptist Church has the largest membership of any white Baptist church in the world. They used to talk of him in America as the "American Spurgeon," and what more fitting than that he should cross the Atlantic to take part in our Spurgeon Celebrations? Before he died in 1944 he had presided at three of our Congresses. Dr. Truett was succeeded in the presidency by J. H. Rushbrooke whose record of service to the Alliance is unique. He was successively Commissioner for Europe, Eastern Secretary, General Secretary and President. Those who were present at the Copenhagen Congress will not easily forget the remarkable tributes paid to him at the memorial service. Perhaps I may be allowed to quote now what I said then:

"Politicans knew that when Dr. Rushbrooke knocked at their doors they had to face up to the rights of oppressed minorities. In his presence it was not possible to ignore or to obscure the principles of democratic freedom. Many were the battles he fought for oppressed Baptists in various parts of the world; many were the victories he won. Some day we shall know more fully the debt we owe to his vigorous championing of our rights."

It is a great satisfaction to us that the life and achievements of Dr. Rushbrooke have been so excellently surveyed by Dr. E. A. Payne in the brief biography he published last year.

Clifford, MacArthur, Mullins, MacNeill, Truett, Rushbrooke . . . all these are gone. They are numbered among the great cloud of witnesses. But there remains one ex-President, C. Oscar Johnson, whose magnificent ministry in Third Church, St. Louis, has given him a place unequalled in the land of his birth. But far beyond that land he is affectionately remembered. We in the Alliance owe this great master of assemblies a special debt; it was due to him more than to any other that we were able to secure our Headquarters in Washington, D.C.

I wish I had time to pay tribute, no less deserved, to many other valued servants of the Alliance, for we have been greatly blessed in our secretaries and leaders of youth and women's work. I have, indeed, tried to express our appreciation in the history of the Alliance published this year; but inasmuch as there is one group of our Alliance officers whose work necessarily lies in the background, I may be allowed to pay special tribute to them. I refer to the men who have presided over our Alliance finances. They are a noble band, and we salute them all—H. K. Porter, E. M. Sipprell, Herbert Marnham, the Hon. Albert Matthews, C. T. Le Quesne, George B. Fraser. To all these servants of our common cause I would apply the words with which Milton, in *Paradise Lost,* described the Seraph Abdiel—"His loyalty he kept, his love, his zeal."

II

But I must pass on to draw attention to some of the events of the past fifty years which have given colour and thrill to our Alliance story. It would not be difficult to portray the half-century of our witness in a series of dramatic scenes, each embodying something of enduring value in our contribution to evangelical religion: the occasion fifty years ago when Dr. Maclaren called on the Assembly to stand with him and repeat the Apostles' Creed, thus asserting that we stand in the authentic line of apostolic witness; the roll-call in Philadelphia in 1911 when there came to the platform veterans from Russia, one of them having been imprisoned thirty-one times and twice exiled; the London Conference of 1920 which by its pronouncements and its allocation of special areas for our Baptist work was a turning point in our modern history; the first Baptist World Exhibition in Stockholm depicting those who had trodden the Baptist road from 1633 to 1923; the great efforts made in the years following the Stockholm Conference on behalf of Russian and Rumanian Baptists; the wonderful gathering in Berlin, exactly twenty years after war had been declared between Germany and Britain, when the more than 3,000 delegates rejoiced that at last August the 4th had come to possess a new and happier significance; the thousands who gathered at the railway staion in Atlanta to welcome President G. W. Truett to his hotel, escorted by a bodyguard of cyclists; the day in Copenhagen in 1947 when delegates loaded the platform with gifts of money, jewels and clothing, symbols of Baptist compassion towards needy brethren; the opening and dedication of the Altersheim Bethel in Munich at which we expressed our affection for W. O. Lewis and our appreciation of his wonderful services in the administration of relief.

From my own experience I could tell of contacts with our brethren in many parts of the world. I have frozen on the Arctic border and roasted on the Equator, and met Baptists in both places. I have had fellowship with our people amid the lovely lakes and forests of Finland, in prosperous and beautiful Sweden, in heroic Denmark, in war-torn Germany and amid the medieval beauties of Austria, in the snows of Switzerland and amid the classical charms of Italy, in Yugoslavia and even behind the borders of Soviet Russia. I have seen our Canadian churches from the grandeur of the Rocky Mountains to the verdant Maritime Provinces. I have experienced American Baptist hospitality in every state of the Union, and have seen the progress of our work down in Rio and across the Andes, in the humidity and political excitement of Central America and the republics further south. Most recently I have met our people across the broad continent of Australia, in entrancing New Zealand and in the plains of Hungary.

To me more than to most have come the privilege and honour of gathering with our Baptist people under many skies, and hearing their prayers in many tongues. What precious memories these five years have brought: that Saturday afternoon gathering by the shores of Lake Titicaca, fifteen thousand feet above the sea amid the Andes, where our Canadian friends have held aloft the banner of the Cross for more than half a century; that wintry night in the outskirts of Munich where, by the light of candles, I worshipped with two-score Displaced Persons; that little service in an upper room in South America where young men guarded the entrance against the threatened opposition of a Roman priest; that day in Sao Paulo when I rode in a taxi driven by an Estonian and my companions in it were an Italian, a Latvian and a Brazilian . . . all of us Baptists; those crowded services with our people in Moscow and in Budapest and in the towns of Hungary's famous and fruitful plains.

What is it which gathers us together from all the continents, and in a world rent by divisions blends all our accents into one language of Christian praise, and unites all our racial traditions in one mighty stream of Christian witness?

Meeting here in London it is natural for us to recall the emergence and development of Baptist witness in Europe. We acknowledge our indebtedness to a number of great men all of whom had the Christian name "John." They were not all Baptists, but we are able to give thanks to God for them all. There was, for example, in the fourteenth century a certain John Wycliffe who set in process the rendering of the Bible into our mother tongue, and who was in a real sense the "morning star" of the Reformation in Britain. They threw his remains into the river Swift, a tributary of the river Avon; whence the lines:

> "The Avon to the Severn runs,
>   The Severn to the sea,
> And Wycliffe's dust shall be spread abroad
>   Wide as the waters be."

The same century gave us another John, John Huss, who in Bohemia led the movement of reform in the name of spirituality and freedom. The sixteenth century brought us John Calvin without whom English Puritanism cannot be understood, and John Smyth who formed the first English Baptist Church, though on Dutch soil. The seventeenth century gave us John Bunyan who enriched both literature and religious experience and taught the whole world what it meant to be a pilgrim on the road to the Celestial City; and John Milton, organ-voiced champion of freedom. Nor can we in Europe ever forget Johann Gerhard Oncken, father of the German Baptists and even, as Dr. Rushbrook claims, father of Continental Baptists. And you have already heard me mention another John, John Clifford, our first Alliance President, and a champion of evangelical religion if ever there was one.

In this galaxy of famous Johns I turn to John Calvin. I could, of course, turn to Martin Luther with equal appreciation, for it was he whose life and work meant so much to our European Protestantism; but I mention Calvin because of his special influence on our British development.

Calvin's theology is seen to rest on two main ideas. I will not say that he was consistent in either of them (but, then, who among us is always consistent?) It is when we recall the mighty writings of this prince of theologians that we discover two great principles with which Baptist people have always had the closest possible sympathy. One is Calvin's belief that through the Bible alone can God be known in His completeness as Creator, Redeemer and Lord of all life. The other is his insistence on the centrality of Christ. Again and again as you read the writings of Calvin, you hear the clarion cry, "Sola gratia, sola fide": "By grace alone. By faith alone." Not all Baptists have been Calvinists, but they have all echoed this great evangelical insistence of the Reformer. But if we ask how it came to pass that John Calvin laid such stress on the place of the Bible, the answer comes, "Because he declined to put in the central place any other figure than the Jesus of the Gospels." Listen to what Calvin wrote in his Commentary on Colossians:

"There is nothing Satan tries so much to effect as to call up mists so as to obscure Christ; because he knows that by this means the way is opened up for every kind of falsehood. This, therefore, is the only means of retaining as well as restoring pure doctine; to place Christ before the view such as He is, with all His blessings, that His excellency may be truly perceived."

I have not quoted this because I want to set before you some aspects of Reformation theology, though that, indeed, were well worthwhile. I have quoted it because, many centuries after Calvin, another John, our own John Clifford, the first President of the Baptist World Alliance, gave the same Christocentric emphasis. Here let me quote from John Clifford's great address in Philadelphia.

"Jesus Christ holds the first place and the last. His word is final. His rule is supreme. The deepest impulse of Baptist life has been the upholding of the sole and exclusive authority of Jesus Christ against all possible encroachments from churches, from sections of churches, from the whole church at any special moment of its life, from the traditions of the elders, from the exegesis of scholars, and from the interesting but needless theories of philosophers. It is the momentum of that cardinal idea which has swept us along to our present position."

I can see the old man now; a frock-coated, slim figure; his deep-set eyes glistening with conviction. Can't you hear that clarion voice as it might have rung through this very Hall?

"Jesus—His word is final—His rule is supreme." Towards the end of his long life John Clifford wrote:

"All the conceptions I have formed of God, the answers I am able to give as to what is religion, human duty, human destiny, all that man may hope for I get from Him who is the way, the truth and the life."

There spoke our first President. He spoke for us all.

"We owe it all to Him." That is the cry which still rises from loyal lips in Arctic wastes and amid Africa's burning sands, in the great churches of America and in the awakening countries of the Orient. The course of our history since 1905 has vindicated the claim once made by Dr. E. Y. Mullins:

"The Baptist World Alliance is a brave gesture of Baptists to prove to mankind that we are not a miscellaneous group of sects, some under Paul, some under Apollos, and some under Cephas; but rather that we are one group under Jesus Christ, supremely loyal to Him and His revealed word."

III

Twenty-seven years ago Dr. Mullins, in his Presidential address, read for him at Toronto by Dr. Truett, put a question which it is still pertinent to consider. He asked, "Is our life in Christ strong enough and constructive enough to survive?"

There are here, you will observe, two questions. Is our life in Christ strong enough? Is it constructive enough? As to its numerical strength, our Baptist progress since the day when Dr. Mullins posed his question supplies an impressive answer. According to the *Directory* published in 1928 Europe had 638,000 Baptist church members: to-day that membership is nearly double; Asia had 343,000 church members: to-day that membership has about doubled; Africa had 72,000 church members: to-day that membership is three times as great; North America had 8,500,000 church members: to-day that membership is more than double. These are examples of extraordinary growth. I mention them not to exult in statistical tables, but merely to point out that our movement has seen remarkable advance during the lifetime of the Baptist World Alliance.

Our distinctive principles, however men may regard them, have succeeded in winning the allegiance of great multitudes both among English-speaking peoples and even more among other language and missionary groups. We do not profess to have the whole truth, nor do we unchurch those who differ from us; but we believe that our witness has been vindicated by the remarkable response to it during the past half-century.

I suppose that most people outside our Baptist tradition, if they were asked to describe us, would say that we are the people who, in the ordinance of baptism, restrict it to believers and use a lot of water. There have been jocular references to us as those who belong to the navy rather than the army. Well, even in matters of theology it is good to retain a sense of humour, for we can afford to bear these and other criticisms with a smile when we remember that the past fifty years have brought an ever-increasing chorus of support for the New Testament foundation of our distinctive rite. Fifteen years ago a Methodist, H. G. Marsh, broke with the teaching of his Church on the question of baptism. Nine years ago Karl Barth startled his colleagues in the University of Basle by declaring that believers' baptism is the only valid baptism. In the same year an Anglo-Catholic, Dom Gregory Dix, while feeling that the Church might afford to retain infant baptism provided it was regarded as an abnormality, roundly declared (I quote his words): "Christian initiation in the New Testament is described and conceived of solely in terms of a conscious adherence and response to the Gospel of God, that is, solely in terms of an adult initiation." We are not therefore to be described in terms of an idiosyncrasy, but rather in terms of a New Testament loyalty.

But we have never been the devotees of a mere rite. If we have held tenaciously to believers' baptism it is because of its meaning both for the individual and the Christian fellowship of which the individual forms a part. We define the Church as a spiritual society of converted men who acknowledge the supreme Lordship of Christ. Those are the words of my teacher, Henry Wheeler Robinson, and while they might be expanded, they contain the substance of our Baptist affirmation.

In Free Church theological circles recent years have brought renewed attention to the doctrine of the Church. We welcome this, for we believe that what we have to say on the subject of the Church is central to our effective witness. I am thinking now of the thousands of Baptist churches scattered throughout the world and of the more than twenty millions of men and women who compose them. Take, for example, our Baptist Church in Moscow, which some of us were able to visit last year. Is that a true church? It has nothing to do with a Pope. It pays no attention to the Council of Trent. It has no episcopacy. All it has is a few Bibles and a very few hymnbooks—but they are in the hands of four thousand five hundred church members who, led by consecrated leaders, are devoted followers of the Master, and who have been sharers in His tribulations as well as in His joys. That is a true church as the New Testament understands churches. It would not satisfy Cyprian. It would not satisfy Thomas Aquinas. But I reckon it would satisfy the men and women who were in the Church in the middle of the first century, for in the year 50—and on this there is not the slightest doubt—he was a valid member of the Church who had received baptism and the gift of the Holy Spirit and who called Jesus Lord.

We build our theory of the Church not on Papal claims or episcopal orders, but on the idea of a regenerate community. This idea, we believe, was adumbrated in the Old Testament, for the great Hebrew prophets looked to a community within the nation to constitute the true Church of God. This idea is certainly dominant in the New Testament. There you do not find a Church equated with a nation. You do not find there a Church constituted by ecclesiastical orders or sacramentarian grace. But you do find communities of men and women who accept Jesus as Lord and confess Him in baptism and who are all, in the deepest sense of the words, called to be priests and saints.

These are the values of the spiritual life which are safeguarded in our practice of Believers' Baptism. They are the values of the spiritual life acknowledged wherever our Baptist people meet, no matter in what clime, no matter in what stage of development. As to-day I recall the fellowship I have had with our people in every continent I realize what John Clifford meant when he described the Baptist World Alliance as "catholic" with a wider catholicism than that of Rome, and "orthodox" with an orthodoxy more spiritual and Biblical than that of the Eastern Church.

But I can hear someone saying, "Ah, this is no more than the beating of the denominational drum, and in view of the new conditions which the twentieth century has brought denominational emphasis should now give place to ecumenical ideas."

I recall that twenty-seven years ago Dr. E. Y. Mullins in his Presidential address to the Alliance said that the question of Christian unity was becoming a burning one among some of the denominations. Since then it has come into the forefront of Christian consideration. On the question of participation in the World Council of Churches our Baptist people are divided. In this country for a long time now we have been predisposed to the warmest possible co-operation with other Christian Communions in concerted attacks on the problems which affect us all. The record of British Baptists in such joint efforts as the Free Church Federal Council, the Christian Endeavour movement, the Sunday School Union and many evangelical movements has shown our willingness to practise cooperation where we can. But if I understand my own denomination aright, we decline to equate brotherly co-operation with the sacrifice of essential principle. We will pray with anybody for the extension of Christ's Kingdom. But we do not share the views of those who talk about the organizational divisions of Christendom as "sin." Nor do we think that the words of our Lord in His prayer in John XVII "that they all may be one" can, by any species of exegesis, be brought to mean a vast organization based either on papacy or episcopacy.

There is a danger, I think, of taking the idea of unity in abstraction, as if it were the one shining and resplendent idea which spells salvation in our modern perplexities. The New Testament does not regard unity in such abstraction. At least two other ideas are there found in conjunction with it—liberty and loyalty. And I know that our Baptist people, whether they are in the World Council or remain outside it, would agree on that. In any arrangements which the followers of Christ may make for their more effective witness in the world there can never be any denial of liberty nor any jeopardizing of loyalty to convictions.

IV

The second of the questions put by Dr. E. Y. Mullins, twenty-seven years ago, was: "Are Baptists constructive enough to survive?" We may remind ourselves that there can be no resting on our laurels. We may be excused a certain pride as we reflect on the contribution Baptists have made to the life and witness of the whole Church: in the battle for liberty in which our fathers were pioneers; in the missionary impulse, which our fathers restored to the eighteenth century Church; in the sphere of evangelism where we have shown, I think, that here lies a great part of our genius; in our traditional devotion to humanitarianism in its application to social problems. Pride, yes, and gratitude for the clear-sighted wisdom of our fathers. Yet are we like the men and women pictured by John Masefield when he wrote:

> "We travel the dusty road till the light of the day is dim,
> And sunset shows us spires away on the world's rim.
> We travel from dawn till dusk, till the day is past and by,
> Seeking the Holy City beyond the rim of the sky."

What did Dr. Mullins mean when he asked whether the Baptists of the world were constructive enough? We can see his meaning in a fine passage with which he brought his Presidential address to a close.

"We need the imagination of the architect because we are building a human temple with living beings as stones. We need the passion of the great poet because divine fire alone can fuse human spirits into the unity and glory of the image of God. We need the patience of the great painter and sculptor because the human material on which we labour is refractory and yields but slowly. We need the inspiration of the great composer because it is only as we are swayed by the eternal music that is sounding itself forever through the heart of God that we can do His work in the world. . . . We need education and culture because our method of winning men is the appeal to reason and conscience."

To-day, a quarter of a century after Dr. Mullins, I would underline his plea for education and culture in our constructive witness. In such an emphasis twentieth century Baptists are in line with their great traditions. It is insufficiently recognized that many of our pioneers in early days were men of cultured mind. John Smyth was a Fellow of Christ's College, Cambridge. Thomas Helwys had the considerable advantages of education at Gray's Inn, then the largest and most fashionable of Inns of Court. Roger Williams was educated at Charterhouse and Pembroke College, Cambridge. Not all our great leaders had academic advantages, but our Baptist achievements have left their mark in Biblical scholarship. We have every reason for pride in the contribution of Baptist scholars in the work of Biblical translation, for while in this field William Carey stands alone he has had many notable Baptist successors. And as we look around the Baptist world to-day we cannot fail to be gratified by the eminence of Church historians like K. S. Latourette in the New World and Gunnar Westin in the Old. In this country I can think of eight persons who have held or hold university appointments in Old Testament studies. More than three hundred years ago John Robinson, Congregationalist pastor of the congregation at Leyden, was responsible for a fine sentence with which his name is always linked: "I am certain the Lord hath more truth and light yet to break forth out of His holy Word." That dynamic thought from the great Puritan epoch has continued to inspire Baptist scholars. A denomination such as ours, which claims in all things to base its position on the Word of God, must continue to bring to the study of the Divine Word its best and finest scholarship. That is why, in recent years, one important feature of Alliance activity has been through various Commissions to give careful study to such important themes as The Church, Baptism and Liberty.

This is all the more necessary because the world in which Baptist young people are growing up is already the scene of great intellectual argument. "Ideology" is not an attractive word, but it is a key-word of our time. Ideas are abroad in the earth, and ideas have power. Many of the ideas most vocal in the twentieth century are definitely hostile to the Christian tradition in theology and ethics. The rising generation is assailed by concepts which violate all we know of the revealed will of God. Our children are encouraged to dethrone the God of their fathers in favour of the nebulous deity of humanism. Sin they are advised to regard as the flimsy creation of theologians, an outmoded concept which will disappear in psychological analysis. They are told that mankind no longer needs a saviour—a little psychoanalysing will do all that is necessary. Add to these the ideas current over one-sixth of the earth's surface that the economic theories of Marx and Engels will replace the Sermon on the Mount as the directive for human happiness, and you have the intellectual atmosphere in which the Faith of our fathers is challenged. It is said by one of our Baptist scholars, T. R. Glover, that the progress of the Gospel in the ancient world was explained by one great fact: the Christian out-thought, out-lived and out-died the pagan. It looks as if, once again, the followers of Christ will have to out-think their critics in the twentieth century.

But there is an even more ominous factor in the modern situation which dwarfs all others. I refer to the greatest menace history has ever known . . . the hydrogen bomb. One of these, we are told, released in its destructive flight, would have a lethal effect over an area as big as Wales. In face of such a menace, which would mean not losses here and there from which a resilient society might recover, but the obliteration and extinction of all we hold dear, all men of goodwill must strain every effort to prevent this Gargantuan monster from passing out of the realm of scientific theory into that of human tragedy. I do not know where these bombs now are. But I do know that they must not be permitted to emerge from their secret hiding places, or there will be an end to all our discussions, and the fair glories of our culture will be lost in a darkness whose depth and intensity no man can conceive.

Thus a new and unexperienced urgency sends all Christian men back to the eternal verities which in our time have been overlooked if not defied. Now we look no longer to the winged emissaries of death, speeding their way through the skies, but to something which shone in the sky centuries ago, the star that hovered over Bethlehem. It is to God we must turn, or we are lost. Said the Russian, Nicholas Berdyaev, before he died in 1948, "Knowledge, morality, art, all must become religious, not by external constraint but freely and from within. I cannot recreate the state and a decayed society otherwise than in the name of religious principles. Not for anything in the world would I be free from God. God must be again the centre of our whole life—our thought, our feeling, our only dream, our only desire, our only hope".

Three hundred and eleven years ago there appeared in England a book by one of the greatest champions of liberty, John Milton. Issued under the title of *The Areopagitica* it was really a plea for liberty in the realm of printing. In the eloquence of his famous plea to the Lords and Commons of England, John Milton had some noble words to say about truth:

"Truth indeed came once into the world with her divine Master, and was a perfect shape most glorious to look upon; but when He ascended, and His apostles after him were laid asleep, then straight arose a wicked race of deceivers, who took the virgin Truth, hewed her lovely form into a thousand pieces, and scattered them to the four winds. From that time ever since, the sad friends of Truth went up and down gathering up limb by limb still as they could find them. We have not yet found them all, Lords and Commons, nor ever shall do till her Master's second coming; He shall bring together every joint and member, and shall mould them into an immortal feature of loveliness and perfection."

I would take a phrase out of Milton's great address to the Lords and Commons of England, and with a slight alteration would apply it to all our

Baptist people scattered now in every continent. Milton referred to the "sad friends of Truth." I would alter that to the "glad friends of Truth," for such we are who have ever come into the radiance of the Truth of God. We are not only friends of Truth. We are friends and followers of Him who is the Truth. Robert Bridges sang:

> "Christ with His lamp of truth
> Sitteth upon the hill
> Of everlasting youth
> And calls his saints around."

It is as we listen to that call, and in dedication respond to it that we claim our noble heritage and transmit it, unimpaired, to the generations that will come.

Our Baptist Faith in the World Today
Herbert Gezork

What are Baptists standing for? What is the distinctive element of their witness to the world and their witness to their fellow Christians of other confessions and denominations? At each of the preceding Baptist World Congresses this question has been put and answers have been given to it, answers that were significant for the particular situation in which Baptists found themselves in that day. And so it is fitting for us to ask the question again and to seek answers relevant for our time.

Let us then say right at the beginning that we as Baptists hold no monopoly on the Gospel. We are a part, and numerically still only a small part, of the universal Church, of the Body of Christ. With many other Christians, all across the world and all across denominational lines, we share the great basic convictions of the Christian faith. With them we believe that God was in Christ reconciling the world to Himself; with them we hold that in the birth and life and death and resurrection of Christ God has revealed Himself as in no other event in all human history; with them we hope and pray and work for the day when at the name of Jesus every knee shall bow, of things in heaven and things on earth and things under the earth, and every tongue shall confess that Jesus Christ is Lord, to the glory of God the Father.

But after that has been said, this also must be stated: in Christian history we see again and again how a great truth, which God had entrusted to His people, became nearly forgotten. But then, under the prompting and guiding of God's spirit, it was rediscovered and brought to life again in the minds and hearts of some of His children. Sometimes this came about in a steady quiet growth, sometimes in a sudden cataclysmic eruption. So as the need arose, God called men and women to bring such a neglected and often half-forgotten truth to light again, not that they should stand before others in arrogant pride, saying: "This which we have is the whole truth and all the truth" but that in humility yet with earnest determination and unflinching conviction they should confess: "This is what God has laid upon our consciences, to witness to and to share it with others so that they, too, might see and acknowledge this truth."

So I believe God has entrusted to us Baptists certain great and vital truths, and we would not be faithful to this trust if we were not willing to witness to them in word and deed, as individuals and as a fellowship.

One of these historic Baptist convictions is our insistence upon the authority of the Bible as a trustworthy and all-sufficient rule of faith and conduct. In its long history of almost 2,000 years, the Christian fellowship has faced various emphases which tended to push the Bible from its central position of authority to the outer rim. One of these has been the emphasis on tradition. Backed by the power and pomp of impressive ecclesiastical systems, all sorts of traditions have developed and the further they were removed from the source, namely the New Testament Church, the less likeness they showed to that Church. And as it was in the time of Jesus when the traditions developed by the Pharisees stood as a wall between God and man, separating them from each other, so it has been again and again with ecclesiastical traditions developed in the course of Christian history.

And others, especially in the modern world which has worshipped man's intelligence, have set up reason as the ultimate arbiter of what is right and what is wrong, what is true and what false, not only in secular life but also in the realm of religion. Thus the worship of man's intelligence has replaced for many the worship of the Eternal God. But now, in our own time, we have had dramatic and frightening examples of how easily man's intelligence can become the maidservant of truly irrational forces, and how readily reason can become subject to evil and diabolical powers. And so the tragic events of the last generation have had at least one valuable result: they have shaken and weakened modern man's faith in his reason.

And so there is in our time a great hunger for authority, an authority not based on tradition nor on reason, but based on an eternal and unchangeable truth. This truth we find in Christ, and the message of this Christ we find in the Bible, both the Old and New Testament. And so Baptists ought to join whole-heartedly in the demand of Biblical scholars: "Back to the sources," not only to study them, to understand them, to interpret them to modern man, but also to pattern our life, individually and collectively, after them. And it is my conviction that the closer we shall come to the sources of our faith, the closer we shall come to each other.

As we study Christian history, we can readily see that again and again a renewal of the Church began with the quest, "What say the Scriptures?" This was true in the Reformation. When Martin Luther was asked to recant his teachings, he laid his hand on the Bible and said, "I am bound to the word of God." And we find many examples, especially in our Baptist history. Here was Adoniram Judson, going out as a Congregational missionary to India, studying his Bible on the long journey half across the world. And as soon as he had arrived in India he asked to be baptized and then became the first missionary of the newly-founded American Baptist Foreign Mission Society, laying the foundation of the great missionary work in Burma.

Or think of the beginning of our Baptist work in Germany. Here was Oncken, not a theologian, but a businessman. He and his wife and a small circle of friends studied their Bible night after night, and they arrived at certain convictions which they found irrefutably stated in their New Testaments. Out of that small Bible study group grew the first Baptist churches on the European continent in modern times.

From this emphasis upon the authority of the Scriptures has come our traditional reluctance to establish any creeds and impose them as coercive upon our people. Now creeds and confessions have their distinct value in the life of the church. They are banners of the faith, to proclaim to all the world the beliefs of the Christian fellowship. But when they are laid on men's consciences by ecclesiastical command, or by any other form of human authority, then they become instruments of coercion, clubs held over men's consciences, shadows standing between the soul and its God.

But as we re-affirm our great Baptist conviction of the Scriptures as our authority for faith and life, let us beware of one peril: namely that we become stagnant and sterile in our appreciation and interpretation of the Scriptures. Let us remember that our understanding of Christ's revelation ought to be a steadily deepening and growing one. For that reason I believe that Baptists need a re-vitalizing of their theological interest and work. I am thinking here of the great new concern with the question of Baptism which has in recent years been sweeping the theological world. The two greatest living theologians, Karl Barth and Emil Brunner, have both wrestled with the problem of Baptism and have called infant-baptism scandalous, confused, un-biblical. But it should be a reason for distress for us Baptists that so many of the best books on Baptism in recent years have been written by non-Baptist scholars. Are we as Baptists, while rendering lip-service to the Scriptures, perhaps too much like the servant in Jesus' parable who buried his talent in the ground? Is it not well for us to remember the word that John Robinson spoke to the pilgrim fathers: "I am verily persuaded that the Lord hath more truth to break forth out of His Holy Word?"

And here is a second great Baptist conviction: the Church, a fellowship of believers gathered from the world and committed to live under the guidance of the word and spirit of God.

All through the pages of the New Testament you will find that at the beginning of true discipleship there stands an experience of personal conversion, of personal commitment, of personal confession of faith. The Christian life begins always where an individual soul experiences Christ as Saviour and surrenders to Him as Lord. In this encounter with Christ, man finds his own true destiny, the meaning of his existence. But he also finds his place in that new fellowship which is already here and now a foretaste and a forerunner of the new community which is the goal of all history, the Kingdom of God.

It is in this basic conception of the Church as a gathered fellowship of committed believers, set apart from the world, that we Baptists may well be called the most consistent and radical Protestants. Luther and Calvin knew only too well that the church of the Apostles was one of regenerate membership. But they felt it necessary to compromise and to fall back upon the old scheme where new-born babes without any chance of ever making a decision of their own were added to the Church, thus making it a great all-embracing institution, where the baptismal certificate issued by the Church could practically take the place of the birth certificate issued by the State. Thus to be a Christian was not a matter of personal decision and commitment, but one of tradition and custom. For 1,500 years this concept of the Church has been dominant in the Christian world.

But now in our time, this system is coming to an end; in many countries of the West, the Church is no longer a mighty respected institution, backed and supported by the power and the resources of the State, but it is becoming again what it was in New Testament times: the little flock, a minority, set against the world, often despised, even oppressed and persecuted; again, as in the days of the early church, it means something to be a Christian, it costs something to be a Christian. With other Christians we Baptists may deplore the forces, such as agnosticism and militant atheism, which have brought this about. But at the same time, this is the historic moment when we as Baptists must step forward and renew our witness in word and life of the primacy of personal commitment, and discipleship. This is the time when we must prove that a regenerate church membership is not a Utopian idea but that it is not only Biblical, but also eminently practical and realizable in the life of the Church.

But at the same time we must in all earnestness ask ourselves: are we,

in our own churches, faithful to this ideal? It is a sacred thing to be a
member of the body of Christ. Our forefathers took this with a deadly
seriousness and for them it was literally often a matter of life and death.
But how is it with us? How eager we are to get new names into our
membership books! How quickly we hurry the candidate to the baptismal
waters. And how little we expect of him afterwards to show in his life the
marks of true discipleship. In some parts of the world we have grown
marvellously in numbers, and we are grateful for that. We have become
majority churches, and the world respects us, but is the price which we
have had to pay for this not perhaps too high? Have our churches instead
of invading the world in the name and for the cause of Christ permitted
the world to invade them? Arnold Toynbee, the eminent English historian, sees the hope for any society always in its creative minority. And that
is essentially the same idea as that of the saving remnant which we find
in the Old Testament. That is the hard but glorious task of the Church.
Would our witness for God not be more effective if we were less interest-
ed in numbers and bigness and more in depth of commitment and Christ-
likeness of life? These are some of the questions that we as Baptists should
ask ourselves to-day in the presence of God.

But I must hurry to speak for a few moments on another great Baptist
conviction, in fact the one which by many is regarded as our outstanding
Baptist distinctive, namely freedom of conscience, or as Baptists have
liked to call it, soul-liberty. Others will during this Congress speak more
thoroughly on this subject, but there can be no statement of Baptist
principles without giving this its due.

Baptists have from the beginning of their history been champions of
religious freedom. Others have joined them later in the struggle for this
freedom which is the basis of all liberties; but at first they stood quite
alone. And while others have been quite insistent in demanding freedom
for themselves and their own convictions and their own group, but as soon
as they had enough power were quite ready to deny that freedom to
others, Baptists have a clean record in this respect. And that is something
to be deeply grateful for. So John Bunyan, imprisoned in Bedford Jail,
when he was offered his freedom if he would put his conscience in shackles, replied, "I will stay in prison till the moss grows on my eyebrows
rather than make a slaughterhouse of my conscience or a butchery of my
principles." So Roger Williams stumbled across the snowy wastes of Massachusetts to establish a haven for religious freedom in Providence and
establish those principles which later found their way into the Constitution of the United States. So Obadiah Holmes was publicly whipped on
Boston Common, but said afterwards to his tormentors: "You have beaten
me as with roses." The Baptist position on the matter of religious liberty
is crystal clear. We have no sympathy for the agnostic or the atheist, but

we shall stand for his freedom to hold his religious or anti-religious beliefs, as we stand for our own freedom.

Many of the characteristic convictions which are usually associated with Baptists have their roots in our insistence on religious liberty. Such is our rejection of infant baptism. We reject it on the one hand because of our conception of the Church as a fellowship of believers in Christ. But we reject it also because we refuse to join a child to the Church before he can utter his protest or give his consent. Thus we regard infant baptism as an intolerable invasion of the sphere of man's own most sacred religious rights.

We further reject, on account of our passion for religious liberty, the idea and practice of religious toleration. To put the power and prestige of the state behind one form of religion, and merely tolerate others, is not religious liberty; it is a subtle form of coercion. Toleration is a concession, liberty is a right; and this right is given to man by God Himself.

From this principle of freedom of conscience, we Baptists also derive our traditional insistence upon a free Church, separated from the State. The marriage of Church and State which has a long and tragic history in Christianity has never been a happy one, especially for the Church. It is a kind of shot-gun marriage, with the State holding the gun. It has always had in itself the seeds of spiritual tyranny. Whether the State tries to subordinate and use the Church for its own ends, or whether the Church tries to use the State as an instrument for its purposes, the pattern in either case is irreconcilable with the ideal of religious freedom, and therefore Baptists must resist and reject both attempts. Let the Church be the moral conscience of the State, as of any other organization or institution, but let it keep itself free from any entanglements with the State.

If ever it was imperative for Baptists to guard jealously this great and precious heritage of religious freedom against all encroachments, it is now. For the most terrifying fact of our time and the greatest problem of our civilization is the totalitarian State which does not only aim at the control of all economic, social and political life, but at the control of man's inmost thoughts, his ultimate commitments, his very soul. And this deadly danger does not only exist in lands behind the various so-called "curtains," whether we call it the "iron" or the "bamboo" curtain, but it exists in every land to-day. For the tendency towards increasing power of the State is observable everywhere, and therefore the Christian must be twice vigilant everywhere. He must guard existing civil rights. He must oppose efforts to make people think and believe alike. He must reject the claim of any State to define right and wrong. He will be willing to render to Caesar what is Caesar's, but he will not allow Caesar to determine what is his and what is God's; he will reserve that right for his own free conscience under God. The unforgettable George W. Truett liked to say that religious freedom is the nursing mother of all other freedoms. And how true that is. In our time we have seen again and again that those who have learned to kneel before Almighty God will be the ones best able to stand up before any mortal man, dictator or otherwise. If ever there was a time for Baptists to proclaim in word and life their great principle of soul-liberty, that time is now.

And there is a fourth and last great Baptist distinctive: *Evangelism.* This, of course, is the unfinished task of every Christian and every church, of whatever denomination. But it is especially vital and indispensable for us Baptists. For we do not replenish the membership of our churches through the birth-rate; we can only replenish and expand it through evangelism. Therefore, a Baptist church which does not believe in evangelism condemns itself to death.

That is why Baptists have been in the forefront of the world-wide missionary cause. The new missionary movement really began when a handful of Baptists in Kettering, here in England, after having listened to William Carey preach his historic sermon: "Expect great things from God; attempt great things for God," founded the Baptist Missionary Society and then sent Carey out as their first missionary to India. With that event began what Dr. Latourette has rightly called: "The Great Century of Christian Missions."

It is this Baptist emphasis upon evangelism which made Oncken, the pioneer of the German Baptist Movement, when asked in America how many evangelists and missionaries he had in the German Baptist churches, without hesitation answer, "Seven thousand," naming the total membership of his constituency; for, as he added, "Every Baptist a missionary."

And here is my first concern in this matter: we have come a long way from this ideal: Every Baptist a missionary. We leave the work of evangelism more and more to the professionals, whether ministers or other specialists in this field. And while I do not wish to say one word against their efforts, yet I wish to remind you that Baptists in the past have become strong largely through the work of lay-people who on the place where they stood, in the vocation which they followed, gave their witness for Christ. Let us not forget that the first disciples of Jesus were lay-people, fishermen, peasants, craftsmen. I sometimes wonder if there ever would have been a first Pentecost, if these disciples had been ordained rabbis and preachers. Let us also remember that to-day, in those lands which have come under the sway of totalitarian and anti-Christian governments, we can observe that those churches have shown greatest vitality and staying power which have developed an active, devoted lay-leadership which was able to step into the breach when their ministers and teachers were taken away from them.

And then another thing: our evangelism should be wider, more inclusive. Are we not limiting our appeal for Christ too much to the individual, his personal life, his soul, and not enough also to his social life? I know of the old controversies in our midst about the validity of the so-called Social Gospel, and I am sick of them. They so often miss the real point. For there is, rightly understood, no Social Gospel and no individual Gospel—there is only one Gospel of Jesus Christ, offering redemption to the whole man, in all his capacities and all his relations, his soul, his body, his family life, his economic and his political life. Let us then strive for an evangelism that aims at the redemption of life in its totality, and not just one part of it.

These, then, are some of our basic Baptist convictions, four sturdy pillars undergirding our fellowship: the authority of the Scriptures, the Church as a fellowship of believers, Freedom of Conscience, and Evangelism as the unfinished task of the church. But each of them presents a challenge to every new generation of Baptists. For only as each new generation puts its sweat and toil, and, if necessary, its blood and tears into the work of holding these truths aloft, will they be maintained. In the midst of all rejoicing about what God has given us, there is cause for earnest self-searching and deep repentance. Where we have failed, may God forgive us; where we have weakly stammered, may we, by His power, recover the authentic, firm voice of conviction; "for if the trumpet give an uncertain sound, who shall prepare himself for the battle?" The world of to-day needs the Baptist witness; the universal Church needs the Baptist witness; may we be ready, by God's grace, to give it, unashamed and unafraid.

10
Rio de Janeiro
1960

Introduction

The Tenth Baptist World Congress convened in Rio de Janeiro on June 26, 1960. This meeting of the BWA was unique and distinctive for several reasons. One, this was the first Congress held in South America or in the southern hemisphere. Two, this was the first Congress to elect a president from outside England and North America. The messengers elected Brazilian pastor, Joao F. Soren, as the new president. Three, the place where the Congress met and the person elected president symbolized the needed and growing international character of the Alliance. Four, the staff leadership of the BWA changed after Rio. Arnold T. Ohrn, who had served as general secretary for twelve years, retired, and he was succeeded by Josef Nordenhaug of the USA. Five, the Rio Congress was unique because of its decidedly evangelistic emphasis. General Secretary Ohrn described the meeting in this manner:

No other Congress has provided a comparable contribution to the cause of missions. Workers in Brazil declared that it set the cause forward at least a quarter of a century. Others said that for a long period the churches would have their hands more than full meeting the increased interest of outsiders and dealing with inquirers.[1]

Billy Graham preached at the closing session of the Congress in the Maracana Stadium to an estimated audience of between 185,000 and 200,000 people. His text was John 3:16, and his subject was "God So Loved the World." Graham gave a unique evangelistic invitation to the largest crowd ever to gather in that stadium for a religious meeting. He asked those who would accept Christ to take out their handkerchiefs and wave them as a token of their surrender to Christ. Thousands waved handkerchiefs.

Theodore F. Adams, personable pastor of the First Baptist

Church of Richmond, Virginia, had opened the Congress with his presidential address. His sermon title was an omen of the confession which many would make during the next few days: "Jesus Christ is Lord!"

Jesus Christ is Lord
Theodore F. Adams

We are happy that the Tenth Baptist World Congress can meet in beautiful Rio de Janeiro where Baptists have given such a splendid witness and enjoyed such a remarkable growth. We come from many different countries representing some twenty-three million Baptists on every continent. The moving and dramatic roll call has given a living witness to our oneness in Christ and the prayer of our hearts "That at the name of Jesus every knee should bow, . . . and every tongue confess that Jesus Christ is Lord, to the glory of God the Father."

We think, of course, of some who could not be represented here. Our hearts go out to them, and we shall be faithful in prayer for them. At the same time, we voice our gratitude to God for the joy of our Christian fellowship here and the opportunity for worship and witness together.

It is my purpose now to give a brief report of my stewardship as your president, to tell a little of Baptist life and work as I have seen it around the world, and to discuss some of the issues that concern Baptists everywhere.

It was the prayer of my heart when I accepted this responsibility in London at our Golden Jubilee Congress that God would give me wisdom and strength to serve you faithfully and well and that He would help me always to say the right word at the right time that our fellowship might be strengthened and the work of the kingdom advanced.

I am grateful to God for guidance and health and strength to carry out the mission you entrusted to me. I want also to thank the members of the First Baptist Church in Richmond, for their willingness to share their pastor with the Baptists of the world and for unfailing support in all that I have been called upon to do. I am grateful to the other officers and members of the Executive Committee who have served with me, to our faithful and loyal secretaries and the chairmen of our various departments and commissions, and to all who have labored so well during these past five years as our work has grown and prospered.

During these five years, Mrs. Adams and I have counted it a privilege to travel thousands of miles to visit Baptists in scores of countries. We have sought to serve where we could, to encourage those in difficult places, and to report fairly and objectively the situation as we saw it, so that those in a position to help might do so intelligently. It has been a joy to note our growth from twenty million to more than twenty-three million baptized believers. We now total nearly four times as many Baptists as when the Alliance was organized in London in 1905. This vast throng of Baptists differs in many ways—in language and in color, in culture and customs, in racial origins and national ties—yet we are one in our devotion to Jesus Christ as Lord.

The Baptist World Alliance is becoming more and more a genuine world fellowship. Our eight vice-presidents represent every continent but South America, which was also represented until the death of the beloved Honorio Espinosa of Chile. It was my joy and privilege to greet each vice-president in his or her own land with the single exception of L. A. North in New Zealand. Meetings of our Executive Committee were held in England, the United States, Canada, Switzerland, and Brazil. Thus, we have met on three continents to conduct our official business, which Dr. Ohrn will report in more detail. I am sure all of you share my own personal gratitude to him for his faithful and devoted service as our general secretary for the past twelve years.

Time will permit only a brief word about Baptists around the world. I planned during my years as president to visit so far as possible the areas where no president of the Alliance had ever been or where he had not been able to visit in recent years. Immediately after the Congress in London, it was my privilege to visit Baptists in a number of the Scandinavian countries where our work took root in spite of persecution and has borne rich fruits through the years. Then in the U.S.S.R., I saw the faith and devotion of Russian Baptists. Like their fellow believers in many lands, we found them to be zealous New Testament Christians.

Later when I visited a number of the islands in the Caribbean, I was deeply impressed by the faith and devotion of our Baptist people in the face of poverty and many difficulties. I have had many opportunities during these years to speak before Baptist groups in the United States and Canada and to visit the Mexican Baptist Convention, where I was inspired anew by their co-operative spirit and their devotion to our Lord.

In the summer of 1956, Mrs. Adams and Mr. Denny and I traveled around the world, spending most of our time with the Baptists of Asia, where many new nations are rejoicing in their independence. We can be proud and grateful for able and consecrated national Baptist leaders in many Asian lands and for the splendid fruits of devoted missionary service. It was a joy to share in the First Asian Baptist Youth Conference in Hong Kong. Never will I forget how those young people from thirteen different countries, many of who had been at war with each other, stood together with clasped hands as a symbol of their Christian fellowship and sang "Blest Be the Tie."

I went to Europe three times during these five years to visit Baptists in England and on the Continent and to share in the meeting of the European Baptist Federation. We thank God for the faithfulness and zeal of Baptists in Europe who, in spite of the devastation of two world wars and major economic and social problems, have kept faith and are carrying on their work with growing evangelistic concern.

Last year it was my privilege to visit this beautiful city and to make a quick trip around the continent. Baptists in South America have made remarkable progress in the last half century, and I am confident that the next fifty years will show a major growth in every country where we are at work.

Last summer we visited the Baptists of Africa. This was the first time any Alliance president had ever visited that continent, and I was tremendously encouraged by what we saw. We found Baptists struggling in the face of many difficulties in some countries and yet rejoicing in their opportunities. We are grateful that in the providence of God there are many Christian leaders ready to help guide the destiny of several new nations. This great continent is just now in a ferment, with nations struggling to be born; but it is a continent that will take an increasingly important place in the life of the world. It was heartening in South Africa to hear Baptists say about the present government's unchristian apartheid policy, "If we must make a choice, we will obey God rather than men."

Everywhere we have found the same major concerns and convictions in the hearts of our Baptist people. We face a world of fear and tension, a world with poverty and misery, discrimination and segregation in many lands, and torn by loyalty to a wide variety of faiths and philosophies. Some areas are openly hostile to Christianity, while in other lands we face open doors for the proclamation of the gospel. Ours is a day in which millions of men and women are free for the first time in their lives. They intend to keep their freedom at all costs and ask only an opportunity to learn to govern themselves. Yet we live in an age when we are more interdependent than ever before, for we are all "bound in the bundle of life" and none goes his way alone.

In such a world our living Lord still says, "Ye shall be witnesses unto me." We have a divine commission that has never been repealed, to take the gospel into all the world and to relate the gospel to all of life. In every land Baptists are trying to do just that with an increasing devotion to evangelism and missions and a deepening concern that the blind may see, the deaf hear, the lame walk, and the poor hear the gospel and know the fulness of the life in Christ.

Newer nations are joining with older lands in carrying on missionary work in keeping with the affirmation of Oncken that "every Baptist is a missionary." Many recall the words of Joao Soren of Rio de Janeiro, as he reminded us in the Congress sermon in London, that the same Christ who took from our hearts the burden of sin and guilt put on our hearts a burden of concern for the lost. Baptists are responding to that concern as did one group of believers in India who made this daily vow, "I am a baptized believer in Jesus Christ as Saviour and Lord; woe is me if I preach not the gospel."

Baptists everywhere are concerned about Christian education. They realize that it is not enough to win the lost. We must teach them and train them that they may give the gospel to the world and live it before the world. More and more emphasis is being given to Bible study and membership training. New and enlarged schools and colleges and seminaries are strengthening our program of Christian education. One of these institutions is Central Philippine College, where each year many students publicly confess their faith in Christ in an outdoor baptismal service on the campus. They go out to provide Christian leadership for our churches and for their country. This concern for Christian education is common to all our people, though we regret that in some lands our opportunities are very limited.

A number of other problems weigh on our hearts as Baptists. Racial justice and Christian brotherhood are a primary concern of our believers everywhere. The race problem is not limited to one country or one continent, though it is of special concern in some areas. The Baptist World Alliance, in the spirit of Christ our common Lord, includes all races and will not hold a Congress where all cannot meet as brothers and sisters in Christ without any discrimination or segregation based on color or national origin. We seek to be one in Christ, who has broken down the middle wall of partition between us. In the face of prejudice and misunderstanding, Baptists in many lands are working for brotherhood and justice and striving for better relationships between races and peoples.

Baptists are deeply concerned about the poverty and need in many lands. Through our Relief Department as well as through our mission boards and other agencies, we have sought to help meet these desperate human needs. In this, as in every other area of life, we are our brother's keeper, as was evidenced by our recent medical mission; and we dare not be lacking in concern for those who suffer physically as well as spiritually.

In the hearts of Baptists everywhere, I have found a deep and abiding longing for world peace. Baptists are loyal to their own countries and are proud of their national heritage; and yet in every land, our people hope and pray and work for peace on earth and good will between men and nations. Through our missionary activities, we seek to advance the cause of peace through the Prince of peace. Our best hope of peace in the world lies in the spirit He proclaims and the principles He taught and the kind of people He can help us become—people who can live at peace with others because they have found peace within and have made their peace with God.

These and other problems have been studied by our various commissions, and we shall hear more about them during these days together. We must remember, however, that if the world is to be more Christian, we ourselves must be more Christlike. Well may we say to our living Lord, "In the work you are doing in the world, you can count on me."

To help solve these pressing problems, we stress anew the basic convictions and principles we share as Baptists. To be sure, we are not alone in proclaiming these principles but the emphasis on each and all of them has been a contribution Baptists have made and must continue to make in the life of the world.

Basic to all is the lordship of Jesus Christ. He said, "I, if I be lifted up from the earth, will draw all men unto me." He is the world's only Saviour and to Him we give our full allegiance as the Lord of life and the conqueror of death.

We believe in salvation by grace through faith and that not of ourselves, it is the gift of God. We are grateful for a God who loves us as a father and treats us, not as we deserve, but as we need. We believe that through our faith in Christ His Son as our Saviour our sins are forgiven, and we have already passed from death into life—the life abundant and eternal.

These and all other tenets of our faith are rooted in the Word of God and in the Word made flesh to dwell among us full of grace and truth. The New Testament is to us the sole and sufficient ground for our faith and practice. Hence, we reject such manmade doctrines as the assumption of Mary or the infallibility in matters of religion of any earthly person or power.

Baptists stress the supreme worth of the individual soul. Since Christ died for all, He died for each of us. We are, therefore, not to view lightly or without concern the rights or needs of any individual, and we are to respect the dignity of each personality.

We recognize the competence of the individual in matters of religion, believing that every man is competent to make his own choices in religion when he has been instructed in the Word of God, and also that "every one of us shall give account of himself to God."

For this reason Baptists have long emphasized the priesthood of all believers. We have no priestly hierarchy and no mediator between God and man save only Christ Jesus our Lord. There is none other to whom we must look for the means of grace and salvation.

Since we believe that each individual must make his own choice in matters of religion, we contend that every person must have the chance to make the right choice; for his eternal destiny hangs upon it. No one becomes a Baptist simply because he is born in a particular family or nation. One must be born again to be a Baptist. Because we seek to give every person a chance to choose Christ as Saviour and Lord, we major in evangelism and claim the right and responsibility to proclaim the gospel and to teach and to preach in Christ's name in all the world. There are many graves similar to one I saw at St. Marc in Haiti that indicate the resting place of missionary pioneers. On the stone over this grave, as on many others, are carved the words of the Great Commission, "Go ye into all the world, and preach the gospel to every creature."

For this reason Baptists stress the importance of religious liberty. We believe in freedom of conscience and in full religious liberty, not as a privilege given grudgingly or merely tolerated by some faith or hierarchy, but as our full right under God.

We know that freedom can be lost, for it has been lost in some lands in our own generation. Some of our believers face persecution, and others find their opportunities for worship and witness greatly limited. The problem varies in different countries. Sometimes freedom is restricted because of a state church or by government decree or because of a rising tide of nationalism that calls for devotion of many of our people who suffer persecution, both open and subtle, but who keep the faith and under many difficulties continue to witness for the Lord Christ.

We believe that "where the Spirit of the Lord is, there is liberty," and "If the Son therefore shall make ye free, ye shall be free indeed." In his name we believe in freedom for, freedom from, freedom through, freedom in, and freedom of religion.

We Baptists do believe in freedom *for* religion. By this we mean not only freedom to worship but freedom to teach and preach, to win others, freedom to change one's faith, freedom to print and publish our convictions, and to own property and build churches in which to worship and serve our Lord. We protest the abridgment of these basic rights anywhere, but we claim no rights for ourselves that we do not claim for all others. We believe in freedom for all religions with special privileges for none.

We also believe in freedom *from* religion, that is, we respect the right of the individual to reject religion and take the consequences. He can choose Christ and life in His name and all the blessings of a free faith, or he can choose to reject that faith for another or to be free from any formal religion. There should be no state or ecclesiastical compulsion in religion. No man is a Baptist because someone else has decided that matter for him, nor is any man a member of a Baptist church because of something that was done to him when he was a baby and he had no choice in it. No man should be compelled to support any religious institution through public taxation or to suffer on account of his religious beliefs.

We believe in freedom *through* religion. We are to "proclaim liberty to the captives and recovery of sight to the blind." We know the joy of freedom in Jesus Christ for He has set us free from the bondage of sin and fear and death. We want the whole world to know the blessings of the faith and freedom that is ours in our Saviour.

We believe in freedom *in* religion, that is, in varieties of religious experience and expression. We Baptists differ in many ways in our services of worship and our religious practices. Yet with all our diversities and varieties we are united in "One Lord, one faith, one baptism."

We believe in freedom *of* religion, that is, the right and responsibility of every individual to make his own choice. God waits on man's willingness to accept Christ as Lord and to receive the blessings of His grace. We respect each individual's right to make that choice as he feels led of the Spirit. The only compulsion in this matter is God's love for us in Christ and our love and concern for those who are lost without Him.

When a man has made his choice of Christ as Saviour and Lord, we ask him to join a church and to share in two ordinances that are filled with deep significance and beautiful symbolism. We believe in the baptism of believers by immersion on confession of faith in Christ as Saviour and Lord. I cannot forget two processions I saw in Haiti one Sunday. One was a procession of those who believed in the witch doctor. The other group was going to a nearby river to bury believers in baptism that they might be raised to walk in newness of life.

This interpretation of the ordinance of baptism calls for a regenerate church membership. Our lives must bear witness to our faith lest others see us and not want to believe.

One of our modern missionary martyrs, Dr. William Wallace, was buried in China after dying in prison for his faith. His Chinese friends put over his grave these words, "For me to live is Christ." His life had been such that the best tribute they could give him was to say that he had been like Jesus. God grant that our lives may bear such a witness wherever He calls us to serve.

Baptists observe a second ordinance—the Lord's Supper. At the Lord's table we are reminded of His broken body and His shed blood and of our oneness in Him. Never shall I forget the day I stood with Brother Jacob Zhidkov at the Lord's table in the Baptist church in Moscow. As we stood together, one in Christ, Brother Zhidkov broke the great loaf of bread and passed it to the congregation with the words, "This is my body which is given for you: this do in remembrance of me." Then I took the cup, saying, "This is my blood of the new testament, which is shed for many for the remission of sins." The blood of Jesus Christ, God's Son, cleanses us from all sin. Truly, "if we walk in the light, as he is in the light, we have fellowship one with another."

Baptists stress this fellowship of believers in the local church as the basic unit of Christian life and service. We co-operate as believers in our associations and conventions where we can do together what no individual believer or local church can do alone. In the wider fellowship of the Baptist World Alliance, with all our diversity, we have a remarkable unity in Christ our Lord, "the same yesterday, and to day, and for ever."

We rejoice also that we are part of a far larger fellowship of other Christians in many lands who love and serve our Lord. We are glad to be a part of that great host as well as of the long line of faithful souls who through the centuries have borne their witness to Christ as Lord. We are one in Him.

One Sunday it was my privilege to worship with the great Immanuel Baptist Church in Rangoon, Burma. Five different national groups worship in this church every Sunday. During the day there are services in their own language for Burmese, Karens, Chinese, and Indians. It was my privilege to preach at the English service, when some from all these groups and others worshiped together. As I spoke about our fellowship in Christ and our faith in the living God, I told of two Christian missionaries who were seized and held for ransom by bandits in China some years ago. Early one morning as they awoke bound and gagged, they recalled it was Christmas day. One man with his bound hands scraped bare a place on the floor and then slowly with bits of straw spelled out the word "Emmanuel"—God with us. Telling of it later he said, "As we saw that word and sensed that truth anew, our hearts were lighter and our spirits were braver, for we knew we were not alone."

Because of our faith in the living Lord, we face the future with confidence. God is with us. It is He who has called us out of darkness into His marvelous light. It is He who has saved us and will keep us. It is He who will lead us in the way He would have us go.

As we gather in this World Congress from many lands, the challenge of our times and the love of God call us to renewed devotion to Christ and His kingdom. Our day calls for Christians of the highest order and the finest faith, with the deepest convictions and the greatest devotion, with the deepest undying love and an abiding commitment to the mission entrusted to us by our Lord and by those who have served Him through the centuries. The forces in opposition are strong; but, in such a day, Christianity is not frightened but challenged, not fearful but stimulated. We know that Christianity has lived under all forms of government and that it has and will survive all kinds of persecution. Our noted Baptist historian, Dr. Kenneth Scott Latourette, well says, "Christianity is more to be reckoned with today than ever before." As we serve Christ in our generation, we can say with confidence as did the prophet long ago when he saw the enemies of the Lord round about the city, "Those who are with us are more than those who are with them."

But salvation and service are personal. We are called to cooperate with all believers and to serve together as Baptists to give the gospel to all the world and relate it to all of life. But each of us must stand in his own place and serve the Lord where God has called him. I made my own commitment to Christ long ago in an experience we all have shared. My father, a beloved Baptist pastor, baptized me, asking as I stood in the water with him, "Do you acknowledge Jesus Christ as your Saviour and Lord?" I said, "I do" and was buried with Christ in baptism. Each of us has made that same personal commitment. We know what it can bring to the life of the believer, and we wish that same blessed peace and joy for every one in all the world.

To that end let us here and now renew our covenant to serve Him as we ought. I think of our responsibility in the words of the charge my father gave me when I was ordained to the ministry. I would give you the same charge today as we begin this Congress and as we face the tensions of our times. He said, "I charge you with three things: Keep close to God. Keep close to men. Bring God and man together." We can never do this alone, but through our living and loving Lord we can; and in God's good time the prayer of all our hearts will be answered, "That at the name of Jesus every knee should bow, . . . and every tongue confess that Jesus Christ is Lord, to the glory of God the Father."

God So Loved the World
Billy Graham

Dr. Adams, Members and Delegates to the Baptist World Alliance, Ladies and Gentlemen: It is a joy and privilege to be in Rio de Janeiro. We have had a wonderful week here. Now I am going to ask for the next few minutes that everyone be very quiet. There are thousands of people who have come today with hungry hearts. There is an emptiness in your life. You are searching for something. I want you to listen.

This is the most important hour that many of you will ever spend. As I am speaking you will hear me through your ears but there will be another voice speaking. You have two sets of ears. You have the physical ears on the side of your head but you also have ears in your soul. While I speak to your physical ears, God will be speaking to your soul. So listen carefully.

When I was a little boy, my mother was giving me a bath. I was born on a farm and she had a big tub that she would put in the kitchen and

I would get in the water. And we always took a bath on Saturday night. She would scrub my back and scrub behind my ears. And when I was five years old, she came into the kitchen one night to give me a bath and said, "I want to teach you a passage from the Bible." And here is what she taught me, "For God so loved the world, that he gave his only begotten Son, that whosoever believeth in him should not perish, but have everlasting life" (John 3:16).

For God so loved the world. I want to ask you a question. Listen! Does God love the world? If God loves the world, why is there so much suffering in the world? Why is there so much disease? Why is there so much war? Why do people hate and cheat and lie? Why do we suffer heartaches? If God is a God of love, why does he not stop all suffering in the world? If God is a God of love, why does he allow wars to continue? Why does God allow crime? Why does God allow disease? If God is a God of love, why doesn't He heal everybody? Have you ever asked yourself that question? The world today is in trouble. Many people think we may have another war. There are many evil forces in the world. There are some people who think the world may blow itself apart. Many scientists are thinking about the end of the world. Is God going to allow the world to blow itself up? If God is a God of love, why does He allow death? There are many of you who are afraid to die and yet you are going to die. The Bible says that it is appointed unto a man once to die.

Well, if God is a God of love, why does He allow us to die? Why does He allow your father, your mother, your sister, your brother to die? The Bible says God is a God of love. Is God a God of love? Let us think about God. He is the mighty God. He made the sun. He made the beautiful moon in the sky. He put the green in the grass. He made you. He created the whole world. He is the mighty God of creation. But the Bible tells us something else about God. The Bible tells us that God is a Spirit. He is not limited to one place at the same time. He can be in China, in Russia, in the United States, in Great Britain, and in Brazil at the same time. God is a Spirit. The Bible also tells us that God is an unchanging God. God has never changed. The same God that hated lying and cheating and immorality and war thousands of years ago still hates it today. We may change, but God never changes. He is the same mighty God that He has always been.

The Bible also tells us that God is a holy and righteous God. God has never committed a sin. He has never thought an evil thing. He is the God of holiness and righteousness and He demands holiness and righteousness in His creatures. God is also a God of judgment. We have an idea sometimes that God is a kindly old man, riding on a cloud, with a long beard, and patting everybody on the back. But this is not the picture of God in the Bible. He is going to judge the world. God destroyed the world once with water because of its sins. How is the world going to end? How is this age going to end? The Bible says, in judgment. And when you die, you go to the judgment. God is going to judge men. The Bible also says that God is an impartial God. He has no special pets. He loves all people. He does not look at the color of your skin. He does not look at your social standing. The Bible says there is no difference. The Bible teaches that God is an impartial God.

The Bible also tells us something else. The Bible tells us that God is a God of love. God loves. And that is why God created the human race. God loved so much that He wanted some other creatures in the universe to love. So God created man in His image. God wanted somebody to love. God was lonesome. He wanted fellowship. So He created the human race. He created us because He loved. And when God created us, He gave us a gift that He did not give His other creatures. Now all of you here today have a body. You have eyes and ears and nose and hands and feet. That is your body. But living inside your body is the real you—your soul, your spirit. Now what happens when you die? Your body goes to the grave. But you, the real you, the soul, your spirit, lives on forever.

I read about a man the other day who committed suicide. You cannot commit suicide. You can only kill your body. You cannot kill the soul. Your soul lives forever. It is made in the image of God. But in your soul God gives you a gift. He gave you a will of your own. He gave you the ability to make choices. God said, "I want you to love me." But God did not make us like an automobile. You can't be pushed like a button. God does not push a button and you obey. You are made in God's image. You are a little god. You have a will of your own, and in the beginning man chose to love God. God said: "If you will obey me and love me, we will build a wonder-ful world. There will be no suffering. There will be no disease. There will be no war. There will be no trouble." And God and man were friends.

But one day something happened. Listen. Tragedy came. Trouble came. Man decided he no longer needed God. So he rebelled against God. He said: "I do not need God. I can build my world without God. Good-by God. I don't need you." And in that moment God and man were sepa-rated. Their friendship was broken and that is where all the trouble began. That is where war began. That is where death began. This separa-tion between God and man was called sin. And every person who has ever been born has a moral disease. It is called sin. The Bible says all have sinned and come short of the glory of God. You are a sinner. I have a moral disease and it is going to kill my soul just as surely as cancer may take my body. The Bible says the wages of sin is death.

There are three kinds of death spoken of in the Bible. First, there is physical death. Your body dies. Secondly, there is spiritual death. You may be alive physically but you are spiritually dead. You may be a rich man, you may be a beautiful woman, but you are spiritually dead.

I was in Hollywood a few months ago. I talked to six hundred movie stars. When I had finished, a beautiful young woman came to me. She is one of the greatest film stars in the world. She said: "I am rich. I am famous. I am beautiful. But I am unhappy. What is wrong with me?"

I said, "You are spiritually dead."

There are thousands of people in the United States and in Brazil who have an emptiness in their lives. You have nothing to believe in. You have nothing to commit your life to. You have everything, but you are unhappy. You may become a great film star. You may become a great sports star. You may become the richest person in Brazil, but you do not have happiness and peace in your soul. That is because you are spiritually dead. There are three kinds of death spoken of in the Bible—physical death, spiritual death, and thirdly, eternal death.

Jesus talked about hell and outer darkness. That means that when you die, you will be separated from God forever. This is the result of sin. We have a disease. You have a disease. It is going to damn your soul. It brings unhappiness into your life. What can you do? Which way can you turn? How can you be healed of this moral disease? How can you be cured? That is the question that the whole world is asking. That is the question that Washington and Moscow are asking. And that is the question that you are asking. The Bible gives us the answer. The Bible tells us that in spite of our sins and rebellion, God still loves us. God loves you. No matter how bad you have been, He loves you. God looked down from heaven and He saw the human race with all its trouble and conflict and hatred and war and He said: "I love you. I want to help you." But what could God do?

One day I was walking along the road where I live. I stepped on a small ant hill. I killed many ants. I wounded many others. I destroyed their house. I stopped for a moment and I thought I would like to go down and help those ants. I would like to tell them that I did not mean to do it, but I could not. I was too big. They were too little. And I could not speak their language. God looked down from heaven. He saw us. He saw our sins and our wickedness, our disease, our war, our troubles, our death. He said, "I love and want to help you." Do you know what God did? How could God talk to us? He was the mighty God. We are little ants crawling around in the sand. What could God do? Then God looked down. Do you know what God did?

Listen! The mighty God became a man. And that is who Jesus Christ was. He was God in human flesh. He was God living like a man. He made the blind to see. He made the deaf to hear. He made the dumb to speak. He made the lame to walk. He raised the dead. He fed the hungry. He was God. He taught a revolutionary system of ethics. He said if somebody slaps you on one cheek, turn the other cheek. He said to love and forgive your enemies. He said that all men are our brothers and we are to love our neighbor as ourselves.

He was God, but He didn't come just to teach and heal. He came for another purpose. He came to die. And the real reason that Christ came was to seek and save the lost. And on that first Good Friday He died. He died for you. He died for me. If you go to every Protestant and Catholic church in Brazil, you will see a cross because we all agree on one thing and that is that the cross is the center of Christianity. They took Jesus Christ outside the city. They cut long leather thongs and beat Him across the back. They put a crown of thorns on His brow. They spit on Him, and when they did that, the angels of heaven drew their swords. They were coming to save Him. He said: "No I love these people. I want to save them. I am dying for them." And they nailed Him to a cross. They put nails in His hands. They put a spike in His feet, and then they lifted Him up and He hung and bled and died.

But that was not His real suffering. The real suffering of Christ came when He said, "My God, my God, why hast thou forsaken me?" In that terrible moment God was taking all of our sins and laying them on Christ. He became sin for us, He that knew no sin. All the lies you have told, all the evil thoughts you have ever had, all the bad things you have ever done, God laid them all on Him; and He bowed His head and said, "It is finished." And they put Him in a tomb, but He did not stay there. On the third day He rose again. Christ is a living Christ. He is not dead. He is alive now. His presence is here now and the Bible says that some day He is coming back to rule.

Where is the world headed? The kingdom of God shall rule. Christ the king shall rule. He is alive. He is coming back. The Bible teaches this. Now what can you do to get into His kingdom? The Bible says that God loved so much He gave His Son, that whosoever believeth in Him should not perish. God has given the Son. Now you must do something. I have studied this book for twenty-three years. I do not believe anybody will get to heaven, I do not believe anyone's sins can be forgiven, unless three things take place.

There are thousands of people in the United States who are members of a church. They go to church, but I do not believe they will all be in the kingdom of God. I want you to listen as you have never listened before in your life to anything. You listen for the next moment or two. There are three things that God demands of you. Do you want to be forgiven of your sins? Do you want peace in your heart? Do you want life in your heart? Do you want to know that you are going to heaven? Then listen to these three things!

First, you must repent of your sins. Jesus said, "Except ye repent, ye shall all likewise perish." Have you repented? You say, "Well, what is repentance?" Repentance means that you acknowledge to God that you have sinned against Him. But it means more than that. It means you have changed your way of living. You cannot follow Christ and live your own life. You can't go on with your lying, your cheating and your lust and your immorality. You might have been baptized. You might go to church once in a while, but that alone does not save your soul. "For by grace are ye saved, through faith; and that not of yourselves." You must be born again. It is the gift of God, not of yourselves. You cannot work your way to heaven. We are saved by the grace and mercy of God. But He demands repentance. Have you repented? Have you turned from your sins? I am going to ask you this afternoon to say to God, "I am a sinner and I am willing to give up my sins."

The second thing you must do is this: you must receive Christ by faith into your heart. This is an act of your will by which you say, "I will receive Him as my own Lord and Saviour." Has there been a time in your life when you received Him? You can do it right now where you are. You can receive Him. You say, "How long does it take?" You can repent of your sins that quick [snapping his fingers]. Receive Christ as your Saviour, and then do you know what happens? The Spirit of God comes into your heart. He gives you new life. He give a new strength and a new power. He gives a new peace and a new happiness in your life. God makes you His child.

But there is a third thing you must do. Jesus said, "You must be willing to obey me by self-denial and cross-bearing." Great crowds came to hear him preach. Many people followed Him, but Jesus said "Wait a minute. Stop. You do not know what you are doing. If you are not willing to deny yourself, your selfishness, your ego and if you are not willing to identify yourself with Me, you may not be my follower." There are many of you who want to be Christians, but you also want to enjoy all the evil things in the world. Christ said no, you must make a choice. And listen to me. It is hard to be a Christian. It is not easy to follow Christ. It is difficult. It means persecution. It may mean that some of you will be sneered at and laughed at because you are living for Christ. It will cost you something. All the apostles who followed Jesus were killed for their faith in Christ. Jesus said, "You must be willing to follow me to the death." Are you willing to follow Christ to the death?

There are three things: you must turn from your sins; you must receive Christ as your Saviour; you must be willing to follow Him and to obey Him. Now that means that if you come to Christ today, you must start reading the Bible every day. This helps you to grow in Christ. It means that you take a few minutes every day to spend in prayer. It means that you openly confess Christ. That is the reason that I ask people to come forward to receive Christ; for He says that if you are not willing to openly confess Him, He will not confess you before His Father in heaven. It means that you also get into fellowship with other believers and Christians of like mind, who believe the Bible and preach the Bible and live for Christ.

Do you want your sins forgiven? Do you want Christ in your heart? Do you want to know you are going to heaven? You can know today, but I want to warn you about something. You cannot come to Christ just any time you want to. You can only come when the Spirit of God drives you. There is a danger of hardening your heart once God speaks to you. There is a little voice down in your heart speaking to you now. You need Christ. You want Christ. The Holy Spirit is telling you that you ought to receive Christ. You better do it now because you may never have a moment like this again.

I am going to ask that we bow our heads in prayer. This is the holy moment. I am going to ask hundreds of you to receive Christ in your hearts. You want your sins forgiven. You want to know you are going to heaven. You are willing to repent of your sins. You are willing to receive Christ. You are willing to give up your sins. You are willing to change your way of living. You want Christ in your heart. Here is what I am going to ask you to do. I am going to ask you, if you mean it, to take out your handkerchief, and in just a moment I am going to ask you to wave it. And where you are, you are saying to God: "I am going to receive Christ in my heart. I am going to start reading the Bible. I am going to give up my sins. I want to live for Christ. I want Christ in my heart. I am ready to follow Him from now on."

I want you to lift your handkerchief now. Just lift it up and then you can put it down. Hold it up and wave it. There are many hundreds of you to whom God is speaking. [pause] You may put your handkerchief down. Perhaps you misunderstood. Listen, I want you to lift your handkerchief if you are receiving Christ as Saviour, if you are going to take your stand for Christ in the office, in the shop, in the store, in the factory, on the street and wherever you go. You are going to get in fellowship with other believers. Now wave your handkerchief if you do this. If you mean it in your heart, wave your handkerchiefs. [pause] Now here is what I want you to do. I want you to stand up where you are. Only those who raised their handkerchiefs, stand up where you are. All that waved a handkerchief, stand up. Now I want you to pray a prayer. I want you to pray out loud. Make your prayer very loud. Pray it after me.

Oh God! [The people repeated the words] Oh God! [The people repeated the words] I am a sinner. I am sorry for my sins. [The people repeated the words] I am willing to turn from my sins. I receive Christ as Saviour and Lord. [The people repeated the words.] From this moment on I am going to follow Him and serve Him in the fellowship of the Church. In Christ's name, Amen. [The people repeated the words.]

Now here is what I want you to do. We have some literature that we want to give you. I want the counselors to move in among you quickly and give you this literature. I do not want you to leave without this literature. You who are standing and waving your handkerchiefs, go to the aisle and get your literature. The counselors will get your name and address so that we can send some books through the mail. Now we will bow our heads once more.

Note

1. *Baptist World Alliance: Tenth Congress, Rio de Janeiro, June 26-July 3, 1960* (Nashville: Broadman, 1961), p. 304.

11
Miami Beach
1965

Introduction

The sixties, to say the least, were different. That decade was not simply "secular"; it was, in the words of one American church historian, "tumultuous." Man had come of age! Rational, responsible, competent, and free, he was on the verge of building a new world order. At least that was the thinking of many in the sixties. The idea was to get "freed up" from every inhibiting constraint. A few theologians, wanting to be free of God, proclaimed God's death. Others, young people especially, proclaimed and practiced sexual freedom.

To be sure, many degrading and destructive shackles deserved to be broken. The chains of colonialism, racism, and poverty, among others, needed to be snapped. Probably at no time in its history had the BWA such an excellent opportunity to speak of authentic Christian freedom than at the eleventh World Congress in Miami Beach in June 1965. The Congress text for that year was John 8:32—"and the truth shall make you free."

In that decade when so many grandiose claims were being made for man, an ironic event occurred at the Miami Congress. At the evening session on Tuesday, June 29, Samuel Miller and Ron Nelson's beautiful oratorio "What Is Man?" was halted in the midst of Act II because of a bomb threat! No bomb was found after the 13,000 people evacuated the hall. The event symbolized, however, that man had not really come "of age" and was not authentically free.

Joao F. Soren's presidential address, "The Present Challenge to Witness to the Truth and the Light," was particularly relevant for the mid-sixties. He spoke of four challenges confronting Baptists. They were (1) the challenge of a divided world, (2) the challenge of moral decadence, (3) the challenge of waning freedoms, and (4) the challenge of the quest for abiding realities.

Russell F. Aldwinckle, a Baptist theologian of McMaster Divinity College, Hamilton, Ontario, spoke on "The Nature and Purpose of Our Freedom." He related the concept of freedom to both the contemporary world and to Baptist distinctives. Warning Baptists of the possibility of misunderstanding the term, he insisted that true freedom could only be found in disciplined obedience to God.

The Present Challenge to Witness to the Truth and the Light
Joao F. Soren

The age in which we live is the most challenging time in history. It is an especially challenging time for the Children of Light and for the followers of the Lord of Truth. Baptists of many lands are becoming increasingly conscious of the fact that something very decisive and very far-reaching must be done in this day of unique challenge if we are to bear witness adequately and faithfully to the truth before this world. Baptist churches and Baptist people all around the world are being swept by a heaven-sent restlessness, a disquieting realization that it behooves us to gird our loins and get about our Lord's business with seriousness of purpose and with true spirit of self-denial and sacrifice.

This great Congress would be a blessed and auspicious event if nothing else happened to these thousands of Baptists who have gathered here besides and beyond this: that the Holy Spirit of God might lead us, as we meet here, to realize our responsibility and our task in this challenging hour.

It would be very gratifying for the one who will soon vacate the chair if, before doing so, he might be used of the Lord to lead his fellow Baptists to place themselves anew before the Lord of hosts in prayer and dedication, so that, as they discern the divine call through the challenges that are placed before them, all may answer as the prophet of old, "Here am I; send me."

It would not be fitting to attempt to draw at this time a complete profile of the world in which we live in an effort to portray the full impact of this challenging twentieth century. Four aspects of this present world have been selected, from among others which might have been chosen, to steer our thinking as we consider the present challenge to witness to the truth and the light.

The Challenge of a Divided World

The powers of divisiveness have kept members of the human race apart and have disrupted the unity of the human family. One can still recall the oversimplification concerning the ancient world according to some of the history books of another generation. Many authors of history textbooks left the students under the impression that the world in the time of Jesus was simply divided into two large blocks or units: the Greco-Roman world and the barbarian world. The picture is completely false. The world of that time was very much divided, both within and outside the boundaries of the Roman Empire. The Roman Empire was a heterogeneous agglomeration of a variety of nations and tribes bound together by the Empire's iron military might and political prowess.

History repeats itself in this day. There is a tendency to consider the present world as divided into two great political and ideological blocks, with the several nations of the world aligned homogeneously in one camp or another. This is indeed a false picture of the present world. What prevails in this world today is divisiveness. Divisions are deep-rooted everywhere. This is "one world" in the sense that marvelous modern means of communication and transportation have virtually shrunk the size of this terrestrial globe. Although there is an abundance of information, one still wonders if there actually is communication in this divided world. Approximation does not necessarily mean communication. There are people who profess to love their antipodes on the other side of the world but despise and antagonize their next-door neighbors. Approximation sometimes, in fact, tends to enhance and accentuate differences that distances will obliterate. A good-humored Protestant bishop said recently that he has benefited greatly by meeting with the representatives of other churches in ecumenical encounters, because these meetings invariably confirmed and fortified the doctrinal views and convictions he held before participating in the meetings.

The barriers that separate and divide the human family not only remain through the years, but each generation raises up new and different walls of separation. Fifty years ago some of the divisive forces which are so virulent today were totally nonexistent. Other such forces which were more or less dormant have become reactivated under new world conditions and are undergirding the bastions of suspicion, prejudice, segregation, racism, xenophobia, classism, and just plain sinful human egotism.

Enmity and hate lurk in the shadows of these walls of division. Violence and wars are bred within the citadels of a divided humanity.

Preachers become hesitant at times to broach this subject from the standpoint of the Christian religion. It is evident that something happened somewhere along the course of the history of the Christian Church which deprived it of that marvelous quality it had in the beginning of bringing men together and making brothers of them. It is a marvel, indeed, that the haughty pharisee with all his fanatical racism and theological exclusivism could become, under the impact of the gospel of God's love to all men, the inspired apostle of Jesus Christ, by whose blood he "hath made both one, and hath broken down the middle wall of partition . . . having abolished in his flesh the enmity."

It was indeed a marvel to the world that primitive Christians could sit together at meat in those feasts of brotherly love, called "agapes," where they proclaimed to the eyes of the world that among them, in the presence of the Lord Jesus, there was no difference, there were no castes, nor nationalities, nor colors, nor races, nor divisions, "neither Greek nor Jew, circumcision, nor uncircumcision, Barbarian, Scythian, bond nor free: but Christ is all, and in all." Genuine New Testament apostolic Christianity breaks down the barriers that divided humanity by making brothers and sisters of all men who have the common language of Christian love and belong to one race, namely, the race of those who have been born again of the Spirit of God.

It thrills us to recall that those inspired Baptists who conceived the idea of a Baptist World Alliance sixty years ago were motivated by the need which they felt of expressing Baptist oneness in worldwide dimensions. As we strengthen the ties that make our Christian oneness more than something merely rhetorical or sentimental, but the demonstration of a deep-seated affinity and an effective means for promoting God's Kingdom here on earth, then we will be witnessing to the power of the gospel as the true hope, the only hope, for this divided world.

"Togetherness" is a wonderful new English word which is often used in our Baptist encounters, but this other expression which occurs in the preamble of the Constitution of the Baptist World Alliance—"the essential oneness of Baptists"—stands out like a flag in a military parade. May it be our banner at this juncture of history! Let us make this "essential oneness," which we have learned from the New Testament, something very true and very real and very effective within our Baptist ranks, that we may witness to the world that in Christ and only

> "In Christ there is no East or West,
> In Him no South or North;
> But one great fellowship of love
> Throughout the whole wide world.

> "In Him shall true hearts everywhere
> Their high communion find;
> His service is the golden cord,
> Close binding all mankind.

"Join hands, then, brothers of the faith,
Whate'er your race may be:
Who serves my Father as a son
Is surely kin to me.

"In Christ now meet both East and West,
In Him meet South and North:
All Christly souls are one in Him,
Throughout the whole wide world."

JOHN OXENHAM

The Challenge of Moral Decadence

Much is being said and written these days about "the present moral revolution." One is at a loss, however, to discover in what respect the present moral trend in the world is revolutionary. Revolutions have leaders and heroes. Revolutions uphold ideas and present some kind of program and coordinated action. Revolutions usually mean the substitution of one system by another. Revolution is not a synonym for degradation. Ethically the human race seems to be walking backward and retracing its steps back to paganism, or at least the neopaganism, which sometimes is called humanism. The higher ethical standards are being repudiated by this generation. In all relations of human life today there is a marked tendency toward breaking recognized rules of decency and dignity and relegating completely the ideals and standards of Christian ethics. Modern man prefers not to be encumbered by a sense of moral responsibility. Although we cannot but oppose, as Christians, the veritable flood of obscene, immoral, pornographic literature being produced by modern writers in many countries, we must admit however that this objectionable literature is in itself a realistic and true moral portrait of the generation that produces and consumes this type of printed matter.

The crisis of faith in the world today is the first cause of its shocking moral decadence. It is from God that human life derives its meaning. It is the very nature of the righteous and holy God that gives man a meaningful moral goal and the abiding, absolute standard of righteousness. As the life of man moves out and away from God, his moral discernment becomes impaired and obscured. The Greeks of old, notwithstanding the brilliancy of their intellectual, philosophic, and political achievements, were lacking in moral illumination and motivation, because they knew not the God of righteousness. They worshiped gods of their own making that had the weaknesses of their makers, the sins and the vices of their pagan originators, and lived in the Hellenic mountaintops, giving full reign to their greed and sensuality.

Another cause for moral decadence in this generation is widespread iconoclasm. I do not use the word in its original and etymological meaning, which literally meant to break idols. Rather, the word is used here to portray the tendency to destroy, to disrupt, to demolish.

A few years ago there was a student and labor strike with political implications in the capital of a South American country. Things were pretty well in hand until all of a sudden something sinister and destructive took hold of the strikers. From them it propagated to the mobs. It was as if the demons of destructiveness had possessed the multitude. Mass hysteria took hold completely and impelled the mobs to an orgy of destruction. By nightfall they had made a shambles of the city.

The most respectable and valuable entities and institutions in this world are in the firing sights of the destructive forces of this generation. A Brazilian intellectual said recently that "this is the age of demolitions and much of debris and the rubble of destruction is still to be seen." There is nothing reasonable or coherent in this iconoclastic rapture. Essentially it has nothing to do with just vindications. It is something pathological, morbid, abnormal, such as the insane firing of a rifle bullet that ended the life of that admirable man who was the President of this great country, piercing so many hearts around the world.

This is not the proper time to consider the causes of the destruction-mania which has possessed the modern world. The so-called moral revolution, the moral decadence of this generation, which expressed itself by the rejection of time-proven moral codes and moral standards, is essentially a religious problem.

The purpose of redemption, as interpreted by Jesus Christ, is to call mankind to God. It is God's plan that men enter into communion with Him through faith in His only begotten Son. Man only becomes that which he was created to be as in faith he is born again of the Spirit and lives the new life of obedience, of perfect trust and hope eternal. The godly life, as opposed to the worldly life, is the Bible's formula for man's victory here and hereafter.

The human race has been thwarted and frustrated in its efforts to build a solid structure of living, because it has not built upon the solid foundation of the Rock of Ages. Unless man's life is God-centered, and not self-centered, he is headed for failure and despair. This world is God's world indeed, but apart from Him it has so little worth and meaning that to depend on it is to meet with profound dissatisfaction and confusion.

The gospel of Jesus Christ transforms men, changing sinners into saints, not only by communicating new powers which give human beings an undisputed supremacy over the powers of evil, but also by giving them a new holy moral core around which all life's energies and interests gravitate.

All hopes and expectancies for a better world where peace and justice will prevail are futile and untenable unless they can be built upon a moral recovery and revival. The pillars of true civilization are those moral principles and axioms that capacitate men to apply toward good ends and purposes the values and resources which their intellects discover and produce. The human race is desperately in need of such moral recapacitation, which only the power of God unto salvation can impart and instil. This is the appointed hour for Baptists to realize with a new awareness that this world is becoming acutely conscious of its moral problems. The world is also acutely conscious of its failure and evident incapacity toward solving such problems. This is indeed the time for our witnessing to the transforming and sublimating power of the gospel. The miracle that transformed the cold and cruel Pharisee into the warmhearted heroic Apostle of the love of Jesus Christ to the Gentiles is not merely a wonder of the past or the product of an obsolete faith. The Christ of Paul is the unchangeable Christ of our present faith. He is still the appointed power for the moral renewal and rebirth of sinners in the likeness and in the image of the holy God.

The Challenge of Waning Freedoms

As one scans the horizon in search of the blessed lights of liberty among the nations of the world today, the search must traverse the dark, arid deserts of prevailing despotisms that either openly or covertly combat and despise liberty. It is indeed shocking to have to admit that in this twentieth century of astounding technological progress and of unprecedented advances and conquests in many realms of human life, the conquests in the realm of human liberty have been relatively insignificant. One cannot deny the fact that there are a few cases in this world where freedom flourishes, but it is also a fact that the vast majority of the world's population of almost three and a half billion has not even remotely breathed the invigorating, exhilarating, uplifting atmosphere of liberty.

Never in history has freedom been opposed by such formidable foes as in this century. Violence and torture have been unleashed and used to horrible extent against the basic rights of the human person in this twentieth-century resurgence of medievalistic intolerance and despotism. In no other time in history have there been such brazen anti-freedom philosophies, theologies, and ideologies propagating with such militant efficiency their peculiar brand of viruses as in this generation. If it is true that the fight for freedom is a war without end, then one must admit that the holy crusade for liberty in this world is still in its incipiency.

The picture is still more shocking when one considers the fact that freedom has suffered severe setbacks not only among the so-called underdeveloped nations but even among the super-civilized peoples of the earth. Liberty has not been trampled upon only by the barefooted, illiterate hordes in pagan countries. It has been trod upon also in concentration camps, in ghettos, in segregated slums, by intolerance, by hate groups, by extremists, by disfranchisements, by corruption in law-enforcing agencies, by vociferous demagogism, by racism, by political hooliganism, by discriminatory legislation, and other such enemies of freedom which have been born and bred right in the heart of the most developed nations and in the centers of so-called highly civilized peoples of the earth.

My country is blessed with religious liberty. Brazil is indeed one of those cases of complete religious liberty. The entire nation was shocked a few weeks ago when in one of our largest northern cities there appeared on the walls of schools and public buildings the insignia of hate, intolerance, and discrimination against a religious and racial minority in that city. The local police force was galvanized into action, and within a few days the police had herded into jail a gang of semiprofessional agitators with international connections and affiliations, whose program is the stirring up of racial and religious frictions and antagonisms. Such occurrences have become commonplace in many cities around the world.

This is a time when religious liberty in particular is being trampled upon by both state and ecclesiastical powers. Timeworn, futile arguments and allegations are being used alike by political governments and established religious majorities to justify their despotic suffocation of religious liberty. All too often throughout Latin America religious liberty is resisted and denied to citizens in the name of national interest. National unity, it is alleged, requires religious unity. To breach the religious unity of a nation means disrupting its national integrity and cohesion. Such an inconsistent totalitarian thesis, which makes a strong appeal to national sentiment, has many advocates in countries where religious despotism has stifled religious freedom. It is indeed a most perplexing fact that religious entities and ecclesiastical institutions within the pale of historical Christianity hesitate, procrastinate, and adopt the tortuous strategy of dubiousness, dialectical obscurity, and silent connivance when religious liberty is at stake. It becomes difficult to determine whether the greater foe of religious liberty in the world today is atheistic, despotic civil power or dominant, absolutist, despotic religion.

It behooves those who believe in religious freedom, those who believe that religious liberty is the basic liberty, the "number one" liberty, those who believe that religious liberty has its roots not only in the intrinsic nature of man but even in the very nature of God and in the divine purpose of redemption, to take their stand and fly their colors at high mast.

For over half a century the Baptist World Alliance has been trumpeting the glorious anthem of soul liberty. Down through the years, since that first memorable Congress in London in 1905, the Baptist World Alliance has proclaimed to the world its witness to religious liberty. The adoption of declarations and manifestos on religious liberty in the Congress proceedings is not routine matter; it is indeed a highlight in all of these great Baptist assemblies. Alliance officials and members of committees and commissions have produced an admirable record of service in presenting to governments, to the press, and to the public in general the issues and the ideals of religious liberty. They have championed courageously the cause of oppressed minorities in many lands. The worldwide drama of religious freedom presents in its superb cast such notable personages as Edgar Y. Mullins, George W. Truett, J. H. Rushbrooke, Walter O. Lewis, Arnold T. Ohrn, and others.

One cannot think of the Baptist World Alliance without calling to memory the names of those who in our own time have gallantly unfurled the banner of religious liberty. We thank God for the watchfulness of Josef Nordenhaug and Erik Ruden, worthy combatants who are ever patrolling the border to make sure that all encroachments upon the sacred soil of religious liberty are met with firmness and resistance. Robert S. Denny, through the effective media of Baptist youth work and public relations, Cyril E. Bryant, the untiring and vigilant journalist of Baptist oneness and Baptist worldwide witness, A. Klaupiks, who is forever extending the Baptist hand of fraternal solidarity to those who suffer disaster and persecution—these, too, are living, everyday watchmen for religious liberty in the service of the Baptist World Alliance.

Not only these, however. Many others come to our memory. These distinguished and most honorable past presidents of the Alliance, many now serving in the Alliance departments, in commissions, in study panels, and in other capacities, have added their valuable contributions to the historic Baptist witness through Baptist World Alliance channels. Many other Baptists around the world, with or without direct connections with the Baptist World Alliance, have made momentous contributions toward the advancement of religious liberty.

There is, however, a persistent and disturbing uncertainty gnawing at our consciences as Baptists at this juncture of the twentieth century, when the conquests in the realm of religious freedom have become precarious and are being threatened by new and powerful antagonists: Have we been sufficiently positive and militant and determined in our Baptist witness to soul liberty? Could it be said of present-day Baptists that valuable ground has been lost to the enemies of religious liberty because of our lack of aggressiveness in the faithful propagation of our New Testament conviction? Is there ground for a valid accusation against Baptists that they are playing the role of "The Vicar" in this world of religious intolerance and widespread opposition to religious liberty? Have we perhaps muted somewhat the clarion note of our historic distinctive by conducting our holy crusade for liberty with too great respect for propriety, diplomacy, and protocol, at a time when the enemies of religious liberty are continually and progressively tightening the screws of oppression and persecution?

This decidedly is not an opportune time for compromise and for tactical withdrawals through entangling alliances with those who combat the historical idiosyncrasy of these New Testament, apostolic Christians called Baptists. The Baptist stand through the ages for soul liberty has its roots deeply set in Christian theology. If such a stand is a Baptist distinctive, it is so for the sole reason that it is a genuine Christian distinctive, a New Testament distinctive.

Not many months ago the Rio de Janeiro Symphony Orchestra was presenting Stravinsky's very modern oratorio entitled *Canticum Sacrum.* The most striking part of the oratorio is "St. Mark Preaching to the Sinners." During the interval immediately after this climactic phase of Stravinsky's oratorio, I asked the gentleman sitting beside me how he was enjoying the concert. He hesitated for a moment, then said, "I do not understand this type of music, but one certainly feels the impact!"

Perhaps this faithless generation cannot understand the beauty and the majesty of all we say and preach about soul liberty. To those who do not have faith in God, it may be that our song of freedom may sound as strange and dissonant music to their ears. But if our witness be unflinching, resolute, courageous, ringing with the forcefulness of unstinted loyalty and unwavering conviction, this confused and sin-enslaved humanity will certainly feel the impact of the great oratorio of religious liberty.

The Challenge of the Quest for Abiding Realities

We live today in a world that drinks the bitter waters of disappointment and frustration. Man-made castles of humanistic utopias have crashed to the ground. Man's highest hopes of a better world built upon the foundations of a technological society have vanished amidst the smoldering ruins left in the wake of highly technological and highly diabolical wars. A profound, melancholic anxiety-neurosis and skepticism have become universal. The machinery that constructed the twentieth-century civilization has become also the machinery of power that is gradually grinding into insignificance the value of human personality in this generation. Typical of modern frustrated humanity was the comment made by a young intellectual journalist in South America after hearing the speech of an eminent statesman on the necessity of pooling all our resources toward the preservation of modern civilization. His sardonic comment was this: "But is this modern civilization worth preserving?"

During the Second World War the Brazilian Expeditionary Force served in Italy as a unit of the Fourth Corps of the United States Fifth

Army. Late one afternoon in April of 1945 the First Infantry Regiment of the Brazilian Force advanced upon the ruins of what had been the very picturesque and attractive city of Montese in North Italy. The little city, which was very strategically located, had been bombed continually by artillery and from the air for two days. Fighting lasted for hours, from house to house, after our troops had entered the city. All the buildings had been hit and severely damaged. Most of them had been completely destroyed. Fire raged in many places. The dead littered the streets. The blood of wounded soldiers and civilians was to be seen everywhere. The withdrawing enemy kept up a strong barrage of mortar and artillery fire, which added to the destruction. Finally, all fighting ceased, and a sudden silence fell upon that terrible scene of devastation and death. With bitterness in his voice, my Regimental Commander, a sensitive, intellectual, and God-fearing man, said, "Behold, Chaplain, the ruins of our modern civilization!"

As the amazingly advanced techniques of the atom era reveal their incapacity and inadequacy toward solving the fundamental problems of man himself, it becomes apparent and evident that something is essentially and fundamentally wrong with what we may call the texture of civilization. One of the most lucid thinkers of our age has said that "in the process of building up civilization, man has not taken into due account the most important element, which is man himself." But this statement does not present the complete picture. The historical fact is that in the process of building up modern civilization man has neglected to take into due account the God and Father of our Lord Jesus Christ.

As the gospel itself is the mainspring of freedom, it is also the mainspring of hope and of that buoyant confidence instilled into the souls of men through communion and fellowship with the God of redemption. When men's faith grows dim and God recedes into unreality, then men lose their vision and their conception of a higher destiny and of the abiding value of spiritual realities.

Without faith in a living God men backslide into the quicksand of secularism, where their souls shrivel and waste away in anguish and frustration. Too long now men have placed their faith in the false gods of their own making. They are repudiating those gods which have turned upon them to destroy them. It is one of the strangest ironies of history that in the age in which scientific research is achieving its most spectacular victories there is such generalized skepticism about the efficacy and functional value of such momentous discoveries for promoting true progress in man himself and in human affairs and relations.

Anxiety, tension, chronic dissatisfaction and fear are no longer mere endemic traits of a sin-sick race. They have become epidemic and of worldwide dimension. On the entire human race there seems to be dawning the consciousness that "man shall not live by bread alone." There is a universal quest for abiding realities and for that which can fill the crucial needs of the inner man.

Modern man is dismayed by the uselessness and pointlessness of his highest achievements as applied toward reaching a higher moral and spiritual level of being and of existence. As far as man himself is concerned, the structure of modern civilization has revealed itself to be external, epidermic, lacking in depth. A sense of failure weighs heavily upon the conscience of this generation. Modern man has lost his bearings. Without faith and without God, man is indeed lost, and he is becoming increasingly aware of his tragic plight.

As modern man in this confused world relinquishes his hold on the ties that bind him to the crumbling institutions of the past and repudiates those principles upon which those institutions were built, he gropes in the twilight of uncertainties and in the baffling maze of many paths for a true and abiding light by which he may travel in security the road of life and of true fulfilment. His spirit thirsts for living waters, and he hungers for that bread that nourishes his immortal soul.

One of the most outstanding public men in my country at present was at one time a disciple of that well-known materialistic ideology which preaches the redemption of this world through economic salvation. Quite recently that influential Brazilian made this statement: "I repudiated the impotent gospel of economic salvation, because it offers a false messiah whose image is based on a false conception of the nature and the fundamental needs of the human person." As this generation revolts and repudiates its idols, it challenges those who have found the true Messiah.

The renewed search for abiding realities in this generation has stimulated religious inquiry and has produced serious expectancy concerning what religion has to offer toward the solution of the pressing problems that confront the human race in this generation.

Is this not providential when it occurs to us that, after all, the great problems of this age are ultimately theological in essence? They have to do with man as a living soul, in his relation to God the Creator, and in his relation to other human beings.

A well-known Brazilian economist, recently addressing students of the University of Brazil in Rio de Janeiro, said that food shortages and famines in the world today are not mere social calamities; they are horrible sins against God and against mankind. With the modern techniques that can be applied to agricultural production and distribution, enough food could be produced to feed a world population of ten billion human beings. If the nations of the world would devote to such a program a fraction of the efforts and resources which are being poured continually into the race for power and military supremacy, there would not be food shortages in this generation.

What a time for our witnessing to the truth! If it is our firm conviction that the gospel of Jesus Christ is the power of God unto salvation, if we are certain that the Christ of God is the true Bread that came down from heaven and gives life unto men, then let us proclaim the blessed message unto this desperate human race. We thank God that there is abiding reality in the gospel of Jesus Christ, in the gospel of redemption, in Him who "is the same yesterday, today and for ever."

The Bible says that "the entire creation waits with eager longing for the manifestation of the sons of God." There is an eager longing in the souls of men today. Bible societies around the world cannot supply the demands for the Scriptures. Mission boards and missionary societies feel the need to increase the numbers of those who under divine calling will go out to the fields where the demands are ever increasing. The churches are awakening to the fact that they must respond to the missionary and evangelistic challenge or else drift away from the pattern of apostolic New Testament churches. Evangelists and evangelistic crusades are the order of the day. Books dealing with theology and religion have become best sellers in some countries. Never were conditions in this world so desperate but so propitious to Christian witnessing as in this generation.

Twenty-six million Baptists, showing forth their oneness through the Baptist World Alliance, cannot find a more eloquent and more adequate channel of expressing their oneness than through a united, wholehearted, Spirit-led crusade that will galvanize into militant evangelistic action this formidable militia.

This is the appointed time and the appointed place for us as Baptists to accept the challenge and pledge ourselves before God to join hands and hearts in powerful thrust of global evangelistic endeavor.

To this end may the Spirit lead us.

The Nature and Purpose of Our Freedom
Russell F. Aldwinckle

The very term "freedom" or "liberty" is an exciting and intoxicating one. In the course of centuries of human history, many different interpretations have been put upon it and the most intense passions have been aroused by it. In the eighteenth century, much blood was shed in the name of liberty, equality, and fraternity. In England in the seventeenth century and on this continent in the nineteenth bitter civil wars were fought in which the appeal to freedom played a dominant role. Two destructive world wars have been fought in the name of freedom, to overthrow tyranny and secure the liberties of men and nations. And so the list could be continued.

What have Baptists to do with such an explosive word as this? What do Baptists think of first when they speak of "freedom"? With great boldness we have chosen for the theme of this conference the text—"And the Truth Shall Make You Free." I suspect that most of us would tend to react by talking of our freedom from the tyranny of priesthood or of the state. Baptists were originally most concerned with spiritual liberty, and by this they meant not only human rights but the freedom of the Spirit of God to have free course within the true church. To secure this freedom, they felt compelled to break with a long and venerable Christian tradition embodied in the Latin hierarchical, priestly, and sacramental Church which had dominated Europe for a thousand years. While retaining the priesthood of all believers, Baptists put a radically different interpretation upon the nature of priesthood. They contended that they owed nothing to any man and depended on Christ, the one and only mediator of our redemption.

Yet in our claims to freedom at this point Baptists need to be on guard against a serious misunderstanding of the priesthood of all believers as this was understood by the Protestant Reformers. When Peter applies the phrase "an holy priesthood" (1 Peter 2:5) to the whole body of believing Christians, he reminds us that we are priests only as members of the Christian fellowship. The priesthood of all believers does not mean only the right to private judgment and intellectual freedom, which Socrates and Bertrand Russell would also stoutly maintain, but the freedom within the community of believers to be, as Luther said, Christ to our neighbor, to show forth the special kind of love and compassion which flows from Christ and works in those who are members of His body, the church. When we assert freedom from priestly dominance in a sacramental sense, we are not claiming freedom of thought necessarily in a general sense, though this may be important even for Christians. We are claiming freedom to love, as Christ loved, all those for whom He died, and claiming this freedom as members of his fellowship of believers. In repudiating a certain understanding of the church, we are not repudiating entirely the importance of the church as the redeemed community through which God works.

Or when asked about freedom, we may begin to talk about the separation of church and state and to assert, with our seventeenth century forebears, the crown rights of the Redeemer, insisting that Christ is the only Lord of the conscience and Master of men's lives. Or we may quote with justifiable pride the famous words of Thomas Helwys, one of the first English Baptists, when he declared that King James I of England (and James VI of Scotland) had no sovereign authority over the souls of men or their faith. For this, he was promptly put in Newgate prison and disappears from our sight. Other defenses of religious liberty followed from Leonard Busher; John Buxton, who wrote his pamphlet in milk so that it could be smuggled out of prison and read by his friends; and, of course, the famous Roger Williams, who founded the first Baptist church in America in 1639.

Or we may deduce from these principles a general claim for religious freedom, of a man's inalienable right to join or not to join a religious body, to be free from coercion, threat, torture or legal pressure from either state or church. The Baptist World Alliance has a noble record in the defense of the rights of our oppressed Baptist brethren in many parts of the world. We should be ready to fight for the freedom of all men who thus suffer, even when they do not bear the name of Baptist. Perhaps also we need to remind ourselves that we cannot consistently claim such freedom without the willingness to concede to others the same freedom we claim for ourselves. Provided a man accepts the rule of law which is binding for all citizens, he should be free to be an atheist as well as a Baptist, however much we dislike the views he may hold on the subject of religion. We have no right to expect that radio and television should carry only the views with which we are in agreement, or to suppress books and literature which express antireligious views, provided this is done through proper and legal means. A limited censorship may be justified in defense of children and minors which would not be proper for adults. In any case, Baptists should have no sympathy with the idea of an index of prohibited reading enforced by civil and ecclesiastical sanctions which has marked Roman Catholic thought and practice in the past. It remains to be seen how much the present renewal in the Roman Church will mean a liberalizing at this point.

There is also the delicate point of theological and intellectual liberty in our own ranks. Baptists, in repudiating creeds (and we have generally had in mind the great historic creeds such as the Apostles', the Nicene, the Athanasian creed), have not always been willing to tolerate theological diversity, though our Baptist claim to liberty must involve this. Every attempt to impose a rigid and narrow theological uniformity on Baptists has led to division, schisms, and separation, some of them tragic for our Baptist witness to the world outside. For some people outside our ranks, the very name Baptist is synonymous with division and theological tension. This does not mean that questions of truth and right belief are unimportant. They are, but Baptists must learn to allow diversity in the theological forms and language if they are to maintain their unity behind the common confession of Jesus as Lord. Of course, there must be some real and substantial unity of belief if there is to be a truly common life in the church. If I came to the point when I could no longer affirm the divinity of Christ in any sense at all with a clear conscience, I should think it right to cease to call myself a Christian. I might be a philosophical theist or a humanist or an ethical idealist or what not, but I would not think it proper to claim to be a Christian. It is quite another thing, however, for me to insist that you accept exactly the form of words or exactly the same categories of theological thought to express what I mean by divinity as it would for you to insist that I accept yours. The basic question is whether we are sincere in confessing Christ as Lord and Saviour. If we are, then other matters can be, and indeed must be, left to the individual, as Baptists have always insisted should be the case. Our freedom, then, is responsible freedom and needs to be tempered by the conviction and needs of the community of believers.

Or we may think of the freedom of the local church to organize its own life under the Lordship of Christ, to elect its own officers, call and ordain its minister, preach and teach its members both young and old, as well as engage in public worship without hindrance.

Few among us would wish to question the desirability of the above freedom or deny that such freedoms are properly involved in a true understanding of the gospel. Yet there are profounder questions which continue to agitate our minds. Freedom from external constraint may lead to anarchy. This is true within the state and between states. The only way in which communities can hold together is when the majority of citizens accept certain laws in common and agree to try to abide by them. In the state, the police force and the armed forces exist as a last resort to coercion if normal procedures do not prevail. But who in the United Nations, for example, can enforce the law even if the states concerned can agree as to what the law is? Similar problems exist within the church, with the all-important difference that few Christians would want to fall back on physical force or legal coercion. However, it has long been maintained by the Roman Catholics that since theological differences breed civil strife, it is right to use the civil arm and force to compel religious conformity as the only bulwark against anarchy, both political and religious. It is possible that the Roman Church is on the point of making a major change in its traditional attitude on this point, but we cannot be absolutely sure of this and many of us await with keen interest the report due to be given on religious liberty. In the meantime, Baptists must continue to affirm their own strong convictions on the matter of religious liberty.

Yet Baptists too face the same problems of liberty and authority. If freedom means the liberty to pursue our own selfish and unredeemed purposes, then this means anarchy, whether in church or state. "Live as free men," says Peter in 1 Peter 2:16, "yet without using your freedom as a pretext for evil." If the person who acts freely is only expressing the anarchy of his own unruly desires, the result is bondage, not true freedom.

So-called advanced thinkers talk of free love, a misnomer if ever there was one. Love without discipline can only be lust and can never express true reverence for the other person. It is possible for men to enjoy a wide variety of political and even religious liberties and yet fall into bondage. Political democracy may guarantee to men certain rights by statute and try to enforce them by law, but it cannot save a man by law alone from the bondage to self. A "free" democracy may be satisfied with bread and circuses. "Free" citizens may indulge their lusts, whether of the flesh or of power. A political majority may not be the voice of God but a tyranny, which was why Plato distrusted it so much. Our true freedom, then, is not to do simply as we like, but true freedom is to love with the love wherewith God has loved us in Christ. We are to be free for other men in love and service as Jesus found His freedom in perfect obedience to the will of God.

Yet how do we sinful men and women come to love in this sense? Not by saying, "Go to now, I will love." We need freedom from self before we can be free to love in this deepest Christian sense. How does this come about? If ever we are to be helped at this point, we need truth not in the abstract but in the concrete, and this is precisely what the gospel offers. Truth for Christians is a person, even Jesus Christ our Lord, not a proposition. We are thus driven back to the most fundamental question of all—the nature of true freedom. Freedom is not only freedom from external constraint but the bringing of all our powers and energies into a unity of character which enables us to become what God intends for us.

We sometimes speak as if it is a comparatively simple matter for men to choose between good and evil, but we know that this is not so.

"I discover this principle, then: that when I want to do the right, only the wrong is within my reach. In my inmost self I delight in the law of God, but I perceive that there is in my bodily members a different law, fighting the law that my reason approves and making me a prisoner under the law that is in my members, the law of sin" (Rom. 7:21-23).[1]

This is the crux of the problem. The famous philosopher Immanuel Kant in the eighteenth century says the exact opposite to Paul. Kant believed that because I ought to do a thing, therefore I can. "For when the moral law commands that we ought now to be better men, it follows inevitably that we must be able to be better men." (Religion within the limits of reason alone.) Yet this is what the profoundest religious minds have always denied, and certainly the experience of most of us is on the side of Paul in this respect.

If we are ever able to love in the Christian sense, it is only because God has first made His love known to us.

"Let your bearing towards one another arise out of your life in Christ Jesus. For the divine nature was his from the first; yet he did not think to snatch at equality with God, but made himself nothing, assuming the nature of a slave. Bearing the human likeness, revealed in human shape, he humbled himself, and in obedience accepted even death—death on a cross" (Phil. 2:5-9, NEB).

This is the basis of our true freedom. "We love him, because he first loved us" (1 John 4:19).

Only because God has loved in this sense is it possible for us to have faith in Him crucified and risen and to know that God has accepted us and restored us to His fellowship. Only thus do we know the reality of passing from darkness to light, of what it means to become a new creation in Christ. When we know that God in Christ has borne for our sakes His own judgment upon our sin and made it possible for us to be united with the crucified and risen Lord we are free from self and free for the service of others in love, compassion, and devotion without discrimination of social status, education, class, or race. We cannot do this of ourselves. Only in the *koinonia* of the church as the fellowship of believers do we know the power of the Spirit which enables us to realize this our true freedom.

What kind of freedom, then, are Baptists offering to men in the name of the gospel when we declare that "the truth shall make you free" (John 8:32)? We must remember that behind the New Testament Greek word for truth lies a Hebrew word which survives in our familiar "amen." The root meaning behind "amen" is fix, confirm, establish, hence steadfastness and trustworthiness. The truth we offer in the gospel is not primarily intellectual understanding, though this is included, but the absolute faithfulness and trustworthiness of the God whom we meet in Jesus Christ. The truth that makes us free is the reality of God in His enduring faithfulness to which we can trust with absolute confidence and without any reservations.

In the contemporary world, this has obvious relevance at three points of special tension:
1. In the realm of sexual morality
2. In the revolt against colonial bondage and the dominance of the white man
3. In relation to the deep fears, often unconscious, which affect us all in a nuclear age

Some voices are suggesting that it is no longer possible to speak of moral principles in the area of sexual morality and that young people must trust to the guidance and intuition of love in specific situations when moral decisions have to be taken. We do our young people no service in pretending that there is no moral law; yet it is also true that law alone never made a good man. The freedom the gospel offers is not the mere external imposition of a moral code but the discovery of true freedom in a relationship of trust directed to Jesus Christ. Here we discover not bondage but the truest freedom, because we find ourselves knit to one who is Himself the embodiment of the most abundant life. Only slaves of Christ are the true free men.

Young nations think of freedom often exclusively in terms of freedom from colonial bondage and dominance by the West. This is right, but such nations must be reminded that mere freedom from political domination without personal discipline and the restraint of the urge to power and the lust of the flesh may lead to internal anarchy and the loss of freedom.

We have been reminded that the fight against the tyranny of the white man must not be replaced by the tyranny of the colored man. Our true freedom must be the freedom to love each other in Christ's sense of love, and this means the willingness of us all, whatever our color or station, to submit to the transforming influence of the Spirit of God.

When political liberty leads to anarchy, it always begets tyranny by way of reaction. The only way out of this impasse, to which history bears such eloquent testimony, is to transcend it in the power of the grace of God in our Lord Jesus Christ.

When Baptists make bold claims for freedom of conscience, freedom from the power of the state, freedom from ecclesiastical tyranny, we must continually remind ourselves that it is the liberty wherewith Christ has made us free that should most deeply concern us. When we condemn the Roman Catholic for distorting the nature of the church, have we allowed the Spirit of God to destroy ambition, pride of place, social prestige, or love of money in those churches of ours which claim to reproduce the pattern of fellowship and love which truly reflects the nature of the body of Christ? True liberty will always be humble, ready to repent, free from censoriousness, tolerant of others—in the true sense of consideration and respecting their rightful liberty—eager to love rather than to dominate. Only if Baptists can show forth this kind of liberty do we deserve to survive or to ask God to bless us. We inherit a noble tradition of men and women who knew freedom in this profound sense. Let us pray for strength to walk with fidelity and constancy in their steps, and may His truth make us truly free.

Note

1. *New English Bible.* © The Delegates of the Oxford University Press and the Syndics of the Cambridge University Press 1961.

12
Tokyo
1970

Introduction

The twelfth World Congress of Baptists met in Tokyo in June 1970. This was the first Baptist Congress held in the Orient. It was also the first time a black presided. William R. Tolbert, Jr., then vice-president of the Republic of Liberia, had been elected president of the Baptist World Alliance in Miami Beach in 1965.

From the beginning of his presidential term in 1965, President Tolbert sought "to open new avenues for Baptist expression."[1] He appointed Mrs. R. L. Mathis as the first woman to serve as chairman of the Program Committee of a Baptist Congress, and he told her that he wanted the Tokyo Congress to have "a program fitting the dynamics of the year 1970."[2] Much of the credit for the Congress belonged to Josef Nordenhaug, general secretary of the BWA from 1960-1969. Dr. Nordenhaug died on September 18, 1969. Mrs. Mathis and Robert S. Denney, who succeeded Nordenhaug as general secretary, brought the Congress to fruition.

The theme of the Congress was "Reconciliation Through Christ." One of the most inspiring moments of the meeting came during the always impressive roll call of nations. Cyril E. Bryant described the event with these words:

During the Roll Call of Nations on opening night, a representative from each country walked beside her flag to the platform lectern—each saying in her own language the words of the theme, 'Reconciliation Through Christ.' But when General Secretary Robert S. Denny called the name of South Africa, two women crossed the stage: a black woman and a white woman, holding hands in graphic demonstration that the apartheid laws of their nation cannot destroy the reconciliation and unity they find in their faith in Jesus Christ. The vast crowd applauded—not as people applaud entertainment but as they exclaim a loud 'amen.'[3]

Tolbert's presidential address was entitled "Let Us Go Forth."

He called for Baptists of the world to go forward in evangelism, in obedience to God's commandments, in meeting the issues of the day, and in individual renewal. U Kyaw Than of Burma gave a thrilling testimony on the reality of reconciliation in his own life. It was a personal testimony rooted in solid Christian theology.

Let Us Go Forth
William R. Tolbert, Jr.

On the twelfth day of July, 1970, in this commodious auditorium of the Budokan, in this great city whose growth and development particularly through the last quarter of a century is spectacularly enormous and tremendously impressive, Baptists from the vast continent of Asia and from Europe, North America, South America, Central America, Southwest Pacific, the Middle East, and Africa assembled and were convened in the Twelfth Baptist World Congress. These individual believers hailing from near and distant lands verily are of different languages, cultures, races, social and economic backgrounds, and political ideologies, but indeed *one in Christ Jesus;* and each personally has confessed him as Lord and has been baptized upon his or her profession of faith in him, and is endeavoring to follow him, thus matching their profession with their deeds and actions.

The occasion of this our auspicious meeting in this Congress is indeed historical and unique, in consideration of the very fact that Tokyo Baptists serving as hosts have made possible a BWA convention for the first time on this vast Asian continent. As significant as this is, it can be considered further remarkable to note that this also is the first time an African is presiding over a congress convention of the Alliance. Such significant acts, now part of the brilliant history of our cherished world brotherhood, are self-evident of and articulate much which need not be herein vocally expressed by your humble servant.

This international meeting again makes possible our functioning, as the constitution provides, to achieve the Alliance's objective; and it presents another opportunity for thousands of tongues in many languages to give praises and thanks to Almighty God for his ceaseless blessings multiplied unto them individually and collectively, far beyond their deserving. Most pleasingly are we enjoying another opportunity to meet and fellowship with fellow Baptists dispersed throughout *our one world,* and thereby we become sources and render services to those in need thereof. We most gratifyingly are having another opportunity of clarifying our Baptist convictions, thereby being more prepared to give evidence to the hope that exists in us. Here again will the needs of distressed people around the world be brought more to focus, and our compassion will be appropriately aroused. Thus, we will be timely motivated to channel aid to them, carrying out the blessed injunction "to bear one another's burdens and thus fulfil the law of Christ." We should ever bear in mind that in the beginning of the Christian era "the disciples, every man according to his ability, determined to send relief to the brethren which dwelt in Judea" (Acts 11:29).

Here, by the panorama that will be presented of various areas of our one world, we are hopeful of becoming truly oriented as to existing conditions therein, particularly in regard to religious liberty and human rights. This we cannot but look forward to with significant interest, for as Baptists true to our convictions, it will ever be our serious concern that man's God-given liberty and dignity be safeguarded and maintained; and, accordingly, toward this end our participation in timely activities that make possible the same can never be withheld. It can be only expected, therefore, that we will identify ourselves with legitimate causes and by proper means and procedures seek to occasion for our fellowmen, creatures as we are of our one loving God, the happiness incident to their having and joyfully exercising due human rights and fundamental freedom.

How overjoyed are we for another privilege afforded by this occasion to witness in this land for Jesus Christ, our omnipotent Lord! Indeed we are here executing our great commission to be witnesses in near and distant lands, in familiar as well as unfamiliar areas, in favorable as well as unfavorable environments, and in friendly as well as hostile situations. We are aware that the eyes and the ears of the world are focused on Baptists during this great Congress, and may the impact of our dynamic witnessing to "Reconciliation Through Christ," with relevance to the demands of the age in which we live, be far-reaching, most meaningful, and productive of great good in these days of confrontation, condemnation, hate, strife, revenge, violence, and conflict.

On the day of June 29, 1965, most memorable for me, in the Convention Hall in Miami Beach, Florida, by your most gracious act, the call of the omnipotent Head of the Church to serve in the capacity as president, BWA, was voiced to me. In all humility I answered the call, not knowing what our Lord really had for me to do, but very certain that he would make it known to me and give me needed guidance, strength, and wisdom to execute same. Thus with his mandate expressed through you, I became engaged in a period of service in my life that to me personally has been most meaningful and enriching. In truth, I esteemed this summons as being only an occasion for the continuation of my *mission,* begun at an earlier time of my existence, with the selfsame *message* to be proclaimed on a higher plane, but with identical imperativeness and urgency. Indeed great opportunities and privileges were thereby afforded me, and utilized, to bear witness in an extensive way to "the truth that makes men free" and "to direct the feet of erring men to that way which verily leads not to a dead end, but to eternal life." In this way if we but walk, guided by the all-illuminating light reflected in our souls, ours will be joy and peace, with all gloomy darkness being dispelled as we journey on our pilgrimage in this world of care and toil, with all of its attending conditions.

Upon being inducted into office, the following seven-point program was revealed to me, and I was urged to execute:

1. To strive to *demonstrate* our essential oneness in Christ Jesus as Baptists.
2. To labor at *broadening* and *making more extensive* the glorious fellowship now happily existing in the Alliance.
3. To *vigorously emphasize* world evangelism and urge upon all of this great Baptist family to make a dynamic thrust in this direction.
4. To urge *more study* of the Bible as the revealed and infallible Word of God.
5. To strive to *develop a keen awareness* of the dignity of the human person.
6. To *emphasize the need* for greater relief to areas of our world where victims unfortunately are suffering and in need and distress.
7. To set the *highest goal* in our quest *for peace* in these days of tension, confusion, strife, violence, and conflict.

To execute this program, I have journeyed to thirty countries on six continents, traveling in all 212,420 air miles and 4,788 ground miles.

In the event that I have achieved any success in the execution thereof, I give praises to Almighty God for his enabling graces, and further attribute same to the splendid cooperation I have inspiringly received from the past presidents, officers, and constituent member organizations of the Alliance. We all, with togetherness and the purposes and objectives of the Alliance always in view, have worked in unity to the glory of our omnipotent Lord and for the enrichment of his little ones throughout the world.

It would certainly be inexcusable remissness on my part, yea, an act of immense ingratitude to fail to express my deep appreciation to President Tubman of Liberia for his most enthusiastic and valuable assistance and wholehearted cooperation given me during my tenure of service. I received from him magnificent moral and financial support which greatly aided in facilitating the travel I make from time to time on missions of the Alliance. By constant acts he truly proves himself to be a statesman possessing extraordinary qualities rarely found in other contemporary political leaders. I thank God for him and fervently pray that God will continuingly multiply rich graces unto him.

Within this period of five years (1965-1970) covering our service in office, astounding events have occurred in the history of our world. Of these startling achievements we have hailed and saluted the great discovery in medical science of human heart transplants and the still greater scientific and technological feat of man's lunar landing.

However the materialistic tendencies of our age and the disheartening sophisticated attitude and actions of those affected thereby, thanks be to the great Head of the church, through the instrumentality of evangelism and missions, yea, the dynamic proclamation of the Word by the power of Almighty God, the Baptist denomination has made noticeable gains. According to available statistics, increases in our world brotherhood have totaled 5,175,150, distributed in all regional areas wherein our organization has constituent members.

Our hearts have, in the meantime, been greatly saddened during this period by the tremendous loss we sustained in the untimely homegoing of our most talented, scholarly, versatile, indefatigable co-worker, and friend to all, General Secretary Josef Nordenhaug, and our most vigorous, friendly, resourceful, positive, dynamic past President Charles Oscar Johnson, who with great erudition impressively delivered the Coronation Address on the subject "Our Unity in Christ" at the last Congress. We can always get inspiration from the quality of selfless, untiring, dedicated service rendered by them, who now rest in our blessed Lord from their labors, while their works follow them.

On so great an occasion as this, I deem it timely to suggest that we meditate upon thoughts that can emanate from the theme: "Let Us Go Forth." A passage of Scripture that can be referred to bearing on this theme is found in Hebrews 13:12-14. I quote: "Wherefore Jesus also, that he might sanctify the people with his own blood, suffered without the gate. Let us go forth therefore unto him without the camp, bearing his reproach. For here have we no continuing city, but we seek one to come."

Another passage pertinent to the theme is "They took Jesus, and led him away. And he bearing his cross went forth . . ." (John 19:16-17). "Going forth" in this passage connotes an advance with vigor and fortitude from a given point beyond a certain boundary on to the end.

"Going forth" also suggests advancing without being fearful of consequences and regardless of dangers involved or ignominy to be encountered and/or experienced.

True to such a connotation, the thought intended by me to be emphasized in this message is that we individually and collectively, facing the confronting problems of our day and the ever-increasing challenges of this age, advance vigorously and with fortitude, never retreating or even remaining in static position but pressingly pursuing the forever-forward movement beyond—and still beyond certain limited set boundaries—to the very end that permits no further advance.

It is always to be borne in mind that our blessed Lord bearing his cross went forth and suffered without the gate. The apostle Paul therefore enjoined upon the Hebrews to "go forth unto him without the camp, bearing his reproach."

We in this day should be prepared and, with determination of making our world better, do likewise.

Let us go forth into highways and hedges and bid the wanderer to come into the "fold" of Christ, which promises divine protection, safety, joy, and peace.

The glad tidings of the rich reward, yea, the more abundant life, freely offered to all who are wise enough to accept the invitation to enter, must be proclaimed to the billions in near and distant lands and under all conditions. Ours is the responsibility and obligation, the imperativeness and urgency as never before, to make this known to all mankind that they may have the opportunity of making a choice—eternal life if they accept and eternal damnation if they reject.

In this ever-changing age, let us go forth meeting the challenge of change by the taking of our positive position and the dynamic proclamation of the Living Word that is relevant to all times. An awareness must always exist that to meet this challenge we must be prepared to lay aside, cut off and cast away, and then put on and add to. "Lay aside every weight and the sin which doth so easily beset us" (Hebrews 12:1). "Add to your faith virtue; and to virtue knowledge; and to knowledge temperance; and to temperance patience; and to patience godliness; and to godliness brotherly kindness; and . . . charity" (2 Peter 1:5-7).

Let us go forth into our every individual closet and remove therefrom those frightening skeletons that do not serve to reflect the true Christian image or glorify God and, accordingly, constitute only blemishes to us first as Christlike individuals, whom we profess to be.

In obedience, let us go forth keeping the commandments of God, remembering as the apostle Paul declared to the Corinthians, "Circumcision is nothing but the keeping of the commandments." Our Lord also emphatically stated: "He that hath my commandments, and keepeth them, he is it that loveth me; and he that loveth me shall be loved of my Father, and I will love him, and will manifest myself to him" (John 14:21).

The first and greatest of the commandments is "Thou shalt love the Lord thy God with all they heart, and with all thy soul, and with all thy might"; and the second is like unto the first: "Thou shalt love thy neighbour as thyself."

Further, the new commandment given by Christ is "That ye love one another, as I have loved you" (John 15:12).

He declared further: "By this shall all men know that ye are my disciples, if ye have love one to another" (John 13:35).

Our deeds and actions to one another must bear evidence of our Christlike character; and as we are aware that our Lord went about doing good, so we, too, ought to go about daily doing good to all without discrimination, and evil to none. This will demonstrate our love for God and for our fellowmen.

Let us go forth meeting the issues of our day and not evading them. The answers to questions of youth continuingly being asked the Christian church, however vexing or perplexing, must be given by us. Our society with all of its inhumane character, materialistic tendencies, ever-upward spiraling permissive attitude, escalating immoral behavior, alarming disappointments, disheartening frustrations, and social evils is verily ours to live in, and accordingly, must be standardized and rendered wholesome by Christian principles and not controlled by expediencies of unscrupulous individuals and influenced by unrighteous acts of vain and base men.

With serenity *let us go forth* into our own individual selves and, after thorough searchings, remove all odious elements of hypocrisy, complex prejudice, racism, conceit, arrogance, disunity, bigotry, contention, discrimination, suppression, oppression, negativism, hate, revenge, strife, hostility, and violence found within us. Then with the *trowel* in hand spreading unsparingly the cement of goodwill, human brotherhood, love, and peace, let us valiantly meet every foe bearing the menacing *sword* of human destruction.

With extended vision, *let us go forth* from this lofty mount of great inspiration into every valley of degradation and despair, however low, yea, in every melancholy slum and ghetto wherein dwell those made of the same flesh and blood as we are and created in the same image and likeness that we, too, by the grace of our common Creator have been created, and appropriately contribute, as our resources will permit, to the alteration of their unfortunate suffering condition and substandard existence, that they, too, may timely and in reality enjoy the blessedness of full, free life and really experience true human dignity and respect, which should be the happy lot of all without discrimination.

With determination, *let us go forth* thus challenged as stalwart dynamic crossbearers garbed in the whole armor of the Christian, and not as compromising, mediocre, seasonal combatants having limited boundaries set for ourselves. Every Calvary, however steep or rugged, that stands before us must be ascended to the summit; and all appearing chasms, however wide, must be spanned by the use of implements made not from metallic substance, but from Christlike love, which is unfailing and all reconciling.

In conclusion, like the apostle Paul, I can, not with boasting but in humility and truth, say that, during these five most meaningful years of my Christian ministry, serving in the particular capacity as president of the Baptist World Alliance, to the limit of my resources, *"I labored: yet not I, but the grace of God which was with me"* (1 Corinthians 15:10). I have come to realize more fully that truly in Christ there exists no East or West; in him no North or South but all in him are of one great brotherhood united by the bonds of love. Indeed, iron curtains render no obstruction to passage and do not come within the range of vision of those who have entered into the fold of Christ.

I shall verily terminate my service as your president a few days hence, but I, as a steadfast servant of our omnipotent loving Lord, most certainly shall continue on my mission with the gospel message of love and peace, charged by him to deliver to all peoples of the earth, of all colors and ranks without discrimination.

With an abiding sense of responsibility to God our Father and involvement in causes that affect man our brother, *let us go forth* on a worldwide mission of "Reconciliation Through Christ" our Savior. By our fellowship, service, and cooperation, may there occasion in the decade of the seventies gloriously beneficial results in relatively comparable proportion to man's lunar landing; and in this constantly changing age may the Christlike heart be transplanted in man, thus rendering a change in his outlook, attitude, and actions toward our one world, and cause him never to live in selfishness and isolation but in harmony, cooperation, and peace with his fellowman.

With faith, let us go forth unrelentingly with togetherness, consistency, and tenacity of purpose, executing our objectives, not in our own strength, but with the grace and in the might of our omnipotent Lord and make our one world better by enriching the lives of all men.

May we, at the end of our course, find satisfaction and joy in the fulfillment of our individual mission to the betterment of our one world and the glory of God.

He Is Our Peace
U Kyaw Than

Peace. Harmony. Reconciliation. These are words which grip our attention as we come to this Congress. *Peace:* this is the issue which grips the attention of the world and particularly of Asia at this time. *Harmony:* this is the slogan which rings in our ears as we come to Japan, our host country.

Reconciliation: this is the theme under which we are gathered as a Congress now.

Some parts of my testimony may sound jarring to the ears of some of you and may also bring back some unpleasant memories. But if we are to struggle with the challenge of the theme of this Congress, each of us will have to go beyond pleasant and comfortable thoughts, to the reality and the agony of the cross which stands at the center of genuine reconciliation.

Let me start by telling you a true story of an incident in my life, an incident which happened in a remote little village in northern Burma toward the end of the second world war. It is not an easy story for me to tell here as we enjoy the welcome, hospitality, and fellowship of our Japanese hosts. Those were difficult and dark days of relations between Japan and the rest of Asia. The Japanese military forces were then occupying my country, Burma, and I was a teenager taking refuge along with my parents at an out-of-the-way village in northern Burma. As a family we were trying our best to stay away from the path of war and to avoid any encounter with the Japanese army. It was the twenty-third of December in the last year of the war—a day before Christmas Eve—when the Kimpertai, the Japanese military police, turned up at the gate of the compound where the little house my father had rented was situated. The military police had come because my father was needed to go along with them to their headquarters for an investigation. Some half dozen heads of families who also had taken refuge in that village were arrested, too, that same morning and taken by boat across the river to the headquarters of the Kimpertai. It was the most difficult Christmas in the experience of our family, and to cut a long story short, my father was the only Christian among those arrested. And he was the only one to return home alive to that village. Here was a practical case of the deliverance that is in Christ. When the Japanese forces retreated and the post-occupation administration was set up, my father was called back to government service and the very same building used as the headquarters of the military police in that district was assigned to our family to use as our home. It was on a river bank and as I took an evening stroll as a boy, I came across the open graves where the victims of those difficult days were thrown after being cut down.

After the war and graduation, I was assigned to visit the Christian work done among the Japanese university communities. You will understand how reluctant I was to visit Japan and to undertake that assignment. I shall remember the first encounter with my Japanese hosts and particularly the words of welcome given me by that great Baptist layman, then leader of the Young Men's Christian Association of Japan, the late Dr. Soichi Saito. He expressed the words of Christian fellowship and at the same time asked for forgiveness for what his nation had done to my people during the war. That moment of Christian fellowship was the turning point in my attitudes toward Japan and the Japanese people.

In a small and personal way, but with lifelong significance for me, reconciliation in Christ's name took place there and then. I have been welcomed into the homes of Japanese Christians, and for these past years some of the closest colleagues in the regional interchurch cooperative program are Japanese churchmen whom I have come to love and respect.

At such moments, the text I have read at the beginning comes alive in a special way: "For he is our peace, who . . . has broken down the dividing wall of hostility, by abolishing in his flesh the law that he . . . might reconcile us both to God in one body through the cross, thereby bringing the hostility to an end" (Ephesians 2:14-16, RSV).

Tonight I think of this sincere Japanese Christian who could have taken the comfortable and easy way of disassociating himself from the policies and actions of the Japanese administration during the war, or he could have even denounced it as unrepresentative of the Japanese church or the Japanese nation as a whole. But he identified himself with the mistakes of his nation and vicariously paved the way for reconciliation. My testimony tonight is about Christ the Reconciler whom this late great Japanese churchman adored and worshiped and in whose ministry of reconciliation he participated.

Reconciliation is not something cheap and superficial. Reconciliation does not mean closing our eyes to walls of enmity which divide peoples and nations. Reconciliation in the gospel does not mean a diplomatic compromise nor condoning the wrong done between two parties. Reconciliation is not indulgence in a sweet and easy sloganmongering about promoting superficial harmony. At the heart of reconciliation is the cross of Jesus Christ. Reconciliation is not cheap. It cost God the life of his only Son. The restoration of relationship between holy God and sinful mankind is the outcome of costly grace. Holy God cannot have fellowship with sinful mankind until wickedness is punished and the consequences of sin are removed. Reconciliation does not mean that the righteous God closes his eyes to the walls of hostility that humanity has set up against God and that he decides to coexist with sinful man. Sin has to be judged, and punishment has to be given. But God took upon himself the punishment for sin and the consequences of mankind's assertion to have its own way separate from the very source of life. A creature cannot fulfill its destiny by existing apart from the spirit and power of its Creator. A motor car, the engine of which is made to run on petrol with a driver, cannot decide for itself that it will do away with the petrol and the guide. Surely a motor car without petrol and a guide cannot run except when it runs downhill. Mankind without the life-giving spirit and without the guidance of its

Creator surely cannot make progress unless we mistakenly believe that running downhill is progress!

Modern medical developments help us to understand something of the meaning of the cross and reconciliation through Christ. We may imagine the case of a loving husband and an adulterous wife. Spurning the love, faithfulness, and care of a loving husband, the adulterous wife indulges in sexual perversion and prostitution. Immorally she runs faster and faster downhill till at last her physical and health condition lands her on the operating table of the hospital. Let us further imagine that the only way to save her life is a heart transplant and a complete transfusion of new blood. Who should appear at this stage at the door of the operating theater? There comes her loving husband and offers his own heart for the transplant and his own blood for the transfusion. The heart is transplanted and the blood transfusion given, thus restoring the adulterous wife to a new lease on life and health. The cost of sin is paid and the consequences of the wickedness of the adulterous wife are borne by her loving husband so that she may start a new life altogether.

All human examples have their limitations, but such an example helps me to comprehend what I believe is the crucial significance of the cross of Christ. Reconciliation is the outcome of costly grace. We are not speaking here about a diplomatic compromise or a matter of promoting superficial harmony but about the very depths of true fellowship in which judgement and mercy, justice and love are met together in integrity.

Reconciliation is not ruthless vindication of one's will and way, nor the proud imposition of a devastating conquest. The Bible says: "Have this mind among yourselves, which you have in Christ Jesus, who, though he was in the form of God . . . emptied himself, taking the form of a servant . . . and became obedient unto death, even death on a cross" (Philippians 2:5, RSV). *Reconciliation is the result of the self-emptying love of Jesus Christ.*

We live in a time when awesome things are happening. We are at the beginning of the so-called second development decade, as the United Nations christened the nineteen seventies. We are witnessing in our day the beginnings of the conquest of outer space by man. But we are also living with the realities of wars such as those raging in Vietnam, Cambodia, and Laos. We are living in a world divided by the growing gap between the nations—some are growing richer day by day as their industrial growth expands because of the direct or indirect contributions to the wars, and other nations are getting poorer and poorer because they are devastated by war or are deprived of sharing in the benefits of processing their own primary products. We are living in a world which, though progress and new scientific achievements are being made ever anew in different spheres, human beings as a species have not found a way of sharing and living together. Mockery is made of harmony in human and international relations.

A third of the world population live in affluence, while the other two-thirds live in poverty and undernourishment. Malaria, cholera, trachoma, leprosy, and tuberculosis attack or cripple the children of "the two-thirds world." The rich, because of the means and power at their disposal, are getting richer while the poor, by the very lack of these means and power, and getting poorer. Someone said about the competition and the race that had gone on to reach the moon and the planets-that while two-thirds of mankind are asking for bread, the wealth of nations in a position to provide some bread to them is spent on space conquest to bring back a stone.

Reconciliation is the work of the true Messiah, Christ the Lord of history, who took upon himself the form of a servant. Reconciliation is not the product of false messianisms by which the mighty and the powerful take upon themselves the role of saviors of the world. False messianism led to the second world war, and the history of human tragedy is the history of high-sounding intentions imposed on others for professedly the good and prosperity of these others.

At the heart of reconciliation is not acquisition and self-assertion. Rather you find at the heart of reconciliation the self-emptying love of Christ, who though he was rich, yet for our sake, became poor that we through his poverty might be made rich. May he who through his costly grace, by his cross, brought about true reconciliation between God and man, and therefore between man and man, enable us at this Congress to proclaim Christ the crucified and the risen Lord and true reconciler, so that peoples and nations may repent and turn away from the paths of division and destruction.

It is to Him I bear testimony tonight, and to Him be the glory, honor, and majesty for ever.

Notes

1. Cyril E. Bryant, "Reflections On the Congress," *Baptist World Alliance: Twelfth Congress, Tokyo, June 12-18, 1970* (Valley Forge, Pennsylvania: Judson Press, 1971), p. 400.

2. Ibid.

3. Ibid., p. 401.

13
Stockholm
1975

Introduction

For the second time in its history, the BWA gathered in 1975 for a World Congress in Stockholm, Sweden. The theme of the second Stockholm Congress was "New People For A New World—Through Christ." The original wording was "New Men For A New World Through Christ." Awareness of the women's liberation movement and a "new world" of sexual equality caused the BWA Administrative Committee to request the Program Committee to change the word.

V. Carney Hargroves, pastor of the Second Baptist Church of Germantown, Philadelphia, Pennsylvania, had been elected president of the BWA in Tokyo. His presidential address at Stockholm urged Baptists to believe something and to do something. He told the Congress participants that "to be new people in Christ demands . . . that we do something about what we believe, that we get involved in the world and set some goals for ourselves." Witnessing to the truth, meeting the needs of the poor and the hungry, creating a clean environment, and working for peace were four actions which President Hargroves held before the Congress.

Thomas Kilgore, Jr., pastor of the Second Baptist Church in Los Angeles, California, echoed some of the same themes as Hargroves. In his address, "Fellowship Beyond Frontiers," Kilgore said that Baptists "must be instruments in creating international movements and programs that would promote justice, fair play, and equity in economics, education, and social services." Here was a Baptist urging Baptists to be concerned about something more than Baptists! It was a wide-ranging, socially sensitive, and challenging message, encouraging Baptists to be a "new people" in a "new world."

New People for a New World—Through Christ
V. Carney Hargroves

Before you, in large letters in English and in Swedish, is the theme of our congress: "New People for a New World—Through Christ." Two things I wish to say. One is the importance of believing in something; the other, the importance of doing something about what we believe.

To be new people in Christ demands that we believe in God. We need not simply an intellectual belief or just an emotional belief, both actually, but a faith and a trust in which we commit our very selves to God.

There are some today who say this is not possible. Once traveling in a plane I was seated next to a mineralogist. We talked about several things, and then I asked him what he believed about God. "I am an atheist," he said. "Science has proved that there is no God."

"And your wife and children," I asked, "what do they think?"

"They believe as I do, there is no place for God in our family."

Unquestionably there are some in every country who reflect the same attitude, who for one reason or another deny the existence of a divine being.

But I for one, and you in this congress also, do believe in God. I believe God created the universe, and we are just beginning to understand some of the processes by which he did it. I believe in God as a spirit and a force of love outside ourselves, outside of mankind, yet available to us and present with us. I believe in Jesus Christ as the expression of that love, and the Holy Spirit as the power of it. I believe that to this high purpose God sent Jesus Christ into the world "that whosoever believeth in him should not perish but have everlasting life" (John 3:16).

Reflecting back on my conversation with the atheist mineralogist, let me declare that science is not entirely on the side of the atheist. It was God who made the world and set up the laws of science. Man only explores and uses those laws.

Science is largely familiar with four major forces. One is gravitation. A universal law about this was laid down by Sir Isaac Newton more than 300 years ago. A second force is electromagnetic, which has to do with the propagation of light, sound, and energy. The third is a disintegrative force that causes spontaneous disintegration of particles as in the crushing of an atom. The fourth force, nuclear power, binds atoms together and is the strongest of these forces.

I contend there is a fifth force, to which might be applied the term "pneumaton." There is a biblical reason for my so defining it. John uses the Greek word *pneuma,* which means spirit, several times in his Gospel story of Jesus' ministry. He says that this *pneuma* or spirit is like the wind—unseen—but also like the wind, it can produce great results. Then

John records Jesus as saying, "God is a spirit and those who worship him must worship him in spirit and in truth" (John 4:24).

One sabbath day the apostle Paul was at the synagogue in Antioch. The leader of the service sent a message to him saying, "If you have anything encouraging to say to us, by all means speak up" (Acts 13:15). Paul accepted the invitation, and in the ensuing Scriptures we read how he led his hearers through a historical recitation of God's eternal vigilance and power as a determining force for good in human affairs. This was Paul's word of encouragement to believers in his time. It can be ours today, for God is still at work.

God has a purpose in all his work, throughout history and today. He seeks to bring human beings into harmony with him and his will. We can refer to the process as reconciliation, for the Scripture says, "God was in Christ reconciling the world unto himself" (2 Cor. 5:19).

I believe in a God of love, and love is the power of reconciliation. Genuine love is the world's greatest need. More information, more technology, more know-how are of course worthy, but man's greatest need is love in the best sense of the word. Love has no substitute. It heals, it motivates, it endures. God himself loved in the noblest sense of the word. We are new people in Christ when we accept God's love and make it paramount in our lives.

To be new people in Christ demands, in the second place, that we do something about what we believe, that we get involved in the world and set some goals for ourselves. One of these goals must be witnessing to the truth as we understand it.

This very year we are celebrating the 450th anniversary of a small group of young men who met in Switzerland in the fifteenth century to share ideas and to pray. Among them were Balthaser Hubmaier, Conrad Grebel, Felix Mantz, and Georg Blaurock. Their thinking differed from that of the church of their day in at least two respects. One was the concept of believer's baptism, the other was that of celebrating the Lord's Supper as a simple meal. These emphases represented, in the words of Ernest Payne, a "turning point" in church history. These men and others launched the Anabaptist movement, aptly described by others as "the cutting edge of the Reformation."

Life became extremely difficult for these four men, as they witnessed to their newfound convictions. Each one's faith was stronger than his fear, and each witnessed to the end of his life. Mantz was sentenced to death by drowning. Hubmaier and Blaurock were burned at the stake. Grebel died of the plague. The vision, the dedication, the courage of these and others of our spiritual forefathers is well told in a book, *The Anabaptist Story* by William R. Estep. We Baptists have a greater heritage than we sometimes realize—a heritage of commitment to Christ.

We need not go back to the Anabaptists to view this commitment. I can speak of it in this twentieth century, in fact, at this very time. Some of you in this congress live and witness in difficult circumstances. You are surrounded in your homelands by people who hold to ideologies and practices different from your own. You have, in most countries and in many ways, a minority status. You are sometimes ridiculed because of what you believe and what you stand for. Simply being a Baptist Christian is enough in certain places to limit your freedoms and your opportunities. I personally am encouraged, and I believe our Lord is encouraged, by the way you stand firm in your convictions, by the way you live by faith rather than by fear, by the way you bear witness to Jesus Christ.

Others of us, in fact most of us here, do not suffer for our faith as these other brethren do. We live in lands more hospitable to the Christian faith. I would urge all of us to commit ourselves to keep our brethren who labor in difficult places and sometimes in prison ever in our prayers. And I would urge us also to look to their dedication and to their sacrifices as an encouragement for us all to give our time and talents and our opportunities to the task of witnessing to our faith.

Another goal is to more adequately express our concern for people in physical need. Most of us do not know what it means to be really hungry. Rarely have we been in the position of wondering from where our next meal will come. On the other hand, statistics tell us that more than half the people of the world are always hungry. It is reported that ten million persons died of starvation in 1974, with the probability that even more will die in 1975. It is easy to say that there have always been hungry people and always poor people, but this rationalization cannot satisfy the Christian conscience.

There is enough food in the world—if properly distributed— to feed everybody. Distribution is limited by economic factors and even by political factors, including the vast expenditure of resources for making war rather than for making peace and understanding. In addition to the importance of limiting population growth, we emphasize again the sharing principle which is essential to the offsetting of hunger in today's world.

The past president of the American Baptist Churches in the United States is Dr. Peter Armacost. Recently it became necessary for him to make a plane trip at night. Knowing of the trip, Dr. Armacost's ten-year-old daughter emptied her small bank of the money she had saved—$1.17.

Then she wrote this note: "Dear Daddy, Take this money. It will take care of a snack for you at the airport. Have a safe trip. All my love, Sarah."

Afterwards he questioned her, "Why did you do this?" She replied, "Because I love you and because Jesus taught us to share."

The Baptist World Alliance has a department dedicated to meeting human need in time of emergency—when there are displaced persons, when there are floods, earthquakes, storms, famine. Our resources, however, are very limited. If for every dollar the Alliance now receives for world relief we could receive 100 dollars, we would be better able to feed starving people in the sub-Saharan (Sahelian) countries, in India, Bangladesh, and elsewhere. If we had greater resources we could more nearly do what is implied in Jesus' words, "Feed my sheep."

Still another of our goals demands that we help create a clean environment. God's creation was characterized by beauty and by order. The psalmist declared, "The earth if the Lord's and the fullness thereof" (Ps. 24:1). With justification we rejoice in the words of the hymn, "This is my Father's world,/ I rest me in the thought / Of rocks and trees, of skies and seas; / His hand the wonders wrought."

We human beings appear at times to forget this, and often we misuse the environment the Father has given us. We clutter attractive places with our debris, we pollute the air with harmful ingredients, we appropriate more than our share of energy, we exploit rather than produce. There is too much of the philosophy, "Everyone for himself."

Some are saying that we should get out of it, that the answer lies for certain earthlings to establish colonies in outer space. In February of this year, I heard a distinguished professor propose such a colony at a point in space equally distant from the earth and the moon. He suggested the cost of such an undertaking and even ways to achieve it. On May 12, 1975, a conference was held at Princeton University to consider such a project.

It was said that by 1988 ten thousand people could be ideally living in such a colony, well-fed, well-occupied and free of many diseases which characterize our society; that by 1994 there could be two such colonies, and by the year 2000 enough to care for a million people. That, however, is not for most of us. We shall be living here, and we must be working toward the goal of making it "the good earth."

Our reverence for God and the earth he created demands that we be not exploiters but participants in the environmental system. Our own interests, our concern for humanity, and the moral and ethical implications of Christianity call us to do our part. In this way, today's children and tomorrow's children can look forward to a cleaner world. Let us each begin where we live.

Still another goal requires that we do something for peace. In an international conference I once attended, the speaker seemed to look directly at me and asked, "What are you doing for peace?" He did not expect an answer, but the question caused me to review my own priorities and perhaps alter some of them.

At the Tokyo congress in 1970, there was a symposium on "Peace with Justice." One of the panelists, Mr. Takaaki Aikawa of Japan, said, "Peace with justice means mutual understanding and compassion among people concerned with each other's needs." Mr. Alexsei Bichkov of the Soviet Union said, "Justice is the base of the moral development of our society, and peace cannot be achieved without it."

Mr. Harold Stassen of the United States said, "From the international point of view, peace is the recognition of national boundaries and the right of self-determination. From the national point of view, peace is the recognition of the right of minorities to equality and protection. From the personal point of view, peace is the recognition of the rights of others."

However it is defined, peace is an objective long desired by the people of the world. Some of the prejudices or conflicts in recent years should never have happened in the first place and should never happen again—the maiming of little children, the destruction of vast areas of productive land, the displacement of great numbers of people. We are sad, humble, and regretful of any part we had in these things.

There can be many agencies for peace—the United Nations, the Christian church, the Baptist World Alliance. In the last analysis it comes back to each of us. Our obligation is to consciously work for understanding among people and between nations, and it begins where we live. As a result of our commitment to Christ these four things, among many others, we must do: witness to our faith; help those in need; create a better environment; become instruments for peace.

The theme of this congress is "New People for a New World—Through Christ." It is not an impossible vision. Let me tell of one incident in which God's spirit, the force we referred to earlier, actually the Holy Spirit, worked miracles in human lives.

The story began in 1872 when Edward Clark and his bride Mary Meade Clark went from Indianapolis, in the United States, to an isolated part of the world called Nagaland. Within this remote country of hills and valleys on India's northeast frontier, there lived tribes of people who were largely animist and to whom head-hunting was a way of life.

Exactly one hundred years later, in 1972, Mrs. Hargroves and I were invited to Impur, in Nagaland, to join 50,000 Baptist Christians in a centennial celebration of the coming of Christianity to their land. We met in a huge building especially erected for this purpose. The building was 300 meters long and 150 meters wide, and still it could not hold all the people who came. Over the platform was a banner, "Jesus Christ Is Lord." There were 1,000 young people in the choir, all in their colorful national dress. It was a great moment when the choir sang, *a cappella,* portions of Handel's *Messiah* including the "Hallelujah Chorus."

The speakers at that celebration praised God for bringing them from a life of head-hunting to a life of worship and witness and brotherly love in the name of Jesus Christ. The Christ that Edward and Mary Clark gave to them a hundred years ago made them new people, and the new people resulted in a new society throughout the hills and valleys of Nagaland.

It was a miracle wrought by God, but it happened because two people in the last century believed that it could happen. Their faith convinced them that if they invested their lives in the cause of Jesus Christ and made their personal witness, God could produce results beyond their imagination. Today more than sixty percent of all the people of Nagaland and eighty percent of the Ao tribe are Baptist Christians.

God still calls us to brave new frontiers for him. This is our challenge in the days and years to come. The frontiers may be different, but there are ever new worlds to conquer in bringing God's truth to all people and applying that truth to all of life.

Fellowship Beyond Frontiers
Thomas Kilgore, Jr.

We are indebted to the Greek New Testament for the word *koinonia.* It literally means, "fellowship in love and concern." In its broader connotation it expresses an enterprise in which we learn from one another, pray for one another, support one another, and share with one another. This mutual sharing reaches its zenith in the sharing of the word and the sharing of the elements of the Lord's Supper. Whatever roots of any significant depth we may have in Christian faith, whatever foundations we may claim, we must ever be aware that it is with all of God's people that we are to establish the deeper roots and the firmer foundations.

The common task of the worshiping and serving community is to establish deeper roots and firm foundations. For it is from this position that we move from our limited self-interest to universal concern. Only when we are grounded properly in the faith delivered to us by the saints, can we move with a sense of awareness to develop a universal network of concerned Christians. We need to grasp more firmly, with all of God's people, the breadth, length, height, and depth of the love of Christ, and to know it as best we can.

Many are abandoning all religious belief and trying other ways to find reality. There are still some atheists and agnostics around trying their Victorian rationalism in the solution of all life's problems. Still others are trying frantically to rationalize religion itself. Like the Greeks of old, they want to make it a *gnosis* (knowledge) or like the avant-garde of today, they want a religious science. But it is hard to know what "knowing" means. Newtonian physics declared that everything works rationally and predictably, and that science simply confirms what common sense already knows.

Alexander Pope expressed the confidence of the age of reason when he said: "Nature and Nature's laws lay hid in night: God said: Let Newton be and all was light." Two centuries later, Father Ronald Knox replied: "It did not last; the Devil howling Ho! Let Einstein be, restored the status quo."

The ambiguity of existence so often blurs the lines between different kinds of knowing. And so the dogmatism about the certainty of science as compared to the speculation of religion has liberally vanished. Men and women of faith believe in the power and progress of knowledge and science, but beyond that they stake their lives on the power of almighty God in his creative and redemptive process. He and he alone determines the course of history, the mental capacity of the scientist, and the life span of the sparrow. He and he alone is worthy of our complete allegiance and faith.

To understand the dimensions of our *koinonia,* and to find practical Christian ways to develop fellowship beyond frontiers, we must understand the nature of the world we live in, the diversity of its lands, peoples, religions, and customs; and we must, with a great degree of clarity, identify the present-day frontiers. Modern technology in both travel and communications has for all intents and purposes done away with former geographical frontiers. Geographically the world is a community. We can literally eat our three meals a day (those who enjoy this luxury) in any three different continents of our choice. Therefore, as we think in terms of frontiers we must identify areas in which we have not identified with one another, then take into consideration our social, racial, ethnic, and psychological strange lands, as well as those who live in geographical locations other than ours. In some instances these strange geographical new lands are across town, and in others they are across the world.

When we talk about fellowship beyond frontiers, we are really talking about exploring different lands, meeting other peoples, developing a new race consciousness, understanding other cultures and religions, and discovering other dimensions of an old mystery that has given life and vitality to our faith. We are talking about a venture that transcends all selfish economic interest, all limited and conscripted social customs, all bigoted culture-dominated religious patterns and all arrogant intellectual and educational exclusions. We are talking about a community in which the Arab and the Jew will view a common destiny; in which east and west will understand their mutual dependence; in which king and peasant will know a common brotherhood; in which rich and poor can see together the need for justice and equity; and in which the lips of prince and pauper can drink from a common communion cup.

As we attempt to fellowship beyond frontiers, the changes and ambiguities of our globe must be reckoned with. The dynamics of the developing nationalistic movements in Asia, Africa, Latin America, and other parts of the world must be viewed in proper perspective. The powerful technological development of the western nations and others must be carefully analyzed in the light of a proper balance between awesome scientific and technical know-how and our moral, ethical, and spiritual convictions. We cannot talk with any authority or credibility about fellowship beyond frontiers while people in some nations spend millions of dollars trying to reduce from overeating, while in other nations millions are starving. There is no dichotomy in our Lord's teachings or in his commands. His gospel is never self-contradictory. In him we live and move and have our being. Under his judgment are our politics, economics, social orders, culture, educational systems, and religious practices. He is no less concerned with the salvation of societies and human structures than he is with the salvation of individuals. All are under his judgment.

If those of us who are Christians and Baptists from all parts of the world would develop a widening fellowship of believers, would keep our witness from corroding, would certify creatively our credentials as witnesses, and make some difference in a difficult world, we must concentrate on some definite approaches to the task. We must find new and better ways than the ones of the past. We will have to discover and understand as fully as possible the words of our Lord, "Ye shall know the truth, and the truth shall make you free," and, "Work while it is day, for the night cometh, when no man can work."

The frontier of a highly developed technological and materialistic world must be crossed and challenged. We must try harder than ever to coordinate our scientific and technical knowledge with moral wisdom. The Christian witness has to be made boldly as we face the problems of scientific powers and moral quandary. In my own country we are struggling with the question of legal abortion. The global picture of abortion is alarming. The Population Council reports that as many as ten million abortions are performed in one country each year, 2.6 for every live birth. Other nations present statistics just as alarming.

Global decisions will have to be made, so that we can determine whether we will continue to begin life and destroy it, or whether we can and will use our scientific know-how to stop chronic starvation and unconscionable misery by massive emergency aid, agricultural assistance, long-range development and education. Do we have the moral courage on a world basis to move away from the anonymity of "do your own thing" and construct new forms of supportive community life? I hope we have not lost the capacity to care. I hope that the church and secular society can in some way receive a sense of our responsibility to bear one another's burdens.

The arrogance of privilege, based upon material wealth, accidents of history and color and race, must be counteracted by development of a kind of two-way frontiersmanship carried on by developed and underdeveloped nations. The great powers of our world have developed arsenals that have the capability to destroy the whole populations of the world sixteen times. This is an awesome thought. This power has produced arrogance. This arrogant frontier has to be crossed. The message of the Lord is badly needed in this area. These powers and principalities have to be wrestled with. The world can no longer live with great pockets of wealth and great pockets of poverty and misery. "The earth is the Lord's and the fullness thereof." The imbalance caused by the concentration of wealth and power in certain nations, certain races and certain powerful cartels and international monopolies has to be dealt with in the light of our Christian responsibility.

We can no longer permit the so-called developing countries to continue to deteriorate. In the 1960's the per capita income of developed countries increased by U.S. $650.00, while in the developing countries the increase was only by about U.S. $40.00. The share of world trade of the developing countries in exports declined from 21.3 percent in 1960 to 17.6 percent in 1970.

If we would do much more than just broaden the dialogue about new frontiers to cross, we must be instruments in creating international movements and programs that would promote justice, fair play, and equity in economics, education, and social services. Churches and denominations must not be satisfied with developing sophisticated mutual admiration societies and powerful bureaucratic structures. We must be models of simple but profound Christian living. We cannot conform to prevailing cultural and materialistic patterns, we must move to transform societies.

In the process of working for the renewal and change there must be a developed appreciation for different worship and liturgical patterns. The spiritual motivations of various ethnic groups and nations and races must be respected by those of other groups, races and nations.

Developed and underdeveloped nations need to bring closer their understanding of development. Both must cross frontiers. If we who claim allegiance to Jesus Christ would cross these frontiers, we must know that development and social change are set in motion not only by the autonomous processes of science and technology but are subject to the convictions and aspirations of men and women. So within this dynamic and complex process, Christian responsibility is to seek to develop social and positive institutions and processes that embody and enhance human dignity, and that give glory and honor to God.

We recognize that each of us belongs simultaneously to different communities—religious, national, and cultural. But at the same time we are in communities of common concerns that cut across lines of indigenous religious practices, nations, and culture. As we understand community in this sense we realize that we all are concerned about our responsibility to other human beings, and our responsibility to God. Knowing this we move by faith, hope, and love across all kinds of frontiers to witness and fellowship.

With a new sense of mission and evangelism, we must cross frontiers of all kinds. Following our Lord we will know that "the spirit of the Lord is upon me, because he hath anointed me to preach the gospel to the poor, he hath sent me to heal the broken hearted, to preach deliverance to the captives, and receiving of sight to the blind, to set at liberty those that are bruised, and to preach the acceptable year of the Lord." This is a daring position to take, but he took it and faced the consequences. We, too, must take it.

If we move by the Spirit of God, we will have to cross frontiers into other Christian denominations. We will need to learn the truth of true economics. We will need to practice a gospel that leads to cooperation with all Christians. We will have to go further than that. We will have to cross the frontier of other world religions. We cannot ignore the gifts that have come to mankind from religions that have stabilized great civilizations. We must in the name of Jesus Christ know and love those who are not of our fold.

There is a land beyond frontiers. It is the land that our Lord prayed for: "I pray for them. I pray not for the world, but for them which thou hast given me: for they are thine. And all mine are thine, and thine are mine; and I am glorified in them. . . . They are not of the world even as I am not of the world. Sanctify them through thy truth. Thy word is truth" (John 17). We are one in the Spirit. We are one in the Lord.

14
Toronto
1980

Introduction

Baptists of the world met in Toronto, Canada, July 8-13, 1980, and celebrated seventy-five years of BWA existence. This fourteenth Congress of the BWA exhibited the increasing "internationalization" of the organization. David Y. K. Wong of Hong Kong, the first Asian and first layman, to be elected as president of the Alliance presided over the Toronto gathering. He had been elected president at Stockholm in 1975. Gerhard Class of West Germany replaced the retiring Robert S. Denney of the USA as general secretary. A secretariat of eight multilingual, multicultural staff persons was elected to help lead the BWA.

The Toronto Congress adopted resolutions on evangelism, religious freedom and human rights, family life and the rights of children, world peace and disarmament, world hunger, refugees, and ecology. Because the violation of human rights was a pressing worldwide issue in 1980, the BWA's Commission on Freedom, Justice, and Peace issued a statement on human rights. That statement is printed in full.

William A. Jones, pastor of Bethany Baptist Church in Brooklyn, New York, preached a moving and memorable sermon on the Congress theme, "Celebrating Christ's Presence Through the Spirit." Speaking of the role of the Holy Spirit in the contemporary world, he identified sin as the universal reality, righteousness as the universal possibility, and judgment as the universal inevitability. The sermon is an excellent example of Baptist preaching in the latter half of the twentieth century. Rooted in a biblical text, the sermon relates to human experience in the 1980s.

Declaration on Human Rights

We the Commission on Freedom, Justice, and Peace gathered for the 1980 session of the Baptist World Alliance in Toronto, Canada, July, 1980, being aware of the widespread violation of human rights and being convicted of our responsibility to apply the biblical mandates for justice, freedom, peace, and love, do hereby issue this statement on human rights.

Theological Foundation

Human rights are derived from God—from his nature, his creation, and his commands. Concern for human rights is at the heart of the Christian faith. Every major doctrine is related to human rights, beginning with the biblical revelation of God. Justice and mercy are used in the Bible to describe God's ways with human beings, but they are also set forth as the responsibility of human to human. Why? Because God, the sovereign Lord of all, commands it. The Bible declares, "What does the Lord require of you but to do justice, and to love kindness, and to walk humbly with your God?" (Mic. 6:8) Human rights are rooted in the nature of God. God is just, merciful, and loving. He requires of humans also to be just, merciful, and loving because they are made in his image and thus are created to be like God in his moral nature.

The Bible presents certain basic truths about mankind which indicate that human rights are intrinsic in the nature of the world as created by God. Humanity has been created for a relationship with God, for social relationships in which human potentialities can be developed to the fullest, and for a harmonious relationship with nature and an enjoyment of her fruits. However, the rights of each individual to enjoyment of these relationships is inseparable from responsible participation in them.

Created by God as *spiritual beings,* persons have the right to worship God individually and corporately and to practice and propagate their faith according to the dictates of conscience. They have the responsibility to renounce all religious coercion and to allow others the freedom to worship, to practice and propagate their faith, or to profess no religious faith. The only authentic worship is that entered into freely.

As *moral beings,* God gives persons freedom of choice and responsibility for that choice. Persons have the right to respond freely to God and neighbors, and they have the responsibility to love God and neighbors.

As *psycho-physical beings,* persons have the right to life and the enjoyment of nature, including adequate food, shelter, clothing, and medical care as well as the right to be free from physical abuse through torture or slavery. They have the right to work. They also have the responsibility for working, if able, to provide these necessities for themselves and for others and for refraining from abusing and depriving others of the basic necessities of life.

As *social beings,* persons have the right to belong or not belong to social groupings, including familial, religious, economic, and political, and to express the identity and aspirations of such groups. They have responsibility to participate constructively in such groups and to refrain from hindering the activities and expressions of other groups. Therefore, human rights are both individual and corporate.

Jesus Christ came to reveal not only the nature of God but also the true nature of humanity. Our standard for what it means to be fully human—and thus for understanding human rights and responsibilities—is Jesus Christ. Jesus' life was dominated by self-giving love and was marked by a strong partiality for the poor and the powerless, for those whose rights are often denied. In defining his mission, Jesus declared, "The Spirit of the Lord is upon me, because he hath anointed me to preach the gospel to the poor; he hath sent me to heal the brokenhearted, to preach deliverance to the captives, and recovering of sight to the blind, to set at liberty them that are bruised" (Luke 4:18).

At the heart of Jesus' teaching was the command to love God and to love one's neighbor as oneself (Luke 10:27). Biblically, love is pictured not as a mere emotion, but as goodwill in action; love calls for doing something about the plight of one's neighbor. For a Christian to observe the violation of another's rights and do nothing is contrary to God's command (Jas. 4:17). The Bible reveals that all persons are made in "the likeness of God" (Jas. 3:9). The Scriptures declare that God "hath made of one blood all nations of men to dwell on all the faces of the earth" (Acts 17:26). Therefore, human rights are not for a few but for all.

Violations of human rights stem from humanity's turning away from God which results in the turning of human beings against each other and against nature. Throughout the Bible God's prophets strongly condemn the injustices and suffering which result from this. Nevertheless, they also proclaim God's continued concern for humanity and promise the ultimate fulfillment of God's original intention for the human race.

Practical Application

The theological foundations of the Christian faith and the direct teachings of the Bible indicate a number of specific human rights with implied responsibilities which ought to be of concern to persons everywhere and especially to those who follow Jesus Christ. Among these are the following:

(1) The right to choose a religion freely and to maintain religious belief or unbelief without political advantage or disadvantage.

(2) The right to meet together for worship and to share religious

faith publicly with others; the government's protection of these rights without discrimination among the faiths.

(3) The right to remain single or to form families in which children are born and religious education is provided for those children.

(4) The right to a healthy environment, including clean air and pure water, sanitary living quarters, and an earth which can support and nurture present and future generations.

(5) The right to be employed and to receive a just return for one's labor.

(6) The right to the fruits of labor, including adequate food, clothing, shelter, and health care.

(7) The right to participate in the political processes, to have a voice in the decision-making apparatus of government, and to be secure from the fear of governmental persecution.

(8) The right to privacy.

(9) The right to express convictions according to the dictates of conscience even when contrary to the prevailing norms of government or society.

(10) The right to cultural identity.

(11) The right to be free from violence against one's person, including slavery, torture, and inhuman or degrading forms of punishment.

(12) The right to be free from arbitrary arrest and imprisonment.

(13) The right to a just and open trial with an opportunity to confront accusers.

(14) The right to equal protection under the law against discrimination on the grounds of age, sex, race, religion, class, national origin, cultural background, marital status, economic condition, or handicap.

(15) The right to a nationality, to freedom of movement and residence within the borders of one's nation state, and the right to travel from one's country and return.

(16) The right to own property individually as well as in association with others.

(17) The right to freedom of peaceful assembly.

(18) The right to freedom of association and freedom from being compelled to belong to an association.

(19) The right to leisure, rest, and recreation and to a reasonable limitation of working hours.

(20) The right to an education.

Implementation

To declare human rights is not enough. To strive to promote and to defend human rights within churches and society at large is also our responsibility. Human rights are universally applicable, but in today's world they are universally violated. We confess our own involvement in the violation of human rights, and likewise our silence, often neither protesting nor interfering when we witness violations. We pledge ourselves to the following efforts to advance human rights in our world.

Evangelization is the key ingredient in advancing human rights. Because human rights are derived from God, all persons everywhere need to know him. Bringing persons to God through Jesus Christ opens to them both the possibility of understanding what is right and the power through the indwelling Spirit of God to do what is right.

Education is a necessary ingredient in the protection of human rights. The Christian message concerning such subjects as racism, sexism, poverty, war, and corruption needs to be taught within churches and without. Christians everywhere need to understand that they are endowed with certain rights and also have definite responsibilities to defend and promote the rights of all persons.

Declaration to the world of our concern for human rights and of our determination to see those rights promoted is imperative. In the light of the world's condition, silence is sin. With prophetic courage we should point to violations of human rights and bring pressure to alter the attitudes and systems which produce them.

Action, therefore, is part of our responsibility. In light of the Bible's teachings concerning human rights, pastors should preach the word of God without fear or favor as it highlights human rights. Churches should champion justice for the oppressed, provide food for the hungry, support changes in laws and systems which harm human beings, and do the things that make for peace. Christians should assume responsibility for ministering in Jesus' name to individuals whose human rights have been violated. Christians should endeavor to defend the rights of all persons no matter how far away or how weak they may be. Baptists everywhere ought to be involved not only in the proclamation of the gospel but also in the application of biblical truth in all areas of life.

Conclusion

Because we are being set free by the power of God through faith in Christ Jesus as Lord, we pledge to use our freedom responsibly to help free others. Individually as well as through our churches and institutions we promise to pray and work for the defense of human rights, to strive to avoid violating the rights of others, and to serve him from whom all human rights come, the only One who is Righteous, Just, and Merciful, the Father of our Lord Jesus Christ.

Celebrating Christ's Presence Through the Spirit
William A. Jones

"I tell you the truth; It is expedient for you that I go away: for if I go not away, the Comforter will not come unto you; but if I depart, I will send him unto you. And when he is come, he will reprove the world of sin, and of righteousness, and of judgment: Of sin, because they believe not on me; Of righteousness, because I go to my Father, and ye see me no more; Of judgment, because the prince of this world is judged" (John 16:7-11).

George Buttrick wrote regarding the presence of God in history in the person of Jesus Christ: "Ours is a visited planet." Buttrick was speaking pointedly and precisely about the Christ-event, the breakthrough of God in time and space by way of Bethlehem.

"Ours is a visited planet." What an apt description of the incarnation. For a few years God lived at our level for our liberation. For thirty-three years he walked our walk, talked our talk, and participated in our pain. And for three of those years he engaged in the most merciful mission this planet has ever witnessed. He showed us not only how to live but also how to die and the purpose of both living and dying. He joined days and destiny. He placed heaven and hell in proper perspective. He made utterly clear the ineluctable ties between earth and eternity. Over and over again he separated shadow from substance and showed that the good life is infinitely more than getting and gaining. Declaring the good news of the kingdom, Jesus articulated the everlasting significance of what we do with our nowness.

What a visit it was and what a visitor he was. Those lyrics often sung by the young in age echo the feelings of all the elect:

> "I should like to have been with Him then,
> I should like to have been with Him then;
> When He called little children as lambs to His fold,
> I should like to have been with Him then."

Divinity visited our humanity, and he did it in the garb of our mortality. But—it was only a visit. And a visit is not forever. Some visits are longer than others; but a visit, irrespective of length, does not last. The hour comes when a visitor must bid farewell. No matter how fruitful or how delightful, a visit does not last.

The day came when the visit of God Incarnate reached a sorrowful end. Its announcement was not abrupt. It did not come without early warning. Jesus had informed his friends more than once that the time would come when they would see his face no more. To their consternation he, one occasion, had engaged in crucifixion conversation. So then his decision to depart was neither precipitous nor spontaneous. He sounded early warnings. Every now and then he spoke in grave (but not fearful) tones concerning his date with death and his prescheduled encounter with calvary. When the time drew nigh, our gracious and glorious Visitor described his departure in as much detail as loving hearts could take. On cruicifixion eve, the night before that fateful Friday, while seated at the Passover table, he announced his imminent exit. He pointed out the perils to be experienced in his absence. He was open, honest, candid, straightforward! "They shall put you out of the synagogues. The time will come when whosoever killeth you will think that he doeth God service. I didn't tell you these things before because I was with you. But now, I depart, I go my way to him that sent me, I return to the Father." And then, as though he anticipated a plea for him to stay or to delay his departure, he moved quickly to put it in the category of necessity.

"I notice," says Jesus, that "sorrow has filled your hearts. Nevertheless, I tell you the truth. It is expedient for you that I go away. My going is for your good. My exit makes possible another entry. My visit terminates in order that another visit might commence. If I do not depart, then the Comforter will not come. If I remain, the Paraclete, the Helper, the Spirit will not come. But if I go, I will send him unto you." That's what Jesus said at supper on crucifixion eve. The Savior departed that the Spirit might arrive. Jesus promised that this planet would not be without a Presence. "If I do not depart, the Comforter will not come. I go that I might send him."

Traditional African religion is replete with interesting proverbs. There is one out of West Africa which says, "If you want to talk to God, tell it to the wind." There's tremendous truth, as well as poetry, in that utterance. It expresses not only a basic sensitivity to the Eternal but it also reflects a sure understanding of God as Spirit. "If you want to talk to God, tell it to the wind."

The proverb, born in the land of my own elders, suggests that the wind is God's messenger—that invisible zephyrs carry the prayers of people to the heavenly presence. Ancient is the idea that God is identified with wind. In the Hebrew it is *ruach*. In the Greek it is *pneuma*. "If you want to talk with God, tell it to the wind." Wind is air in motion. Wind is air marked by activity, moving freely without restriction. And so it would be with the Spirit.

Jesus was God's particular Presence. The Holy Spirit is God's pervasive Presence. Like the sky covering the circumference of earth, the Spirit covers the whole of humanity. "I send him," said Jesus. "He will represent me everywhere to everybody. No parcel of the human landscape will be off-limits to his presence. No segment of society will have special claim on him. He'll be accessible and available wherever the curse is found. He will not speak a language different from my own. He will not speak of himself. He will say that which I tell him to say. With us there is no communication gap. There's no static and no interference. He will glorify me, for he will draw upon what is mine and disclose it to you. He'll bear witness to me. I send him unto you. And when he comes he will convict the world. He will convict the world of sin, of righteousness, and of judgment. What I have accomplished on location, he will perform universally."

Sin, righteousness, and judgment—conditions with which every soul must deal—are within the Spirit's purview.

What a sweeping assignment. It covers the gamut of human experience. Sin—the universal reality! Righteousness—the universal possibility! Judgment—the universal inevitability! The real, the possible, and the inevitable—that's the sphere of the Spirit's function. That's also the church's witness.

The Spirit, working in and through the people of God, extends the incarnation to every generation in every age. This does not allow for a worldless witness. This vitiates the notion of saints existing in solitude. This undercuts every theogony which divorces faith from ethics. The Spirit operative in and through the church is holistic, speaking in redemptive manner to the totality of human experience. Therefore, authentic celebration is conditional. It cannot occur if our witness is truncated or bifurcated.

People possessed of the Spirit will, of necessity, deal plainly and pointedly with the real, the possible, and the inevitable. The real is the starting point. How tragic is the tendency to avoid the real, to be oblivious to the harsh and brutal realities which hurt our humanity and even seek to deface our divinity.

Emil Brunner was clearly correct in his solemn declaration that "the greatest sin of the Church is that she withholds the Gospel from herself." Our Lord, speaking through the Spirit, bids us be honest in our self-scrutiny and in our appraisal of the human predicament. How often we Christians have capitulated to culture. How many times along the pathway of our pilgrimage have we put Caesar before Christ. How many times have we accommodated our lives to the prevailing political arrangement. And since there can be no celebration in the absence of confession, we ought, every day of our lives, to confess our contributions to the world's madness.

How grave is the human situation even as we meet this night. Commentators from within and without the church paint our predicament in poignant strokes. Amos Wilder has characterized our age as one that is "marked by the loss of absolutes." LeComte DuNouy has written, "The true values, dimmed by the glitter of a new star, have been relegated to second place." Colin Morris, a British cleric, has declared concerning the powerful few who rule the world, "They can, at will, reverse the miracle at Cana and turn wine into water; they are so decadent as to make ancient Byzantium seem like the New Jerusalem, and yet so decent that even when they are clubbing you to death you feel impelled to apologize for spilling blood on their carpets."

The witness of the Spirit, in and through us, begins always with a recognition of the real—the reality of sin, broken fellowship, rebellion against God, structured evil, and institutionalized iniquity.

Maxie Gordon, longtime professor at Benedict College in South Carolina, USA, tells of a little girl's bedtime prayer. Her mother stood in the doorway to the child's room, looking and listening with loving concern. The little girl uttered her prayer, said "Amen," and rose to her feet. But she immediately returned to her knees and added this postscript—"By the way God; don't forget to take good care of yourself, 'cause if anything happens to you, all of us will be in a mess." Recognition of the real, no matter how ruthless the real, is the point of departure on the pathway to glory.

Emerson once remarked, "When it is dark enough, men see the stars." The real is the prelude to the possible. Righteousness is the postlude to repentance. The clear testimony of the gospel is that, by God's grace, we can triumph over every tragic aspect and consequence of the real. Righteousness is within reach. Sinners can be saved. The saved can be sanctified. Peace is possible. Pain and pleasure can be democratized. The lion and the lamb can lie down together. The Holy Spirit, Christ's vicar in the earth, is the agent of righteousness, the instrument of the possible. All who participate in the possible, as a result of redemption, are qualified to celebrate.

But what is the nature of the celebration? Well, it is three-dimensional. It includes the soul's delight over what God has already done; joy in what God is now doing; and the thrill of that victory which is yet to come. God has not left us to ourselves. He made the world; he's redeeming an alien humanity. He shall judge the world. His people know that evil's doom is certain and that judgment is fixed. "The prince of this world is judged." Already "the victory is won." Already "the middle wall of partition" is down. Already there is heard "the song of saints on higher ground."

In spite of the world's madness and regardless of the degree of demonism, a remnant rightly rejoices. A company properly celebrates. It's a strange crowd, a peculiar commonwealth—"not many mighty, not many noble, and not many wise." They wind their way through the centuries with a strange seriousness. They pray without ceasing; they sing anthems of grace. They declare with gratitude, "Redeemed! Redeemed! I've been redeemed by the blood of the Lamb." They live in the Spirit and show forth the fruits thereof—love, joy, peace, longsuffering, gentleness, goodness, faith, meekness, and temperance. Daily they declare, "Come Holy Spirit, heavenly Dove, in all thy quickening power."

I know whereof I speak, for I belong to their company. Thirty-nine years ago in the church of my rearing in Lexington, Kentucky, USA, I felt the Savior's embrace through the Spirit's urging. "I came to Jesus and I drank of that life-giving stream; my thirst was quenched, my soul revived, and now I live with him."

That's the testimony of the twice-born. That's their song even in the midst of storms. What is the clue to this peculiar capacity for celebration? Well, they've been empowered. The Paraclete is the provider of power. Power? Yes, power! How does one define it? It's *dunamis* in the Greek. But how do you define divinity? You don't. You simply describe the divine. Power! The power of the Holy Spirit! It's illumination for ignorance. It's insight and inspiration. It's strength for the struggle. It's calm for our worries, comfort for loneliness, and strength for weariness. The Spirit provides power for every inadequacy and insufficiency.

The late Lucy Campbell captured it in verse and set it to music.

> "Preachers and teachers would make their appeal,
> Fighting as soldiers on great battle fields;
> When to their pleadings, my poor heart did yield,
> All I could say, there is something within.
>
> Something within me that holdeth the reins,
> Something within me that banishes pain;
> Something within me I cannot explain,
> All that I know there is something within.
>
> Have you that something, that burning desire?
> Have you that something that never doth tire?
> Oh, if you have it, that Heavenly fire;
> Then let the world know there is something within."

Sing it! Shout it! Tell it! Swell it! The Comforter has come, and we celebrate his coming because he is Presence, Peace and Power. Hallelujah! Hallelujah! Hallelujah!

Conclusion

In the September 2, 1983, issue of *Christianity Today,* Martin E. Marty, a Lutheran and America's best-known church historian, wrote an article with an intriguing title, "Baptistification Takes Over." *Baptistification* is a word Marty created to describe what he called, "the most dramatic shift in power style on the Christian scene in our time."

What did Marty mean by *baptistification* and by "dramatic shift"? He did not mean by *baptistification* that people of other Christian denominations are shifting to join *only* Baptist churches. Nor did he mean that people are accepting the Baptist mode of baptism in dramatic new numbers. Marty meant that there is a new religious mood among such groups as Catholics, Lutherans, Anglicans, and others. This mood, he said, stresses *freedom, choice,* and *voluntarism* in matters of faith. Correctly and significantly, Marty identified these themes as hallmarks of the Baptist identity and focal points of the Baptist vision. They constituted *the essence of Baptist life* and the stackpole around which Baptist convictions emerge.

Baptistification is a specific *style* of faith, a distinctive *posture* of faith, a particular *attitude* toward the issues of faith. Baptistification does not refer to an isolated doctrine. It does not specify a theological or ecclesiological concept, such as salvation by grace, believer's baptism by immersion, or a regenerate church membership. Baptistification is a *spirit* that pervades all of the Baptist principles or so-called Baptist distinctives. It is the *spirit of freedom.*

The documents taken from BWA Congresses give overwhelming documentation for the idea that freedom is the essence of Baptist life. Baptists have honestly admitted that there is a risk in this style of faith. In his masterful address in 1911 in Philadelphia, John Clifford confessed for all Baptists when he said, "We know our insistence upon freedom has its risks: but they may be avoided; whereas the stagnation and death that follow enslavement of the human soul are inevitable."

And in 1928, E. Y. Mullins said, "Individualism is a dangerous principle but so is every other great principle of enlightenment and progress." He went on with this confession which was really exhortation for the Baptist spirit:

The right of private judgment is a dangerous word, but it is a winged and emancipating word. It is the sole guaranty that man will press out of childhood to the manhood stage of religion. It is the key that Hubmeier and Bunyan used to unlock the door of the dungeon wherein man's intellect had been so long imprisoned. It was the hammer with which Roger Williams broke the chain which united church and state. It was the word which inspired the heroic courage of Oncken, and the stubborn, passive, resistance of a Clifford. The right of private judgment kindled the vision of world evangelization to the faith of William Carey and transformed Western Christianity. The right of private judgment: yes, a dangerous word, but a word which started man on a new voyage of spiritual discovery, a word which gave his spirit wings to soar among the angels in its flight upward to God.

Thus Baptists have stressed freedom rather than control, voluntaryism rather than coercion, individualism rather than the "pack mentality," personal religion rather than proxy religion, diversity rather than uniformity.

While confessing the risks, and even the limitations, of freedom, Baptists have nonetheless pursued it passionately. And they have because they sense that there are forces inherent in the life of the world which would gladly jettison freedom. The conflict between freedom and tyranny—of all kinds—is a perennial one. So, repeatedly the Baptist World Alliance speakers called for relating the spirit of freedom in Baptist life to the spirit of tyranny in the life of the world.

At the first World Congress in 1905, J. D. Freeman launched the BWA emphasis on the need to relate the freedom of Baptists to the needs of the world. He said,

The world has not outgrown the need of Baptist principles. It was never in greater need of them than it is today. Our principles have not yet manifested the full force that is in them. New light and power are to break forth from them in days to come. *Loose them and let them go.*

E. Y. Mullins spoke on the Baptist theme of freedom at both the 1923 and 1928 World Congresses. Much of George W. Truett's 1939 address, "The Baptist Message and Mission For The World Today," focused on the same concept. In 1950 C. Oscar Johnson called on Baptists of the world to "stand our ground for the truth, for the freedom of the individual against the hierarchies in government and church. We must stand our ground against all opposition to the worth of an individual and the right of access of every person to the God who created him."

Herbert Gezork in 1955 echoed Johnson, Truett, Mullins, and Freeman. Speaking of his own day, Gezork said, "If ever there was a time for Baptists to proclaim in word and life their great principle of soul-liberty, that time is now." Ten years later Joao F. Soren referred in his address to "the challenge of waning freedoms." Acknowledging that "perhaps this faithless generation cannot understand the beauty and the majesty of all we say and preach about soul liberty," he went on to encourage an "unflinching, resolute, courageous" witness by Baptists to freedom and liberty.

So if there is a single, recurring, and almost monotonous theme in these BWA documents, it is that of *freedom.* While the word itself is used repeatedly, the idea behind the word is found in numerous other phrases—*the voluntary principle, soul liberty, self-determination, religious liberty, democracy, autonomy, individualism, believer's baptism, the undelegated sovereignty of Christ, spiritual Christianity, separation of church and state, freedom of conscience, an open Bible, human rights,* and *personal conversion.* The list is almost endless!

The Baptist spirit of freedom as mirrored in these documents fans out into almost every area of life and faith. In closing, I want to identify five specific types of freedom which Baptists have stood for through the BWA. These five freedoms are Soul Freedom, Bible Freedom, Civil Freedom, Church Freedom, and Human Freedom. Each deserves comment.

Soul Freedom is also called "soul competency," "freedom of conscience," and "priesthood of believers." John Clifford, the greatest British Baptist to see the dawn of the twentieth century, dubbed it "sanctified individualism." E.Y. Mullins thought soul competency to be the distinctive contribution of Baptists to the religious thought of the world.

Soul Freedom is the inalienable right and responsibility of every person to deal with God herself or himself. It is based upon the following ideas: people are made in God's image with the capacity to choose; God is able to reveal himself to individuals; and individuals have a capacity for God.

George W. Truett, the "American Spurgeon" and long-time pastor of First Baptist Church, Dallas, Texas, argued that the principle of the competency of the soul "is the keystone truth of the Baptists." "Out of this cardinal, bed-rock principle," he continued, "all our Baptist principles emerge."

Soul competency is not human self-sufficiency. It is the individual's competency *under* God. Excluding all human interference between the person and God, soul competency is a safeguard against coercion and intimidation of any and all kind. Several years ago a popular song stated something like, "If you want to see me do my thing, all you gotta do is pull my string." The late Grady Nutt, Baptist preacher/humorist from Texas and Kentucky, countered with the spirit of soul freedom when he shouted, "Wrong! If you want to see me do my thing, keep your hand off my cotton-picking string!"

The polar opposite of soul competency is, of course, soul incompetency. And soul incompetency is inherent in all forms of rigid authoritarianism, theological totalitarianism, and doctrinal imperialism. It was just such imperialism that Baptists of the seventeenth century sought to escape.

No paragraph in BWA annals puts it better than John Clifford's in his stirring address of 1911.

Therefore we preach soul Liberty, and contend against all comers that the spirit of man has the privilege of direct conscious relation to God in Christ and through Christ. Nothing may come between the soul and God. Not the priest, whatever his claims; he will cloud the vision of Christ, and put a fetter on the soul's freedom; not the theologian; he may help, if he keeps his true place; but he may check individual search for truth and emasculate the man; not even the church, for it may wrap the spirit in conventions, and tie it up with red tape; not the State, it will imprison energy and check growth. The soul must be free. All the Lord's people are potential prophets and liberty is the vital breath of prophecy. To every one is given the spirit to do good with; and the first law of the spirit is that there must be no quenching of its fires. Grace is free from first to last, i.e., God is free in His advent to the soul and His work within, to redeem it, to renew it, to raise it to the heights of moral energy, and fashion it after his likeness. Freedom is inherent in the very conception of the spiritual life, and therefore there must be ample room and verge enough within the territories of the Church for the full expression of an eager, intense, and sanctified individualism.

Where does the Christian life begin? That is one dimension of the issue of soul freedom. The Christian life, Baptists contend, begins where an individual soul experiences Christ as Savior and surrenders to Him as Lord. In this meeting with Christ, people "discover themselves," their destiny, and the meaning of existence. Stand-ins will not do. Proxy faith is no faith. Soul Freedom means that the individual must be free for faith to be authentic. Soul Freedom also means that the individual must be *alone* "before God."

Soul Freedom is not selfishness clothed in Baptist dogma. It accents the value of the individual. Soul Freedom, rightly understood, issues into a concern for the rights and needs of other individuals. The dignity of each is to be respected. Given the depth and implications of the meaning of soul freedom, there is little wonder that J. D. Freeman said of Baptists, "We did not stumble upon this doctrine. It inheres in the very essence of our belief."

These BWA documents also testify to the historical and universal Baptist call for *Bible Freedom*. Baptists have had a profound belief in the power of the "open Bible." They have, therefore, uttered vigorous objection to a "closed Bible," whether closed by state, church, creedal restrictions or any form of tyranny.

The Baptist emphasis on freedom of all kinds is rotted in biblical principles. "Our fathers," said Clifford, in 1911, "were advocates of freedom because they were men of the Book." The authority of the Bible, especially the New Testament, is central to the life of the believer because it reveals the mind and will of Christ. George W. Truett spoke for all Baptists when he said:

I would here frankly say that for Baptists there is one authoritative and final source of religious truth, and that source is the Bible. Our contention is that God's will for mankind is fully expressed in the Bible, and to that Will we are bound to conform, in all matters relating to doctrine, polity, ordinances, worship and Christian living. How shall we find out Christ's Will to us? He has revealed it in His Holy Word. The Bible, and the Bible alone, is the rule of faith and practice for Baptists.

The Baptist cry for freedom is rooted in the Bible and the Bible alone. But Bible Freedom means more than that for Baptists. It also means that the individual believer, unencumbered by tradition or creed, must be free to interpret the Bible. Only that kind of freedom is able to produce Thomas Helwys's passionate proclamation of religious liberty. Only that kind of freedom can produce Carey's vision of the church's worldwide responsibility. Only that kind of freedom can produce a Judson or an Oncken or a Martin Luther King, Jr.

Thus these documents echo throughout the theme of unrestrained freedom of access to the Bible. Bible Freedom has meant anticreedalism for Baptists. Confessions of faith, voluntarily framed and voluntarily accepted, have been acceptable to Baptists if these confessions were not used to coerce conscience. "But when," as E. Y. Mullins said, "they are laid upon men's consciences by ecclesiastical command, or by a form of human authority they become a shadow between the soul and God, an intolerable yoke, an impertinence and a tyranny." The Bible, say Baptists, must be free. And Baptists must be free to interpret the Bible.

Civil Freedom is a third manifestation of freedom which prevades the documents of the Baptist World Alliance. It is through this expression of freedom that Baptists have made one of their most enduring contributions to the life of the world. What is meant here by Civil Freedom? At least three things: freedom *of* religion, freedom *from* religion, and freedom *for* religion.

Baptists have been champions of freedom *of* religion. This is worship freedom, commonly known as religious liberty. Beginning with John Smyth and Thomas Helwys, Baptists have consistently—and persistently—argued that conscience must not be compelled by state or church to follow any prescribed religion or form of worship.

Baptists such as Herbert Gezork loved to quote John Bunyan on this issue. Imprisoned in Bedford jail, Bunyan was offered his personal freedom if he would only behave religiously. Said Bunyan, "I will stay in prison till the moss grows on my eyebrows rather than make a slaughterhouse of my conscience or a butchery of my principles."

In pleading for religious liberty, Baptists made it clear that they were not advocating mere religious toleration. They distinguished between religious liberty and religious toleration for several reasons. Religious toleration is a concession; religious liberty is a right. Religious toleration is expediency; religious liberty is principle. Religious toleration means special privileges for some; religious liberty means equal rights for all. Religious toleration implies a state church; religious liberty affirms separation of church and state. Baptists have not sought a condescending toleration from the state. Baptists have wanted, and they still want, absolute religious liberty!

And they want this not only for themselves but for *all* people. The Baptist insistence on freedom *of* religion, therefore, includes freedom *from* religion. One's right not to believe is as sacred as one's right to believe. "While we have no sympathy with atheism or agnosticism or materialism," wrote E. Y. Mullins, "we stand for the freedom of the atheist, agnostic and materialist in his religious or irreligious convictions."

Baptists have also stood for freedom *for* religion. This is evangelistic freedom. Religious freedom is far more than the right to worship according to the dictates of conscience. It is the freedom to share one's faith with others, to teach and preach without molestation. It is the freedom to seek to persuade in an open marketplace of ideas. To curb such freedom is to abridge one's civil rights. Evangelistic freedom is crucial for Baptists because they do not replenish themselves through birth but through rebirths. Again, however, what Baptists have asked for themselves—the right to propagate their faith freely—they also have asked for all people of all faiths as well as for those without faith.

The Baptist appeal for civil protection for religious freedoms expresses itself politically in the concept of separation of church and state. Contending that any alliance between church and state is a misalliance, Baptists have rejected the domination of either by the other. The church must not court the powers of Caesar. And Caesar must not seek to control the church. One church must not receive preferential treatment above other churches. On this ground, George W. Truett voiced strong Baptist opposition to the establishment of diplomatic relations between the United States and the Vatican. Baptists' contention for the separation of church and state is inexplicable apart from the Baptist passion for freedom.

A fourth freedom is stressed throughout the history of the Baptist World Alliance. It is *Church Freedom.* Baptists are a major part of what is known in Christian history as "the free church tradition."

The church must be free, Baptists contend, to determine its own membership. One is not "born" into a local Baptist church. Rather, one is "born again" into the church. Just as the individual must be free to choose Christ as Lord, the local congregation must be free to determine its membership based upon spiritual commitments.

This Church Freedom has obvious implications. It means that neither civil nor other ecclesiastical bodies can dictate terms of church membership. Moreover, infant baptism is replaced by believer's baptism and the "parish church" concept is replaced by the "gathered church" concept. Here is a good place to note that the Baptist conviction regarding believer's baptism is not rooted primarily in the amount of water used. It is rooted in the spiritual nature of the church and the nature of authentic religious experience. Defining the church, therefore, F. Townley Lord described it as "a fellowship of believers gathered from the world and committed to live under the guidance of the word and spirit of God."

Church Freedom also includes the local congregation's right to govern itself. Baptist churches are "autonomous" and "independent"; they are "congregational" and "democratic." These are treasured words to Baptists because they speak of the freedom of the church from all outside interference.

Each local congregation is free to choose and ordain its own officers. Ministers and deacons cannot be imposed; they must be selected by the people of the congregation. When selected, the officers do not have any more authority than any other member of the congregation. All believers have a right to equal privileges in the church. Truett said that a local Baptist church "is a pure democracy, without disbarment of franchise to any member, on the ground of nationality, race, class or sex."

Just as the local Baptist church is free from the state and ecclesiastical bodies, from bishops and magistrates, it is also free from the control of other Baptist organizations. The Baptist World Alliance has been especially careful to safeguard the autonomy of local Baptist churches, recognizing that church freedom is basic to Baptist life.

Finally, there is an urgent appeal within the Baptist World Alliance documents for *Human Freedom*. This is what Theodore Adams had in mind when he spoke of "freedom *through* religion." He meant that the gospel helps to liberate human beings from all the forces that would restrict potentiality. This includes economic oppression, racial, and sexual discrimination, and political totalitarianism. Human Freedom means freedom from war, freedom from hunger, and freedom from exploitation.

In the earliest years of the BWA, John Clifford, after extolling the Baptist virtues of individualism, unapologetically called upon Baptists to "advocate and work for the Social Gospel." Baptist ideas, said Clifford, "carry us with tremendous momentum to the side of the common man." A concern for liberty, equality and fraternity came straight from "the heart of the Baptist faith," he argued. The results were obvious: poverty must be dealt with at its causes; charity cannot be accepted as a substitute for justice; those who have been "flattened out by the long tramp of misery, must be rescued, healed, strengthened and set on their own feet"; international peace must be sought; and all that injures God's creation must be broken up. Clifford ended his appeal with a sentence on Human Freedom. He said, "Man must be free to work out his own salvation, to realize himself, and to enthrone God in Christ, in the whole life of mankind."

This compassionate cry for Human Freedom echoes in each of the Baptist World Congresses. At the 1980 Congress in Toronto, the Baptist World Alliance received a report from a group with the significant title of the Commission on Freedom, Justice, and Peace. Also significantly, the report was entitled "Declaration on Human Rights." John Clifford, though long dead, surely must have enjoyed it. Among other things, the document said, "Human rights are derived from God—from his nature, his creation, and his commands. Concern for human rights is at the heart of the Christian faith." Then there followed a list of twenty specific human rights "which ought to be of concern to persons everywhere and especially to those who follow Jesus Christ." Human Freedom is a basic Baptist concern.

Baptist life is built on these five freedoms: Soul Freedom, Bible Freedom, Civil Freedom, Church Freedom, and Human Freedom. The world today needs this witness. The universal church needs this witness. But Baptists need to "discover" this witness where it is not known among them, and they need to "recover" this witness where it has been lost among them.